MORE
IMPORTANT
THAN
MONEY

...AN ENTREPRENEUR'S TEAM

MORE IMPORTANT THAN THAN MONEY

...AN ENTREPRENEUR'S TEAM

ROBERT KIYOSAKI

AUTHOR OF THE INTERNATIONAL BEST-SELLER *RICH DAD POOR DAD*
AND THE RICH DAD ADVISORS

Published by RDA Press, LLC

Rich Dad Advisors, B-I Triangle, CASHFLOW Quadrant and other Rich Dad marks are registered trademarks of CASHFLOW Technologies, Inc.

The Kolbe A™ Index, Action Modes® and Kolbe Strengths™ are the trademarks of Kathy Kolbe and Kolbe Corp. All rights reserved. Used with permission.

RDA Press LLC
15170 N. Hayden Road
Scottsdale, AZ 85260
480-998-5400

Visit our Web sites: RichDad.com
                     RDAPress.com
                     RichDadAdvisors.com

For more information on Kolbe Corp visit: kolbe.com

Printed in the United States of America

First Edition: May 2017

ISBN: 978-1-937832-87-2

052017

In this book you will learn why going to school
drains the natural entrepreneur out of us.

And more importantly, in this book, you will
learn how to get your spirit back.

We are all entrepreneurs.
We all can build a lemonade stand.

This book is about the differences between
entrepreneurs who build lemonade stands
and entrepreneurs who build
global businesses like Apple and Facebook.

Step 1 To Building a team is establishing a code of honor. This is Vital Because its what keeps The Team together during hard, challenging times, keeps People in line and thinking and acting for whats best for every one. Rules are established for good reason without them discord is sown.

"You can't connect the dots looking forward;
you can only connect them looking backwards.

So you have to trust that the dots will somehow connect in your future.
You have to trust in something—your gut, destiny, life, karma, whatever.

This approach has never let me down,
and it has made all the difference in my life."

— Steve Jobs

Dedication

To the entrepreneurial spirit…
in all of us.

CONTENTS

CONTENTS

PREFACE

Robert Kiyosaki

Many people have million dollar ideas. They believe their new product or service will make them rich and that all their dreams will come true. The problem is, most people do not know how to turn their million-dollar idea into millions of dollars.

Q: Why can't people turn their ideas into millions of dollars?

A: Because most people went to school to learn to be employees, not entrepreneurs.

That's why most people are told, "Go to school and get a job." You never hear, "Go to school and learn to create jobs," which is what successful entrepreneurs do.

Most people go to school to learn to *work for money*, a steady paycheck. Few people *learn to create money*, so that they never need a paycheck. If you read *Rich Dad Poor Dad*, you may recall that rich dad's Lesson #1 is, "The rich don't work for money." Entrepreneurs understand that lesson well and they find ways to put money to work for them and build assets that deliver both cash flow and equity.

David, Goliath and Pee Wee

There are three distinct types of entrepreneurs in the world: Davids, Goliaths, and Pee Wee Hermans.

Goliaths are entrepreneurs like Steve Jobs, founder of Apple, Inc., one of the richest companies in America. Other goliaths are Larry Ellison, founder of Oracle, Henry Ford, founder of the Ford Motor Company, Bill Gates, founder of Microsoft, Thomas Edison, founder of General Electric, Richard Branson founder of Virgin, and Walt Disney founder of The Walt Disney Company.

An important point to keep in mind is that all of these Goliaths started as Pee Wee Hermans.

Another important point is that they were all, once, Davids—Davids who took on Goliaths in a battle for the top spot. The movie *Pirates of Silicon Valley* is about young guns Bill Gates and Steve Jobs taking on the Goliaths, IBM and Xerox. The movie explains how Bill Gates "stole" the PC business from mainframe giant IBM and Steve Jobs "stole" what would become the mouse and the Macintosh from Xerox. *Pirates of Silicon Valley* is a must-see for Pee Wees and Davids, little guys with the courage to take on giants… and, possibly, one day becoming Goliaths themselves.

The story of Richard Branson has a similar theme. Branson, a rock and roll entrepreneur, became David when he had the audacity to take on world airline giant British Airways with his start up company, Virgin Airways. Today, Virgin businesses are "giant killers," going after fat, lazy, bloated, and expensive corporate giants. For example, when Richard saw the "fat" (known as *margins*) in the cell phone business, Virgin Mobile was created. Today, Virgin Mobile is the featured brand at Walmart stores across America and ranks among the top carriers in the United States.

Not all Davids are Goliath killers. Some Pee Wees become Goliaths by inventing products that change the world. For example, Thomas Edison went from Pee Wee to David to Goliath when he invented the electric light bulb, an invention that led to the creation of General Electric.

Mark Zuckerberg started as Pee Wee in his dorm room at Harvard, working on Facebook. He became David when he expanded Facebook from Harvard to other college campuses and then became Goliath when he took Facebook to the world.

Elon Musk went from Pee Wee to David to Goliath when his company SpaceX took on NASA.

Elon then took on the automotive giants like General Motors with his company Tesla, making electric cars sporty and sexy.

Pee Wee Changes the World

You do not have to be a David or Goliath to change the world.

Pee Wees can change the world by being *trim tabs*. In my book *Second Chance*, published in 2015, I wrote about Dr. R. Buckminster Fuller and how he changed my life. If not for Dr. Fuller, or "Bucky" as he was called, there would not be a Rich Dad Company. I would probably still be in the rock and roll business, like Richard Branson, and I would never have become a teacher or an entrepreneur in education.

I had the good fortune to study with Dr. Fuller three times, in the summers of 1981, 1982, and 1983. Dr. Fuller passed away a few weeks after the class I had with him in 1983. His passing inspired me to let go of the rock and roll business and become a *trim tab*, a Pee Wee in the business of education. The Rich Dad Company produced a video titled *The Man Who Could See The Future*, a mini-documentary on the financial crisis, and it is free to anyone who is interested in learning how to see the future and how to solve the economic crisis via financial education. To view this documentary visit: RichDad.com/RDTV

Today, The Rich Dad Company is taking on the old, out-of-date, out-of-touch, and extremely expensive education industry. Our job is not to kill Goliath. Our job is to be a trim tab on the SS Titanic, also known as the education system.

Q: What is a trim tab?

A: A trim tab is a tiny surface on the trailing edge of a larger control surface on a boat or aircraft. A trim tab is like a rudder on the rudder of a ship—and it's how ships are stabilized to stay on course without the operator constantly applying a control force.

Fuller often asked himself, *What can I do? I'm just a little guy...* That was when he decided to become a trim tab. Rather than becoming a Republican or a Democrat and running for political office—hoping to become captain of the ship—he became a trim tab at the back of the ship. A small but strong force that could affect direction and change. In 1927, he became a Pee Wee, a little guy who changed the world. In the video *The Man Who Could See The Future* you will see a few of Fuller's lifetime accomplishments, accomplishments such as the Geodesic Dome at Expo '67, the 1967 World's Fair in Montreal, Canada. You will see how he influenced me to become a Pee Wee, a trim tab in education.

The Rich Dad Company is taking on the school system as "little guys"… as a trim tab that can change the world. That's what entrepreneurs do. Today, the *CASHFLOW* game is played all over the world as a teaching tool that bypasses the school system.

This book is written for anyone who is interested in becoming an entrepreneur and changing the world by being a rich and smart business leader. Whether you take on the big guys or stake your claim to uncharted territory, success as an entrepreneur is not an easy path. It takes strength, commitment, and discipline, and it takes the vision and confidence to surround yourself with a team of smart, experienced, and trustworthy advisors.

I think you'll find, as I have, that your team can be among your greatest assets. And they can make the difference between simply having a million-dollar idea and turning it into a multimillion-dollar business.

PART ONE

Who's On Your Team?

"Business and investing are team sports."

– Rich Dad

INTRODUCTION
Robert Kiyosaki

A few months ago I was talking with my doctor who proudly told me, "I'm a millionaire. I've finally made over a million dollars."

I congratulated him and, since we are close friends, I felt comfortable asking, "How much did you pay in taxes?"

"About $700,000," he replied sheepishly.

"That's a lot of money." I said, choking and gagging.

"Well, how much do you pay in taxes?" he asked. "I know you make more than I do."

"I pay a lot less than $700,000," I replied. "And I do make more than you do. Quite a bit more… yet what I hand over to Uncle Sam is significantly less."

"What do you suggest I do?" he asked.

"Fire your accountant."

Bad Advice

I have had to fire many accountants, attorneys, CEOs, presidents, and other so-called professional advisors over the years. I have had accountants and attorneys from prestigious, big-name firms who were hopeless. So I meant what I said, when I told my doctor, "Fire your accountant."

If you have read my other books, you know I often write about the importance of having a team. In this book you will hear from my team. They are the real deal. The Rich Dad Advisors, along with other entrepreneurs on the Rich Dad team, will share their expertise as well as the successes, challenges and failures, of being an entrepreneur.

My team is much more important than money, because without them, I probably would not have any money.

In this book, my team will *not tell you about what they do.* They will tell you *why* what they do is important. For example, my accountant, Tom Wheelwright, will explain *why* the rich pay much less in taxes, and how you can too. The reason Tom's wisdom is more important than money is because Tom's advice saves me millions of dollars in taxes, legally. Garrett Sutton will do the same on the subject of corporate entities and asset protection.

You may be saying to yourself, *I don't make millions. In fact I don't make very much money. Will this book be any good for me?* The answer is: Absolutely. For many people, the reason they aren't making more money is the same reason they pay more than they need to in taxes— bad advisors and bad advice.

The Most Important Thing

According to many social scientists, the most important thing in life is a person's social and professional network. In other words, the people around you, your team, and the people you work with. If you have poor people around you, you will probably be poor. As the saying goes, "Birds of a feather flock together."

The CASHFLOW Quadrant represents the four different people in the world of business. Remember that there are entrepreneurs found in three of the four quadrants—the S, the B, and the I.

E stands for employee

S stands for self-employed

B stands for big business (500 employees or more)

I stands for investor

My doctor is an entrepreneur in the S quadrant... and S can also stand for specialists, small business, smart, and star, such as professional athletes and movie stars.

Before firing his accountant he asked, "Who should I talk to if I fire my accountant?"

I gave him three names: Tom Wheelwright, my accountant, Garrett Sutton, my attorney, and Ken McElroy, my partner in real estate.

Why do I have to call all three?" he asked.

"Because business is a team sport and they are all part of my team," I replied. "We have been together for years. We have made millions together. I trust them with my life."

"But why three?" asked the doctor.

Because it takes three different advisors to make money, protect what we make from taxes, and protect our money from predators. If not for the three of them, I would be like you, making millions but paying excessive taxes and worried about predators who want steal my wealth through the court system.

"Do you mean lawsuits?" he asked.

I nodded. "Lawsuits and taxes. You see, if you have plans on becoming rich, you need to know how to protect yourself —before you get rich."

My doctor had another question: "Why didn't my accountant give me this advice?"

That really is the million-dollar question, isn't it? And the answer is that I don't know. My friend would have to ask his accountant that question. What I *do* know is that my previous accountants did not really know how to protect my wealth either. They were smart and expensive. When I realized they did not know or understand why I invested in real estate, I let them go. When another accounting firm suggested I sell all my real estate and invest in mutual funds, I fired them immediately. They may have been smart accountants in the E quadrant, but they were not smart accountants in the I quadrant.

In this book, you will learn from my team so you can build your own team. Being an entrepreneur is no big deal. Almost anyone can be an entrepreneur.

There was a young girl in my neighborhood who had a babysitting business. Her parents allowed her to use the family home to take in young children of different ages, in the evenings. Parents would drop their kids off and gladly pay her fee to be able to enjoy an evening without the kids. Once her charges were asleep, the young entrepreneur would do her homework while she made $10 an hour per child. On a Saturday night, her busiest night, with seven kids to watch, she earned $70 per hour, plus tips. Not bad for a 15-year-old girl.

She used her earnings to pay for most of her college tuition and expenses. In other words, she reinvested her money, which made her a richer entrepreneur. I do not know if she paid taxes. That is between her, the tax department, and her conscience.

The point is that anyone can be an entrepreneur. The problem is, very few entrepreneurs become rich entrepreneurs.

Statistics show that most entrepreneurs do not become rich. In fact, many small business owners earn less than their employees. The small business owner earns less because their work continues after the employees go home and they work even when the business is closed. When you calculate the number of hours the small business owner puts in and how much they are paid, many earn less, per hour, than their employees.

A friend, an entrepreneur, recently had a news article written about her. The newspaper stated she made $80,000 a month. I am sure many people gasped at hearing that amount. Later, when I had a coffee with her, I asked, "How much of that $80,000 a month do you keep?" Smiling she said, "None of it. I reinvest every penny of it to grow the business. We survive on my husband's paycheck."

Being an entrepreneur is a 24/7 job. Even when they are not working physically, most are working mentally, or worrying emotionally. Employees can go home, or go on vacation. Most entrepreneurs cannot. I've heard that Bill Gates did not take a day off for eight years while he was starting Microsoft.

I stress this because many employees think being "the boss" is easy. Many employees think they do all the work and the boss has it easy and makes all the money. The reason many employees think the boss is not working as hard as they are is because employees and entrepreneurs do different types of work, work that requires different skills.

Statistics show that the reason nine out of 10 small businesses fail in the first five years is because most employees, even college graduates with advanced degrees such as MBAs, do not possess the essential skills to be entrepreneurs. Making matters worse, of the one in every 10 that does survive the first five years, nine out of 10 fail in the second five years. I know. I have been one of those statistics. I have had far more failures than successes.

I am quite certain that the reason most employees do not become entrepreneurs is because the thought of failing— and of being without a steady paycheck—terrifies them. For those that cannot control that fear, it is best they keep their day job, their benefits, and paid holidays... punching out at 5:00, having dinner, watching TV, enjoying their three-week vacation each year and appreciating the security of being an employee.

What Is an Entrepreneur?

Entrepreneur is a big word that means different things to different people. Barron's publishes a book titled *Finance and Investment Handbook*, and it offers this definition of an entrepreneur:

> *Entrepreneur: a person who takes on the risks of starting a new business. Many entrepreneurs have technical knowledge with which to produce a saleable product or to design a needed new service.*

Nice try Barron's. On the surface their definition is accurate. Yet the word *entrepreneur* runs much deeper. As stated earlier, most entrepreneurs fail in the first five years because they lack the skills that entrepreneurs needs. My neighbor, the young babysitter, has the *technical skills* to be a successful babysitter. For someone her age, she made a lot of money, and put herself through school. But she lacks the entrepreneurial skills to build a business and become a rich entrepreneur, even after she received her college degree. Today, she is a high-paid employee in a large medical corporation.

For those of you who have read my other books, you already know that my rant is that our schools teach young people to become employees, not entrepreneurs. That is why we are all trained to memorize and regurgitate, much like Pavlov's dogs were trained to salivate every time the dinner bell was rung, the admonition, "Go to school and get a job." We are *not* trained to say, "Go to school to start businesses and create jobs."

A young friend of mine recently graduated with a Master's degree in entrepreneurship. He said the many instructors spent a lot of time teaching his class how to prepare a resume… to get a high paying job. Are you kidding? True entrepreneurs do not focus resumes. True entrepreneurs review resumes and hire employees whose resumes reflect the skill sets the team needs.

Different Entrepreneurs

Entrepreneurs come in many, many different shapes, sizes, and styles. Another one of my neighbors is a medical doctor who is in private practice. He is an entrepreneur. Another man, in the same neighborhood, is a medical doctor who quit his job at a large hospital to become an entrepreneur working on a new drug to cure a disease of the brain. He and his wife have been struggling financially for over six years as their new drug goes through the government approval process. Three other neighbors are large real estate developers. Another neighbor is a real estate broker who does not develop real estate, but sells it. She is an entrepreneur and owns a medium-sized real estate brokerage. Two other neighbors own professional sports teams, baseball and basketball. They are sports entrepreneurs who employ professional athletes and coaches, paying some of the athletes millions of dollars each year. A few of my neighbors are the coaches of these teams, employees hired by the sports entrepreneurs.

Artists tend to be entrepreneurs. Many artists are professional painters, musicians, and actors. The Beatles were entrepreneurs who earned fortunes in the world of music.

Many choose the path of entrepreneurs because they hate being employees. They want to be their own boss, they want to do their own thing, and they do not like being told what to do. Many became entrepreneurs because they cannot get or keep a job.

There are many people who are called "serial entrepreneurs." They start a business and sell it. They start another business and sell it. They are much like people who flip real estate, buying real estate properties only to re-sell them as quickly as possible.

And a few entrepreneurs become entrepreneurs to change the world. I put Henry Ford, Thomas Edison, Walt Disney, Steve Jobs, Bill Gates, Oprah Winfrey, Sergey Brin, Jeff Bezos, Richard Branson, and Mark Zuckerberg in this category. Their impact on the world will last for decades.

Related to this book, it is important to point out that Henry Ford, Walt Disney, Thomas Edison, Steve Jobs, Bill Gates, Oprah Winfrey, Mark Zuckerberg, and Richard Branson did not finish school. These entrepreneurs may not have finished school because they did not want to "go school to get a job." They wanted to become entrepreneurs who changed the world, and they have.

Are We Born Entrepreneurs?

The question many people ask is, "Are people born entrepreneurs or are entrepreneurs created?"

I believe we are all born entrepreneurs. That is why I began this chapter with the story of the high-school girl with her own baby-sitting business. We have all seen kids with lemonade stands or out selling Girl Scout cookies. Anyone can be an entrepreneur—young or old, the highly educated or academic drop-outs.

During the Agrarian Age, most farmers were entrepreneurs. They had a small plot of land, tilled it, planted it, harvested the crops, and fed their families. What they didn't consume was sold.

Then came the Industrial Age. Millions of farmers left the farm, moved into cities where the factories were, and became employees.

Today, our schools continue to train young people to be employees. The problem is, we are now in the Information Age and technology is replacing employees. When employees go on strike and demand higher wages, jobs move overseas to lower-wage countries or a new technology replaces the employee. The buzz about the "rise of robots" is real. In our supermarkets today, checkout clerks are being replaced by automated check-out stations.

With the idea of job security for life threatened, being an entrepreneur is the hot new profession. Many forecasters predict that the S&P 500 will be downsized to S&P 300, because new entrepreneurs will make 200 of today's 500 companies obsolete. This means more unemployment for millions of employees who found a job with the wrong company.

You may remember that it was Steven Sasson, an employee of Eastman Kodak, who invented digital photography in 1974. Less than four decades later, in 2012, Kodak—a 131-year-old company—filed for bankruptcy protection. It was their own technology that put them out of business, costing thousands of Kodak employees their jobs.

Today, the mantra of "Go to school to get a safe, secure job" is an obsolete idea. Technology and global competition will one day make all of us, as employees, obsolete. That may be why many college dorms all across the world are "incubators" for student entrepreneurs, hoping to create the next Facebook, the next new thing… the next business that will change the world. The problem is: Most entrepreneurs, even if they get a business off the ground, will never become rich.

The facts are that most entrepreneurs are not much different than an employee, living paycheck to paycheck. The challenge is becoming a rich entrepreneur.

Ask Entrepreneurs

The following is an excerpt from *Forbes* magazine about the importance of a college education and being an entrepreneur:

> *"While 69% of business owners surveyed had attended college (well above the national average), only 68% of this college grad group said they believed this education made a difference in their success. Compare that to 86% of the general population who believe college remains a good investment – albeit an increasingly expensive one. Only 61% of all business owners felt a college education was very or somewhat important for success in today's economy – a number that stands in stark contrast to the general public sentiment on the value of a college degree."*

Translation: If you are going to be an employee or self-employed doctor or lawyer, traditional education is important.

Taxicab Entrepreneur

In 1907, Harry N. Allen, entrepreneur and founder of The New York Taxicab Company, imported 600 gas-powered taxicabs from France. He was the person who coined the word *taxicab*, and millions became entrepreneurs known as *taxicab drivers*.

Today, *Uber* is the word replacing *taxi,* and many independent entrepreneurs are becoming Uber drivers.

The question is, how long will it be before taxi drivers *and* Uber drivers become obsolete? How long before innovations like the Google self-driving car, a car that does not require a human driver, replace both Uber drivers and taxi drivers?

In 2014, I attended a reunion of fellow Marine Corps pilots in Pensacola, Florida. Pensacola is where we went through pilot training, in the 1970s before going on to Vietnam, and we all served in the same squadron. Not surprisingly, the discussion amongst old pilots and new pilots centered on the question, "Do we need pilots?" Many of the new pilots are learning to pilot *drones*, not *planes*.

If the Google car can replace the need for Uber drivers, can drones replace the need for pilots? As a former pilot, I know that today's pilots are doing less and less flying. Today, modern planes can take off, fly, and land without the need of human pilots. Human pilots are back-up pilots, only there to keep the passengers feeling safe, just in case technology fails.

In the world of medicine, robots are capable of doing a better job in the operating room than human surgeons.

We should be asking ourselves: *Who else will be replaced?*

Why Become an Entrepreneur?

These are a few examples of why more and more people are becoming entrepreneurs. Technology and foreign competition are making people obsolete. The ideas of a high-paying job and a paycheck for life are very old—and obsolete—ideas.

Today, millions are realizing that being an entrepreneur may be safer than being an employee.

Andy Grove, one of the founders and CEO of Intel Corporation, is known for his guiding motto "only the paranoid survive." This book is written for those who are paranoid, those who are dedicated to growing smarter, and those wanting to grow richer as entrepreneurs.

During the Industrial Age, entrepreneurs were known for creating jobs and business. In the Information Age, entrepreneurs are known for destroying jobs and businesses.

One example is the book industry. When *Rich Dad Poor Dad* was first published in 1997, the bricks and mortar book business was thriving. Then came Amazon and many Industrial-Age bookstores, like Borders, disappeared.

A few days ago, I was in a food market, and one of the people stocking groceries stopped me and asked, "Do you remember me?" When it was obvious that I didn't, she said, "I was the manager of the Borders near your home. I use to set up all your speaking engagements and book signings."

The conversation broke my heart. I did my best to stay cheerful and thank him for all he did for my books, my business, and me. As we talked about old times, Andy Grove's mantra—"only the paranoid survive"—kept echoing in my brain.

Again, entrepreneurs are not creating jobs. Today, entrepreneurs are destroying jobs and businesses at high speed.

The problem is that our schools are still training students to be employees who look for job security, rather than entrepreneurs seeking financial security.

The good news is schools are now offering courses on entrepreneurship. While I applaud their efforts, I am afraid schools still have employees attempting to teach students to be entrepreneurs. That would be like learning how to surf or play golf by reading a book. If you have never been "wiped out" by a giant wave, how would you know what it feels like, as an entrepreneur, to have your business "wiped-out" by the competition?

Simply said, *employees* see the world through the mindset of employees. *Entrepreneurs* see the world through a different set of eyes. This book is about seeing the world through the eyes of real entrepreneurs.

One of my favorite quotes by Steve Jobs is presented at the opening of this book. It is a powerful insight that merits repeating:

> *You can't connect the dots looking forward; you can only connect them looking backwards. So you have to trust that the dots will somehow connect in your future. You have to trust in something – your gut, destiny, life, karma, whatever. This approach has never let me down, and it has made all the difference in my life."*

Most people fail to become entrepreneurs because they went to school, and learned to drive through life, looking in the rear view mirror. Entrepreneurs can see the future.

Real Entrepreneurs

Kim, my wife and business partner, is the real deal when it comes to being a real estate entrepreneur. She and our Advisors have all contributed to this book—because it's the team we've created, at The Rich Dad Company and with our personal investments, that has been the foundation for our success. Our Advisors are real entrepreneurs who are in the trenches. They are seasoned and successful and passionate about teaching they've learned. Kim and I thank them for their contributions to this book.

The entrepreneurs in this book share their successes and, perhaps more importantly, their mistakes—and how their mistakes became priceless lessons. While a college education can be important, nothing replaces real world business experience as the best teacher.

One of the problems with traditional education is that our schools still believe making mistakes is bad. Traditional teachers punish students for making mistakes, which means the person who makes the fewest mistakes is the labeled the smartest student.

In the real world of entrepreneurship, the entrepreneur that makes the most mistakes and learns from their mistakes win. For example, Thomas Edison failed over 1000 times before inventing the electric light bulb. Henry Ford went bankrupt five times before the Ford Motor Company succeeded. Steve Jobs was fired from his own company, Apple, before he came back and rescued it from bankruptcy. Today, Apple is one of the richest companies in the world. Bill Gates was charged by the U.S. government for monopolistic practices and won. And Mark Zuckerberg, was sued by the Winkelvoss twins, who claimed they created Facebook.

I mention the trials and tribulations of these giant entrepreneurs because this is what real entrepreneurs go through. They can be the lessons that determine the future of a business—if we look for the lesson in every mistake or failure.

In this book, you will learn what is important, what is valuable, and what you may need to learn to be an successful entrepreneur. Most important of all, you'll learn why having a "great idea" is only the beginning...

Team Code of Honor

Blair Singer

We watch it on Sunday afternoon. We read about it in amazing stories of valor and accomplishment. We wear the jerseys of our favorites. It's the magical dynamic of a group of committed individuals who come together to produce something extraordinary and even unpredictable on a given day. We call it championship team play.

For many, it is something that they only hear about, but never experience. But for any successful entrepreneur, second to sales, the ability to recruit and build a championship team is the most important skill to master in order to bring your idea or dream to life and success.

Why is it critical? By the mere fact that you only have a limited amount of time, energy and resource to do things yourself, you need a team to be able to deliver a promise to a waiting public. But more than that, there is a magical synergy that happens on great teams that over deliver and create results beyond expectations again and again. Dr. Buckminster Fuller defined synergy as whole systems "unpredictable" by the sum of its parts.

Building a great team in business is not something that happens by luck. It also is not just the "perfect" mix of talent and personal chemistry. Herb Brooks, the legendary coach of the 1980 U.S. winter Olympic hockey team told his young players that they did not have enough talent to win on talent alone. Yet they beat the world's best in Lake Placid that year. It is something that can be created with inspired leadership and some very definitive steps.

For the last 25-plus years I have built my own business teams in the trucking business, teaching business, franchising, licensing business and have been part of some great teams. I have also coached thousands of organizations to build their teams. Companies as large as Singapore Airlines, L'Oreal, HSBC, and IBM to small businesses of 5 to ten people. In all cases, the principles of successful teams remains the same.

The first step is to make sure you are clear on your definition of "team." For some, team is family, for others, a group that takes on a common goal, for others it entails a level of transparency and honesty that many do not even experience in their primary relationships. There is no right or wrong definition. It is important however that all members are on the same page.

To make this simple… let's boil it down to a few key steps:

Recruiting

Recruiting is the promise that attracts the right players to the team. And in order to do that there's an important first step: Get clear on the mission. What is it you are trying to achieve—and why? Probably the *why* is the most important. Years ago Robert introduced us to one of his friends, a retired General in the Marine Corp.

He was fascinating to talk with, especially because he had been in charge of recruiting for the Marines.

He stressed one of the most important things about building teams. He said that the Marine Corp pay scale is very low. So clearly new recruits do not come for money. He said they enlist because of *who they hope to become* in the process of becoming a Marine.

He said that young recruits want to be part of something bigger than themselves.

Now think about that for a moment. There are no promises and no money. Only the desire to grow and BE part of something significant.

As a business owner, can you make that same offer? That is why I say that your number one skill is the ability to sell. Without that, you will find it difficult to inspire people to work for you or with you for the right reasons. Think about a franchise. Franchisees actually pay to be part of a team.

As an undergraduate attending Ohio State University, I had the privilege of being a student manager for the Ohio State Buckeye football team under the leadership of legendary coach Woody Hayes. It was there that I learned the importance of discipline, hard work, selfless team play, and playing for something bigger than a trophy. Most players on the team knew they would not play at a professional level, but they wanted to be "part of something."

In my first trucking business, we were not the highest-paying employer, but we had minimal employee turnover and an amazing team who pulled our business from the brink of disaster time and time again and helped us become one of the fastest-growing air freight trucking operations of its kind at the time.

As captain of a high school cross country team that was in contention for a state championship, our mantra was to "stay together and push each other." If you know anything about cross country running, you know that one or two superstars will not win it for you. We prided ourselves on running together close to the front of the pack. That is how we won. Every day we asked, "What kind of a team would we have to become to run in the state championships?"

The Code

I learned a long time ago and from watching Coach Hayes that all great teams have one thing in common. As a matter of fact, this is true of any great business, religion, civilization, or family.

The ones who last and who succeed have rules. A simple, understandable set of rules that we call a Code of Honor.

It is a set of rules that take the core values of any group— values like hard work, honesty, accountability, and team play—and protect them with a set rules. Think of the Ten Commandments.

That is a classic Code of Honor. It was designed to take a group of wandering Israelites and keep them together and strong as a culture.

In a business or a marriage, when the rules are ignored or not enforced, chaos and disorder soon follow. Coach Hayes would go ballistic if a player broke curfew, was late to practice, swore on the practice field, disrespected a coach, or failed a class. The Code held the team together. Every player wanted to be their best and Coach Hayes' promise was that if you followed his rules you would become your best.

The first thing we do when we start a company or when we coach a company, is to establish a Code of Honor. Why? Because in the absence of rules, people make up their own rules.

And when the heat goes up, people revert to their instinctive behavioral patterns… and, most of the time, that is not good for the team. It's not because they are bad people, it's because everyone has their own experiences, backgrounds, and conditioning.

In school, we are taught to do things on our own. Not great for team play. Cooperation in school is considered cheating, but in business collaboration is often the key to success. I was taught to be a strong individual and someone who did not have to ask for help or support. That won't work if you are trying to get a whole group to pull together. That is why you have to have rules.

As a Rich Dad Advisor team, we have a Code of Honor that we all subscribe to. In our own individual businesses, we have different rules because we have different teams. My wife and I have a Code. We have a Code for our kids and family. I have a Code for myself. Why?

In 2012, my 16-year-old son and I went to Tanzania to climb Mt. Kilimanjaro. The first night on the mountain my son got very sick. The next day, though he tried to move on, he got worse. He could no longer hold anything in his system. It was clear he had to descend and find a doctor. I was faced with a decision. Take him down or let one of the porters take him down. I wanted so badly to climb that mountain! The oxygen was low, my emotion was high, and my intelligence was low. That is a bad combination, but not unlike lots of situations we face in business and relationships.

Yet in the middle of that decision, one thought shot through my mind. It was, *I wrote a book about this!* It's called *Team Code of Honor.* And the first rule he and I had created before embarking was, "We start together, we finish together." Our Code was clear: Never abandon a teammate in need. Decision made; I took him down.

Without those rules, I might have made a catastrophically bad decision at 10,000 feet. I operate by a Code to protect me from myself!

After an eight-hour decent, he laid in a questionable third-world clinic with me lying next him until he recovered. It cemented our father-son relationship forever. So much so that he decided to go back the next year and on July 3, 2013 at

11:27 on a glorious morning, he and I hit the summit of Kili together. I handed him a key chain with a pendant that I had been carrying the whole way that said,

"We start together, we finish together.
I will always have your back."
– Dad

I learned that there was something bigger and more powerful than a mountain. It's called love. And luckily we had created a rule to protect it. Believe it or not, other families on other expeditions did not make those decisions and it ripped them apart.

Performance

One of the rules of teams is this: The higher the performance, the tighter the tolerances—and the rules. Championship teams call it pretty tightly. They leave little room for weaseling out of responsibility. Once rules are in place, everyone on the team has to play by them and everyone has the responsibility to enforce them. This is not always easy. It can be uncomfortable. That is why we have to work on Little Voice Mastery—that little voice in our heads that's constantly second-guessing and chattering about what we can and cannot do.

I have seen many teams that wanted high performance results, but operated with loose tolerances and wondered why they did not achieve their expectations. It's like trying to tune a Lamborghini the same way you would tune a Vespa.
I can also give countless stories of businesses and teams where the true courage was not in taking on the task at hand, but in being vulnerable and open to other team members. Being able to tell the truth with compassion and receive feedback in order to make the team better are critical to the success of a team.

It's Not about the Summit

I have now summited Kilimanjaro several times. Each time the challenge is how to take ordinary people (non-climbers from all walks of life) and forge them into a team that supports one other to become the best they can be, exceed their own perceived limitations, and take them to 19,341 feet. Here is what I have learned:

Enjoy the Process

There are two parts to every team goal: the preparation and the task itself. As a leader, you teach your team to love both parts and to **enjoy the whole process**. When climbing Kili anything can happen. You could twist your ankle. The weather may shift. If you were only focused on the summit you will be severely disappointed and energy can drop precipitously.

Celebrate all Wins

But if you **celebrated all the wins** along the way, there is no way to lose. Those who only focused on the Summit worked hard, but did not enjoy it as much. As a matter of fact, they became more fatigued than the rest of us. They did not have the energy of daily wins to push them on. They only had a Little Voice worrying about the end result.

Stay Focused

It's important to **remove extraneous distractions and keep your team focused.** On Kili we had over 60 porters carrying our gear, preparing the campsites, cooking, and breaking camp. All we had to do was focus on climbing. The most powerful team lesson on Kili is something I have taken onto every team in my life...

It's one step at a time. One breath at a time.

Don't look up at the summit. It can intimidate you. Stay focused on what is happening right now. We were not allowed to ask about what would happen tomorrow or the next day. The result was five and a half days of being 100% present. Our minds were quiet. Our intentions were focused. We were in the zone.

Before every championship or Super Bowl game, the interviews with the competing teams are always the same. When asked about how they feel about playing in the biggest game of all, they always say: "We aren't worried about that. We are just playing one play at a time, doing our best, making corrections, and at the end hopefully we have a great outcome." This is the language of champions.

In business, you set the goals, do the work, and take it one step at a time. Break it down to manageable parts. As a leader you must keep your team in that zone. If you do, before you know it, you have reached the summit.

There is another (very similar) thing that all champion teams say after they win or achieve their goal. When asked how or why they did it, they rarely say it was for the trophy. They say they did it for each other. A great championship team, particularly in the face of adversity, comes together to support each other… committed to not let the other person down.

The night before we summited Kili, the whole team shared that they were a bit sad that we were going to summit the next day. Why? Because we knew that after summiting, the journey would be nearly over. Everyone wanted it to go on because of the wins and incredible lessons we were all getting and the amazing depth of the relationships we were building.

Great teams do not happen by accident. And it's not about the summit. The purpose of a team goal, is to keep the team moving, learning, and growing together. And a Team Code of Honor is the foundation for that. The true wins and gifts come along the way if you are paying attention to them. If you can move your team in this way, nobody will ever stop you.

The B-I Triangle:
The 8 Integrities of a Business

Robert Kiyosaki

Mission | Leadership | Team
Product | Legal | Systems | Communications | Cash Flow

"I have a great idea!"

Great. We all have them. It's what we *do* with them that will determine if this "great idea" can make it in a highly competitive marketplace. As the Preface of this book stated, many of us have had a million dollar idea. The problem is that most of us do not know how to turn that million-dollar idea into a million dollars.

That is precisely why the diagram that my rich dad called the B-I Triangle is important. The B—in B-I—stands for Business owner, and the I stands for professional Investor. True entrepreneurs "live" on the right side of the CASHFLOW Quadrant pictured on the next page.

When an entrepreneur "builds a business," what they build is a B-I Triangle, or a system of systems. My rich dad called these eight components the 8 Integrities of a Business.

If the entrepreneur cannot put these 8 integrities together, the business fails or suffers financially. And if any of these components are weak or dysfunctional, the business is likely to struggle or fail. That's how important the components of the B-I Triangle are.

This book will teach you how to put together these 8 critical components of a business—and the team that will take your million-dollar idea into a million-dollar money-maker. One reason why most entrepreneurs fail, even those with genuine, million-dollar ideas, is because all they have is top of the triangle. Most are missing one or more of the other integrities.

Notice that the Product, or the "great idea," is the least important part of the B-I Triangle.

Why Many Entrepreneurs Fail

One reason why most entrepreneurs fail, even those who did well in school, is because schools teach us to be *specialists* or *experts* in only one of the integrities. For example, a person who graduates from law school is well educated in the Legal integrity of the triangle. They are not experts in the other integrities, although most lawyers believe they are.

Another example is the bottom line of the inside section of the Triangle—the Cash Flow line. Most accountants are trained for his line in the Triangle. They may be great accountants, but most are not good at the other seven integrities.

If an accountant is in charge of the business, and when the business has "cash flow problems," the accountant will often "cut back" or "downsize." The accountant will often cut back on the Communications line, cutting funds for advertising, marketing, and sales teams. Often, this causes the business to fail faster.

In many instances, if a business is having cash flow problems, rather than cut back on spending, the smarter move would be to spend more on sales, marketing, and advertising.

In other words, the reason so many entrepreneurs fail is because their education trained them to be *specialists*, employees on only one of the eight integrities.

To be a successful entrepreneur, the entrepreneur must think like a *generalist,* looking at all 8 integrities, the big picture, the whole business, not just their specialty.

This is what makes this book different. Rather than learn from just one entrepreneur you will be learn from many entrepreneurs who are specialists from all 8 Integrities of a Business. My team.

To be a great entrepreneur means I need to have a great team. Today our team consists of 8 Rich Dad Advisors as well as members of The Rich Dad Company team who are both skilled and experienced in specific components of the B-I Triangle. What they all have in common is a commitment to the mission of The Rich Dad Company and the fact that they all place a high value on education and life-long learning. We meet often, we study books together and discuss what the author is saying and how we can apply those lessons to our lives, our businesses, and our teams.

Part Two of this book will feature Profiles of Kim, Ken, Blair, Garrett, Tom, Andy, Josh, Lisa, and Darren. In Part Three, we'll focus on Mastering the B-I Triangle and that section includes sections on all 8 of the Integrities of a Business, those critical elements that make up the B-I Triangle. Mike, Shane, and Mona (as well as Kim, Garrett and Tom) have contributed to Part Three with very targeted sections related to the components of the B-I Triangle that they support and strengthen. They all contribute specific—and essential—talents and skills.

The old adage that you're only as strong as your weakest link certainly applies here. We have all heard the abysmal stats on new business failures and, in my experience, the challenges a business faces are directly related to the B-I Triangle. If any of the components is missing—or weak—it can seal the fate of the business.

Rich Dad's Team

When I was a little boy, my rich dad would invite his son and me to sit in on his Saturday morning meeting with his business team. Sitting around the table were his attorneys, accountants, bankers, managers, executives, and other team members essential to his business.

By the age of 10, I realized business, especially entrepreneurship, was a team sport. You do not have to be the smartest person to be a smart and rich entrepreneur. In fact, rich dad often said, "If you're the smartest person on your team, your team's in trouble."

That's what this book is about. It is written as a guide to assist you in building your own team of smart and rich entrepreneurs.

Change is a fact of life in today's fast-paced world. What worked yesterday, may not cut it today. And a product or service that was in high demand today… may be obsolete tomorrow.

With that thought, here is a quote from Alvin Toffler, that sets the stage for Part Two of this book…

> *"The illiterate of the 21st century*
> *will not be those who cannot read and write,*
> *but those who cannot learn, unlearn, and relearn"*

> *— Alvin Toffler,*
> *American writer and futurist*

In Part Two you'll find Q&A-style Entrepreneur Profiles of all the contributors to this book. The questions were created to give you personal insights into our backgrounds and personalities. You'll see that some were "A students"… while others struggled through school. You'll also find, I think, lots of common ground: How we all view mistakes as opportunities to learn and how frustrated we are with the traditional school system and how poorly it prepares people for the real world.

I believe that each of us has talents and strengths—special gifts that make us unique. You'll find our Kolbe Index charts included in our Entrepreneur Profiles because that assessment tool has helped us identify our natural strengths, as individuals and as a team, so we can leverage those assets.

PART TWO

Real-Life Entrepreneurs

*"If you're the smartest person on your team,
your team's in trouble."*

– Rich Dad

Robert Kiyosaki

Personal Background and Entrepreneur Profile

Name   Robert T. Kiyosaki
Date of Birth   April 8, 1947
Place of Birth Honolulu, Hawaii

Traditional Education

U.S. Merchant Marine Academy at Kings Point, New York
Degree: Bachelor of Science

Professional Education

3rd Mate's License – any ocean, any tonnage, specializing in oil
tanker operations
Marine Corps pilot – single engine fixed wing and helicopter
gunships

Grade Point Averages

High School: 1.8
College: 2.01

Value of traditional education… relative to becoming an entrepreneur

Not very valuable

Subject I liked most in school

English – because I had a great teacher, Dr. A.A. Norton
(and, ironically, I flunked out of high school with an F in… English)

Subject I hated most in school

Eighty percent of what I was taught in school was a waste of time.

First entrepreneurial project

Making nickels, dimes, and quarters out of old toothpaste tubes at age nine. (Venture was aborted when I found out what *counterfeiting* meant.)

The key entrepreneurial skill I was *not* taught in school

Collaboration and cooperation... in school it's called *cheating*

Why and when I became an entrepreneur and my first major venture

I became an entrepreneur just to find out if I could be like my rich dad, rather than an employee like my poor dad.

I knew I could be a high-paid employee—sailing oil tankers for Standard Oil, or as a pilot flying for the airlines, or climbing the corporate ladder at Xerox. I found out I hated being an employee in a big corporation. I wanted my freedom more than job security.

I did not know if I could become a rich entrepreneur, and I wanted to find out if I could make it. I wanted the challenge.

My first major venture was bringing to market the first nylon and Velcro® surfer wallets in 1977. The name of our company was Rippers and we were based in Honolulu, Hawaii. We manufactured our products in Korea and Taiwan, and warehoused and distributed from New York. In 1978, Rippers was voted the #1 new product in the sporting goods industry.

Rippers then began producing products for the Rock 'n' Roll industry. Rippers produced hats, wallets, and bags for bands like Pink Floyd, Duran Duran, Boy George, Iron Maiden, Ted Nugent, and The Police.

Rippers went up like a rocket in 1978 and came crashing down in 1981. We were not able to handle—or finance—our success.

Best Lesson from first business

I learned I had a lot to learn. I knew I could thrive as an employee, sailing oil tankers or flying for the airlines. I wanted to give up as an entrepreneur, go back to school for my Masters degree, get a job and a paycheck.

It was my rich dad who encouraged me to keep going. He reminded me that most great entrepreneurs failed many times. For example, Henry Ford went bankrupt five times. He reminded me that failure is the path to success and that making mistakes is how we learn.

Rich dad also said, "School is important. The problem is that in school you're taught not to make mistakes. In the real world, if you don't make mistakes you don't learn. Getting a job is good, if you need a paycheck. The problem is you're fired if you make mistakes. So you receive a paycheck, but you don't learn much."

Rather than go back to school and get a job, rich dad recommended I go back to the wreckage of my business, write down every mistake I made, learn from my mistakes, and rebuild the business. It was by facing my creditors, investors, and fears—learning rather than defending, and taking the feedback—that I became a better entrepreneur. Today, I continue to fail, take feedback as it comes in, learn, and grow richer because I am constantly learning from my mistakes.

The best lesson was to learn to have faith in myself.

What I learned about myself from my Kolbe Index

ROBERT KIYOSAKI
Kolbe A™ Index Result

CONGRATULATIONS ROBERT
You Got a Perfect Score on the Kolbe A™ Index

You are terrific at stepping into tough situations and concocting daring solutions, making the seemingly impossible, possible. You lead the way out of dilemmas as you blaze uncharted trails and improvise inventions until you get them working.

Kolbe Action Modes®

Fact Finder   Follow Thru   Quick Start   Implementor

2   2   6   9

©1997-2017 Kathy Kolbe All rights reserved

Reprinted with permission from Kolbe Corp.

My Kolbe explained to me why I did not do well in school. Traditional education is designed for Fact Finders and Follow Thrus. As you can see from my chart, I am a Quick Start… which means I become bored easily.

I am also an Implementor, which means I learn by doing, rather than by reading or lecture. After my Kolbe assessment was done, I understood why my career in traditional education began going down hill in the first grade, the year they took away the wooden blocks.

I learned from my Kolbe that my "genius" is to simplify. Today, I take the complex and make it simple. That is why *Rich Dad Poor Dad* was a success. It took complex financial concepts and made them simple.

Traditional education takes the simple and makes it complex. Traditional education takes a simple 1+2=3 and turns it into calculus. One reason why so many smart people are not rich is because they take complex things and make them more complex. They think complexity makes them smart. Unfortunately, complexity makes them poor.

Today, The Rich Dad Company continues to make the complex simple. That is why we are a rich company.

We use the Kolbe Index at Rich Dad to make sure we have the right people in the right jobs, using their natural strengths.

My role in the B-I Triangle

Contribution to the Mission, Team and Leadership comes from the Communication line. My job is to clarify the Rich Dad message to our customers as well as our employees in support of our Mission.

Skills that are essential for entrepreneurs—but not taught in schools

The power of making mistakes. Our schools punish students for making mistakes. Hence, many young people leave school thinking they are stupid, because they have made too many mistakes.

The same is true in corporate America. The employee who makes the most mistakes is usually fired.

In the world of entrepreneurs, the entrepreneur who makes the most mistakes—and learns from his or her mistakes—is richest and most successful. Entrepreneurs who make mistakes and pretend they don't make mistakes are soon bankrupt or poor.

When I look at the Cone of Learning, the second line from the top is the most important: Simulating the Real Experience.

Cone of Learning

After 2 weeks we tend to remember		Nature of Involvement
90% of what we say and do	Doing the Real Thing	
	Simulating the Real Experience	Active
	Doing a Dramatic Presentation	
70% of what we say	Giving a Talk	
	Participating in a Discussion	
50% of what we hear and see	Seeing it Done on Location	
	Watching a Demonstration	
	Looking at an Exhibit Watching a Demonstration	Passive
	Watching a Movie	
30% of what we see	Looking at Pictures	
20% of what we hear	Hearing Words	
10% of what we read	Reading	

Source: Cone of Learning adapted from (Dale, 1969)

It is through simulations that a person learns from mistakes. Simulations in sports are known as practice. Simulations in arts and entertainment are known as rehearsals.

Every successful person spends far more time at the second line of the Cone of Learning than at the top line, doing the real thing. For example, every professional golfer has practiced putting many more times than he or she putts in tournaments.

When I was nine, my rich dad began teaching me about money playing the game of *Monopoly*®. We played that game for hours and hours. Today, most of my wealth is in the I quadrant, where I continue to play *Monopoly* in real life.

Playing *Monopoly* and doing real things inspired me to be a life-long learner. I was interested in learning from teachers who did the real thing, teachers whose experience earned my respect and inspired me to learn more.

This is why Kim and I and our team of Rich Dad Advisors have 3-day Advisor seminars twice a year, learning from people who do the real thing and practice what they teach.

My Most Important Lesson for Entrepreneurs
Bad partnerships lead to finding great partners.

How I learned to raise capital
One word: desperation. I was out of money and needed to learn—fast.

How I learned to overcome fear and failure
I fought failure and fear of failure… with failure. "Fail faster," rich dad told me. We all learn from our failures if we look for the lessons they can teach us.

My personal strength
I am mission driven. At military school and in the Marine Corps, I learned the spiritual power of mission. In Vietnam, I learned the importance of having a team with the same mission. Having a strong mission helped me to overcome my laziness and made me a stronger member of the team.

My personal weakness
I am lazy. My laziness is one reason why I went to military school in New York. I needed the discipline and a system that forced me to study.

The Entrepreneurial Skills I Teach best
Marketing, branding, and positioning

The Entrepreneurial Lesson I Teach
Building a Business into a Brand

Building a Business into a Brand
by Robert Kiyosaki

"If you are not a brand...you are a commodity.
If you are a commodity, then price is everything
and the low-cost producer is the winner."

– Ancient Wisdom

A brand can be far more valuable than a business. For example, the trademark Coca-Cola is more valuable than all of the company's physical plants, equipment, and real estate used to produce Coca-Cola products for the world. I have heard estimates that the Coke trademark alone is worth an estimated $90 billion to $120 billion. That means the Coca-Cola Company could be paid $90 billion to $120 billion... just for its name.

Take a moment and think about the brands in your life. What brand of cell phone do you use and why? Probing further, ask yourself:

- What is your favorite make of car?
- Do you have a favorite fashion designer?
- A favorite hotel chain?
- Favorite restaurant?
- What TV programs do you watch?

If someone asked you, "What's the name of a fast food restaurant?" what brand would come to mind? What about these questions?

"Let's talk over a cup of coffee. Where do you want to go?"
"Where do you want to go to on your next vacation?"
"What is the best university in the world?"

Whatever business or brand you responded with, that business has done a great job of putting their name in the front of your brain.

Years ago, I read a great book titled *Positioning: The Battle for Your Mind,* by Jack Trout and Al Reis. Although it is an older, pre-Internet, Industrial-Age book, its message is as true today as it was 40 years ago. Positioning is about the battle to be number one in your customer's mind. If you are not number one, then you do not exist. Think about this:

Who was the first person to fly solo across the Atlantic? Charles Lindberg in 1927.

Who was number two? Who cares?

Today, positioning—the battle for the number-one spot—is also known as SEO, search engine optimization.

And today, even terrorists have brands. Hundreds of years ago there was a Hun named Attila. He spread fear throughout the world. There was also Genghis Khan, who invaded Europe using terror as his weapon. His fearful victims were faced with two choices: fight or flight.

Brands have impacted my life for years. During the Vietnam War, I had to decide which branch of service to join. There were five basic choices: Army, Air Force, Navy, Marines, and Coast Guard. Once I knew I was going to Vietnam, I chose the Marines. Joining the Marines was not a spur of the moment decision. The Marines had been branding me since I was a kid. My friends and I knew the Marines were the toughest. When we played war games with toy guns, we all wanted to be Marines.

The Marine Corps hymn is an essential component of their brand. Every time I heard it, I wanted to sign up.

The lyrics are:

From the Halls of Montezuma
To the shores of Tripoli;
We fight our country's battles
In the air, on land, and sea;

First to fight for right and freedom
And to keep our honor clean;
We are proud to claim the title
Of United States Marine.

It is the oldest official song of all the U.S. armed services.

The Marine Corps uniform is another component of the brand. If you see Marine Corps recruiting posters, Marine dress blues are often the focal point of the ad. The Marine Hymn and dress uniform deliver the same focused brand message. When it came time to choose a branch of service, the choice was easy. I had already been branded.

Brands are powerful in combat. When I was in Vietnam, the brand "Viet Cong" struck fear in our hearts. Today al Qaeda and ISIS, are brands that strike fear in hearts and minds all over the world.

Returning from Vietnam and entering the civilian world, I applied for jobs at IBM or Xerox. Although there were other office product companies, such as 3M and Kodak, IBM and Xerox were tied for first place in my mind. Since 3M and Kodak did not exist in my mind, I walked right past them at the job fairs.

I chose to work for the Xerox Corporation because I liked the corporate recruiters who were doing the interviews. IBM recruiters were stiff, boring, dressed in blue suits, white shirts, and red ties. The Xerox recruiters wore more fashionable suits and ties. They were loud, hip, and offered me a beer when I sat down for an interview. Guess which company I chose?

Brand Lesson

*Your clothing, appearance, and personality are important
components of your brand. Just as uniforms are important
for the Marines, the same is true in the business world.
For example, when you go into a McDonald's, all employees
wear McDonald's uniforms. Big corporations like
Xerox and IBM have dress codes for their executives.*

Entrepreneurs like Steve Jobs and Bill Gates have their own styles. They are instantly recognizable. The same is true for Donald Trump, Mark Cuban, Mark Zuckerberg, and of course Oprah. They personify their brands.

I am not able to recall the names or faces of Fortune 500 CEOs. They just don't come to mind. Yet, when asked who my favorite entrepreneurial CEO is, many people come to mind. For example, I can easily picture Steve Jobs, Mark Zuckerberg, Donald Trump, and Jeff Bezos. That is another example of the power of a brand.

Brands Becomes Words

A brand can be so powerful that it can become part of our vocabulary. In other words, a brand can become a word used in everyday conversation to identify a type of product.

During the 1970s, the Xerox brand was so strong that Xerox launched a nationwide campaign asking people to stop saying, "Xerox this." Instead, they were asking the public to say, "copy this." The company was afraid the Xerox trademark would enter the public domain and no longer retain a legal position as a brand or trademark.

The same is true with the Kleenex brand. Millions of people ask for a "Kleenex" rather than "a tissue." Google is in a similar position today. Rather than say, "Search for it," people say, "Google it." Those are powerful brands with powerful brand equity.

How Do You Create a Brand?

The original concept of brands comes from the cattle industry. When ranches and farm land was unfenced, open and free, the only way ranchers could tell their cattle from their competitors' was to brand their cattle. The same is true today in the open range of cyberspace. No rancher would allow his cattle to graze unbranded. Neither should you.

If you are a big corporation and have millions to spend on advertising, promotions, and consumer outreach programs, you have the money to spend to build a brand. But keep in mind that spending a lot of money is no guarantee you *will* build a brand.

During the dot-com boom, many start-ups spent millions trying to get their brand to stick. Pets.com was one of those start-ups. They used a white sock puppet, holding a microphone, rather than a human for their spokesperson. Promotions included an appearance in the 1999 Macy's Thanksgiving Day Parade and TV spots during the 2000 Super Bowl. Their "spokes-pet" was interviewed by *People* magazine and appeared on *Good Morning America*.

The company started in 1998 and spent over $300 million on advertising and promotions. People still remember the sock puppet, but the business died in 2000.

Brand Lesson
Spending a lot of money does not guarantee a brand.

The Lights Go On

During the early 1980s, I was in the rock and roll business. The business owned a manufacturing business with factories in Honolulu, Taiwan, and Korea. We manufactured licensed products for the several bands, including Duran Duran, Judas Priest, Van Halen, Boy George, and The Police.

Although the business was fun and sexy and grossing millions of dollars, I was not making much money. Finally I realized I was on the wrong side of the table. The rock bands were the licensors on one side of the table, and I was the licensee on the other side. I put up all the money to produce products such as hats, wallets, bags, and T-shirts with the likeness of the bands on my products. On top of that, I paid them a royalty for the right to use their name on my products. I took all the risk—while they had all the fun and made all the money.

That was when the lights went on in my head and I began my study of the power of brands. I wanted to change the side of the table on which I sat. I wanted to be the person who created the brand that someone else paid me royalties to use. And that is exactly what I do today.

Brand Lesson:
The B-I Triangle:
The most important of the B-I Triangle's 8 integrities is the mission. The mission determines the product and the brand.

It is the mission of the business that your customers love. When Ford Motor Company was founded in 1903, automobiles were only for rich people. Henry Ford's mission was "to democratize the automobile." In other words, make the automobile affordable to everyone, including his workers.

Ford's mission is reflected in all of his cars. His mission is the reason Ford cars were loved, adored, and bought by millions of people. To this day, millions of people remain die-hard fans of Ford.

Simply put, mission generates brand loyalty.

Following Ford's mission, Sam Walton founded Walmart in 1962. Today Walmart is known for high-quality goods at low prices. Their positioning statement is: Always low prices... always.

That is why millions of people say, "I'm going to Walmart"… rather than "I am going shopping."

Brand Lesson

Your business and products communicate your mission to your customers.

The mission of The Rich Dad Company is: *to elevate the financial wellbeing of humanity.*

Once Kim and I were clear on our mission we began product development. Once the prototype of the *CASHFLOW*® game was beta-tested, and *Rich Dad Poor Dad* was in manuscript, the next step on the B-I Triangle was legal. We needed a patent and trademark attorney to turn my products into property, branded products.

I had learned my lessons from rock and roll. Rather than be the entrepreneur with the factories, employees, overhead, and other miseries of business, The Rich Dad Company was designed to be a brand. That is why the core Rich Dad company is a small company. We do not own factories, printing presses, or warehouses. We have a relatively small staff. We make our money by allowing businesses all over the world—businesses like book publishing companies—the legal right to produce our products, and pay The Rich Dad Company a royalty. In some ways, it's like money for nothing.

Obviously, I make it sound easier than it really is. For Kim and me, it was a trying process. Today, Rich Dad is an international brand working cooperatively with partners all over the world. In many ways Rich Dad is much like Coca-Cola. We own the brand and our partners own the printing presses and organizations that produce our books, seminars, and games under our license.

What Is a Brand?

A brand simply *defines the product value* and *creates relationships*. For example, the world is filled with books, watches, cars, clothes, and other products and services. A brand defines what makes your products different and creates a relationship with the customers who are looking for the differences your product offers. Price often defines products. Some brands are high-priced and others are known for being cheap. If you are going to be the high-priced brand, your customer must feel that the value of your product is worth the price. For example, a brand communicates to a car buyer exactly why a Ferrari is more expensive than a Toyota.

Counterfeiters who sell "knock-offs" often damage the relationship and trust between a business and its customers. Louis Vuitton sells high-end handbags and accessories. Just around the corner in the alley, a counterfeiter may be selling Vuitton "knock-offs." If the business does not actively go after imposters (aka crooks) the brand will eventually suffer or disappear. The same thing happens on the Web. I am amazed at how many people knock off my products and my name. To those who counterfeit other people and their products, I say, "Get a life."

Brand Lesson
You must defend and protect your brand.

How Rich Dad Became a Brand

The Rich Dad Company has spent little to nothing on advertising. So, you might ask, *How did you build a brand?*

The answer lies in the B-I Triangle, in one of the 8 integrities of a Business—Communication. In the world of communication, there are three primary means of promoting your business or products. They are: Public Relations and Social Media, Advertising, and Sales.

We all have met high-pressure sales people. They must use high pressure, or gimmicks, because they spend little time or money on PR and advertising. Pets.com spent $300 million on advertising and went bust. Rich Dad has spent virtually nothing on advertising. But we spent a lot of time (but very little money) on PR.

Once *Rich Dad Poor Dad* was ready to publish, Kim and I found a service that booked authors on radio shows. Every week, I would be a guest on radio stations in different cities around the United States and tell the story of *Rich Dad Poor Dad.* I was not *selling.* By telling the story, I was getting people to want to *buy* the book. At the end of a five-minute or half-hour radio interview, the radio host would ask, "Where can listeners find your book?" My answer was, "…at book stores everywhere."

These interviews sent thousands of people to bookstores in search of the book. People who wanted to buy. The bookstores did very little selling.

Brand Lesson

Behind every great brand is a great entrepreneur with great passion to solve a great big problem. If you do this, you will be a very, very rich entrepreneur.

About Robert Kiyosaki

Best known as the author of *Rich Dad Poor Dad*—the #1 personal finance book of all time—Robert Kiyosaki has challenged and changed the way tens of millions of people around the world think about money. He is an entrepreneur, educator, and investor who believes the world needs more entrepreneurs who will create jobs.

With perspectives on money and investing that often contradict conventional wisdom, Robert has earned an international reputation for straight talk, irreverence, and courage and has become a passionate and outspoken advocate for financial education.

Robert and Kim Kiyosaki are founders of The Rich Dad Company, a financial education company, and creators of the *CASHFLOW*® games. In 2014, the company leveraged the global success of the Rich Dad games to launch new and breakthrough offerings in mobile and online gaming.

Robert has been heralded as a visionary who has a gift for simplifying complex concepts—ideas related to money, investing, finance, and economics—and has shared his personal journey to financial freedom in ways that resonate with audiences of all ages and backgrounds. His core principles and messages—like "your house is not an asset" and "invest for cash flow" and "savers are losers"—ignited a firestorm of criticism and ridicule. Over the past two decades, his teachings and philosophies have played out on the world economic stage in ways that have been both unsettling and prophetic.

His point of view is that "old" advice—go to college, get a good job, save money, get out of debt, invest for the long term, and diversify—has become obsolete advice in today's fast-paced Information Age. His Rich Dad philosophies and messages challenge the status quo. His teachings encourage people to become financially educated and to take an active role in investing for their future.

The author of 19 books, including the international blockbuster *Rich Dad Poor Dad*, Robert has been a featured guest with media outlets in every corner of the world—from CNN, the BBC, Fox News, Al Jazeera, GBTV and PBS, to *Larry King Live, Oprah, People, Investors Business Daily, Sydney Morning Herald, The Doctors, Straits Times, Bloomberg, NPR, USA TODAY*, and hundreds of others—and his books have topped international bestsellers lists for two decades. He continues to teach and inspire audiences around the world.

His most recent books include *Unfair Advantage: The Power of Financial Education, Midas Touch*, the second book he has co-authored with Donald Trump, *Why "A" Students Work for "C" Students, 8 Lessons in Military Leadership for Entrepreneurs, Second Chance, More Important Than Money*, and *Why the Rich Are Getting Richer*.

To learn more, visit RichDad.com

BEST-SELLING BOOKS
BY ROBERT T. KIYOSAKI

Rich Dad Poor Dad
What the Rich Teach Their Kids About Money –
That the Poor and Middle Class Do Not

Rich Dad's CASHFLOW Quadrant
Guide to Financial Freedom

Rich Dad's Guide to Investing
What the Rich Invest in That the Poor and Middle Class Do Not

Rich Dad's Rich Kid Smart Kid
Give Your Child a Financial Head Start

Rich Dad's Retire Young Retire Rich
How to Get Rich and Stay Rich

Rich Dad's Prophecy
Why the Biggest Stock Market Crash in History Is Still Coming...
And How You Can Prepare Yourself and Profit from It!

Rich Dad's Guide to Becoming Rich
Without Cutting Up Your Credit Cards
Turn Bad Debt into Good Debt

Rich Dad's Who Took My Money?
Why Slow Investors Lose and Fast Money Wins!

Rich Dad Poor Dad for Teens
The Secrets About Money – That You Don't Learn In School!

Escape the Rat Race
Learn How Money Works and Become a Rich Kid

Rich Dad's Before You Quit Your Job
Ten Real-Life Lessons Every Entrepreneur Should Know
About Building a Multimillion-Dollar Business

Rich Dad's Increase Your Financial IQ
Get Smarter with Your Money

Robert Kiyosaki's Conspiracy of the Rich
The 8 New Rules of Money

Unfair Advantage
The Power of Financial Education

The Real Book of Real Estate
Real Experts • Real Stories • Real Life

Why "A" Students Work for "C" Students
Rich Dad's Guide to Financial Education for Parents

Second Chance
for Your Money, Your Life and Our World

8 Lessons in Military Leadership
for Entrepreneurs

Why the Rich Are Getting Richer
What Is Financial Education... Really?

Books Co-Authored with Donald Trump

Why We Want You To Be Rich
Two Men | One Message

Midas Touch
Why Some Entrepreneurs Get Rich
—and Why Most Don't

AN EXCERPT FROM

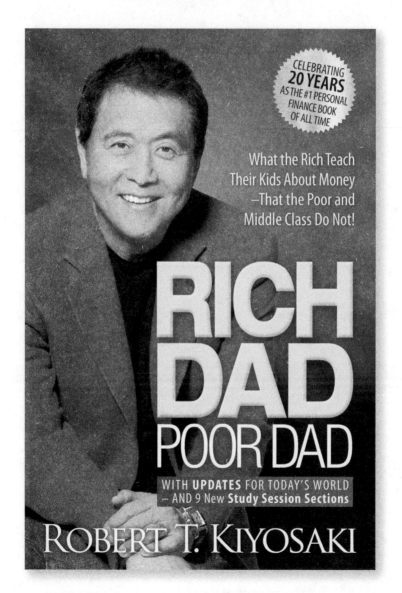

CELEBRATING
20 YEARS
AS THE #1 PERSONAL
FINANCE BOOK
OF ALL TIME

What the Rich Teach
Their Kids About Money
—That the Poor and
Middle Class Do Not!

RICH DAD POOR DAD

WITH **UPDATES** FOR TODAY'S WORLD
— AND 9 New **Study Session Sections**

ROBERT T. KIYOSAKI

Chapter One

LESSON 1: **THE RICH DON'T WORK FOR MONEY**

The poor and the middle class work for money.
The rich have money work for them.

"Dad, can you tell me how to get rich?"

My dad put down the evening paper. "Why do you want to get rich, Son?"

"Because today Jimmy's mom drove up in their new Cadillac, and they were going to their beach house for the weekend. He took three of his friends, but Mike and I weren't invited. They told us we weren't invited because we were poor kids."

"They did?" my dad asked incredulously.

"Yeah, they did," I replied in a hurt tone.

My dad silently shook his head, pushed his glasses up the bridge of his nose, and went back to reading the paper. I stood waiting for an answer.

The year was 1956. I was nine years old. By some twist of fate, I attended the same public school where the rich people sent their kids. We were primarily a sugar-plantation town in Hawaii. The managers of the plantation and the other affluent people, such as doctors, business owners, and bankers, sent their children to this public elementary school. After grade six, their children were generally sent off to private schools. Because my family lived on one side of the street, I went to this school. Had I lived on the other side of the street, I would have gone to a different school with kids from families more like mine. After grade six, these kids and I would go on to the public intermediate and high school. There was no private school for them or for me.

My dad finally put down the paper. I could tell he was thinking.

"Well, Son...," he began slowly. "If you want to be rich, you have to learn to make money."

"How do I make money?" I asked.

"Well, use your head, Son," he said, smiling. Even then I knew that really meant, "That's all I'm going to tell you," or "I don't know the answer, so don't embarrass me."

A Partnership Is Formed

The next morning, I told my best friend, Mike, what my dad had said. As best as I could tell, Mike and I were the only poor kids in this school. Mike was also in this school by a twist of fate. Someone had drawn a jog in the line for the school district, and we wound up in school with the rich kids. We weren't really poor, but we felt as if we were because all the other boys had new baseball gloves, new bicycles, new everything.

Mom and Dad provided us with the basics, like food, shelter, and clothes. But that was about it. My dad used to say, "If you want something, work for it." We wanted things, but there was not much work available for nine-year-old boys.

"So what do we do to make money?" Mike asked.

"I don't know," I said. "But do you want to be my partner?"

He agreed, and so on that Saturday morning, Mike became my first business partner. We spent all morning coming up with ideas on how to make money. Occasionally we talked about all the "cool guys" at Jimmy's beach house having fun. It hurt a little, but that hurt was good, because it inspired us to keep thinking of a way to make money. Finally, that afternoon, a bolt of lightning struck. It was an idea Mike got from a science book he had read. Excitedly, we shook hands, and the partnership now had a business.

For the next several weeks, Mike and I ran around our neighborhood, knocking on doors and asking our neighbors if they would save their toothpaste tubes for us. With puzzled looks, most adults consented with a smile. Some asked us what we were doing, to which we replied, "We can't tell you. It's a business secret."

My mom grew distressed as the weeks wore on. We had selected a site next to her washing machine as the place we would stockpile our raw materials. In a brown cardboard box that at one time held catsup bottles, our little pile of used toothpaste tubes began to grow.

Finally my mom put her foot down. The sight of her neighbors' messy, crumpled, used toothpaste tubes had gotten to her. "What are you boys doing?" she asked. "And I don't want to hear again that it's a business secret. Do something with this mess, or I'm going to throw it out."

Mike and I pleaded and begged, explaining that we would soon have enough and then we would begin production. We informed her that we were waiting on a couple of neighbors to finish their toothpaste so we could have their tubes. Mom granted us a one-week extension.

The date to begin production was moved up, and the pressure was on. My first partnership was already being threatened with an eviction notice by my own mom! It became Mike's job to tell the neighbors to quickly use up their toothpaste, saying their dentist wanted them to brush more often anyway. I began to put together the production line.

One day my dad drove up with a friend to see two nine-year-old boys in the driveway with a production line operating at full speed. There was fine white powder everywhere. On a long table were small milk cartons from school, and our family's hibachi grill was glowing with red-hot coals at maximum heat.

Dad walked up cautiously, having to park the car at the base of the driveway since the production line blocked the carport. As he and his friend got closer, they saw a steel pot sitting on top of the coals in which the toothpaste tubes were being melted down. In those days, toothpaste did not come in plastic tubes. The tubes were made of lead. So once the paint was burned off, the tubes were dropped in the small steel pot. They melted until they became liquid, and with my mom's pot holders, we poured the lead through a small hole in the top of the milk cartons.

The milk cartons were filled with plaster of paris. White powder was everywhere. In my haste, I had knocked the bag over, and the entire area looked like it had been hit by a snowstorm. The milk cartons were the outer containers for plaster of paris molds.

My dad and his friend watched as we carefully poured the molten lead through a small hole in the top of the plaster of paris cube.

"Careful," my dad said.

I nodded without looking up.

Finally, once the pouring was through, I put the steel pot down and smiled at my dad.

"What are you boys doing?" he asked with a cautious smile.

"We're doing what you told me to do. We're going to be rich," I said.

"Yup," said Mike, grinning and nodding his head. "We're partners."

"And what is in those plaster molds?" my dad asked.

"Watch," I said. "This should be a good batch."

With a small hammer, I tapped at the seal that divided the cube in half. Cautiously, I pulled up the top half of the plaster mold and a lead nickel fell out.

"Oh, no!" my dad exclaimed. "You're casting nickels out of lead!"

"That's right," Mike said. "We're doing as you told us to do. We're making money."

My dad's friend turned and burst into laughter. My dad smiled and shook his head. Along with a fire and a box of spent toothpaste tubes, in front of him were two little boys covered with white dust smiling from ear to ear.

He asked us to put everything down and sit with him on the front step of our house. With a smile, he gently explained what the word "counterfeiting" meant.

Our dreams were dashed. "You mean this is illegal?" asked Mike in a quivering voice.

"Let them go," my dad's friend said. "They might be developing a natural talent."

My dad glared at him.

"Yes, it is illegal," my dad said gently. "But you boys have shown great creativity and original thought. Keep going. I'm really proud of you!"

Disappointed, Mike and I sat in silence for about twenty minutes before we began cleaning up our mess. The business was over on opening day. Sweeping the powder up, I looked at Mike and said, "I guess Jimmy and his friends are right. We are poor."

My father was just leaving as I said that. "Boys," he said. "You're only poor if you give up. The most important thing is that you did something. Most people only talk and dream of getting rich. You've done something. I'm very proud of the two of you. I will say it again: Keep going. Don't quit."

Mike and I stood there in silence. They were nice words, but we still did not know what to do.

"So how come you're not rich, Dad?" I asked.

"Because I chose to be a schoolteacher. Schoolteachers really don't think about being rich. We just like to teach. I wish I could help you, but I really don't know how to make money."

Mike and I turned and continued our cleanup.

"I know," said my dad. "If you boys want to learn how to be rich, don't ask me. Talk to your dad, Mike."

"My dad?" asked Mike with a scrunched-up face.

"Yeah, your dad," repeated my dad with a smile. "Your dad and I have the same banker, and he raves about your father. He's told me several times that your father is brilliant when it comes to making money."

"My dad?" Mike asked again in disbelief. "Then how come we don't have a nice car and a nice house like the rich kids at school?"

"A nice car and a nice house don't necessarily mean you're rich or you know how to make money," my dad replied. "Jimmy's dad works for the sugar plantation. He's not much different from me. He works for a company, and I work for the government. The company buys the car for him. The sugar company is in financial trouble, and Jimmy's dad may soon have nothing. Your dad is different, Mike. He seems to be building an empire, and I suspect in a few years he will be a very rich man."

With that, Mike and I got excited again. With new vigor, we began cleaning up the mess caused by our now-defunct first business. As we were cleaning, we made plans for how and when to talk to Mike's dad. The problem was that Mike's dad worked long hours and often did not come home until late. His father owned warehouses, a construction company, a chain of stores, and three restaurants. It was the restaurants that kept him out late.

Mike caught the bus home after we had finished cleaning up. He was going to talk to his dad when he got home that night and ask him if he would teach us how to become rich. Mike promised to call as soon as he had talked to his dad, even if it was late.

The phone rang at 8:30 p.m.

"Okay," I said. "Next Saturday." I put the phone down. Mike's dad had agreed to meet with us.

On Saturday I caught the 7:30 a.m. bus to the poor side of town.

The Lessons Begin

Mike and I met with his dad that morning at eight o'clock. He was already busy, having been at work for more than an hour. His construction supervisor was just leaving in his pickup truck as I walked up to his simple, small, and tidy home. Mike met me at the door.

"Dad's on the phone, and he said to wait on the back porch," Mike said as he opened the door.

The old wooden floor creaked as I stepped across the threshold of the aging house. There was a cheap mat just inside the door. The mat was there to hide the years of wear from countless footsteps that the floor had supported. Although clean, it needed to be replaced.

I felt claustrophobic as I entered the narrow living room that was filled with old musty overstuffed furniture that today would be collectors' items. Sitting on the couch were two women, both a little older than my mom. Across from the women sat a man in workman's clothes. He wore khaki slacks and a khaki shirt, neatly pressed but without starch, and polished work boots. He was about 10 years older than my dad. They smiled as Mike and I walked past them toward the back porch. I smiled back shyly.

"Who are those people?" I asked.

"Oh, they work for my dad. The older man runs his warehouses, and the women are the managers of the restaurants. And as you arrived, you saw the construction supervisor who is working on a road project about 50 miles from here. His other supervisor, who is building a track of houses, left before you got here."

"Does this go on all the time?" I asked.

"Not always, but quite often," said Mike, smiling as he pulled up a chair to sit down next to me.

"I asked my dad if he would teach us to make money," Mike said.

"Oh, and what did he say to that?" I asked with cautious curiosity.

"Well, he had a funny look on his face at first, and then he said he would make us an offer."

"Oh," I said, rocking my chair back against the wall. I sat there perched on two rear legs of the chair.

Mike did the same thing.

"Do you know what the offer is?" I asked.

"No, but we'll soon find out."

Suddenly, Mike's dad burst through the rickety screen door and onto the porch. Mike and I jumped to our feet, not out of respect, but because we were startled.

"Ready, boys?" he asked as he pulled up a chair to sit down with us.

We nodded our heads as we pulled our chairs away from the wall to sit in front of him.

He was a big man, about six feet tall and 200 pounds. My dad was taller, about the same weight, and five years older than Mike's dad. They sort of looked alike, though not of the same ethnic makeup. Maybe their energy was similar.

"Mike says you want to learn to make money? Is that correct, Robert?"

I nodded my head quickly, but with a little trepidation. He had a lot of power behind his words and smile.

"Okay, here's my offer. I'll teach you, but I won't do it classroom-style. You work for me, I'll teach you. You don't work for me, I won't teach you. I can teach you faster if you work, and I'm wasting my time if you just want to sit and listen like you do in school. That's my offer. Take it or leave it."

"Ah, may I ask a question first?" I asked.

"No. Take it or leave it. I've got too much work to do to waste my time. If you can't make up your mind decisively, then you'll never learn to make money anyway. Opportunities come and go. Being able to know when to make quick decisions is an important skill. You have the opportunity that you asked for. School is beginning, or it's over in 10 seconds," Mike's dad said with a teasing smile.

"Take it," I said.

"Take it," said Mike.

"Good," said Mike's dad. "Mrs. Martin will be by in 10 minutes. After I'm through with her, you'll ride with her to my superette and you can begin working. I'll pay you 10 cents an hour, and you'll work three hours every Saturday."

"But I have a softball game today," I said.

20 YEARS AGO TODAY...
DECISIVENESS

The world is moving faster and faster. Stock market trades are made in milliseconds. Deals come and go on the Internet in a matter of minutes. More and more people are competing for good deals. So the faster you can make a decision the more likely you'll be able to seize opportunities—before someone else does.

Mike's dad lowered his voice to a stern tone. "Take it, or leave it," he said.

"I'll take it," I replied, choosing to work and learn instead of playing.

Thirty Cents Later

By 9:00 a.m. that day, Mike and I were working for Mrs. Martin. She was a kind and patient woman. She always said that Mike and I reminded her of her two grown sons. Although kind, she believed in hard work and kept us moving. We spent three hours taking canned goods off the shelves, brushing each can with a feather duster to get the dust off, and then re-stacking them neatly. It was excruciatingly boring work.

Mike's dad, whom I call my rich dad, owned nine of these little superettes, each with a large parking lot. They were the early version of the 7-Eleven convenience stores, little neighborhood grocery stores where people bought items such as milk, bread, butter, and cigarettes. The problem was that this was Hawaii before air-conditioning was widely used, and the stores could not close their doors because of the heat. On two sides of the store, the doors had to be wide open to the road and parking lot. Every time a car drove by or pulled into the parking lot, dust would swirl and settle in the store. We knew we had a job as long as there was no air-conditioning.

For three weeks, Mike and I reported to Mrs. Martin and worked our three hours. By noon, our work was over, and she dropped three little dimes in each of our hands. Now, even at the age of nine in the mid-1950s, 30 cents was not too exciting. Comic books cost 10 cents back then, so I usually spent my money on comic books and went home.

By Wednesday of the fourth week, I was ready to quit. I had agreed to work only because I wanted to learn to make money from Mike's dad, and now I was a slave for 10 cents an hour. On top of that, I had not seen Mike's dad since that first Saturday.

"I'm quitting," I told Mike at lunchtime. School was boring, and now I did not even have my Saturdays to look forward to. But it was the 30 cents that really got to me.

This time Mike smiled.

"What are you laughing at?" I asked with anger and frustration.

"Dad said this would happen. He said to meet with him when you were ready to quit."

"What?" I said indignantly. "He's been waiting for me to get fed up?"

"Sort of," Mike said. "Dad's kind of different. He doesn't teach like your dad. Your mom and dad lecture a lot. My dad is quiet and a man of few words. You just wait till this Saturday. I'll tell him you're ready."

"You mean I've been set up?"

"No, not really, but maybe. Dad will explain on Saturday."

Waiting in Line on Saturday

I was ready to face Mike's dad. Even my real dad was angry with him. My real dad, the one I call the poor one, thought that my rich dad was violating child labor laws and should be investigated.

My educated, poor dad told me to demand what I deserve—at least 25 cents an hour. My poor dad told me that if I did not get a raise, I was to quit immediately.

"You don't need that damned job anyway," said my poor dad with indignation.

At eight o'clock Saturday morning, I walked through the door of Mike's house when Mike's dad opened it.

"Take a seat and wait in line," he said as I entered. He turned and disappeared into his little office next to a bedroom.

I looked around the room and didn't see Mike anywhere. Feeling awkward, I cautiously sat down next to the same two women who were there four weeks earlier. They smiled and slid down the couch to make room for me.

Forty-five minutes went by, and I was steaming. The two women had met with him and left 30 minutes earlier. An older gentleman was in there for 20 minutes and was also gone.

The house was empty, and here I sat in a musty, dark living room on a beautiful sunny Hawaiian day, waiting to talk to a cheapskate who exploited children. I could hear him rustling around the office, talking on the phone, and ignoring me. I was ready to walk out, but for some reason I stayed.

Finally, 15 minutes later, at exactly nine o'clock, rich dad walked out of his office, said nothing, and signaled with his hand for me to enter.

"I understand you want a raise, or you're going to quit," rich dad said as he swiveled in his office chair.

"Well, you're not keeping your end of the bargain," I blurted out, nearly in tears. It was really frightening for me to confront a grown-up.

"You said that you would teach me if I worked for you. Well, I've worked for you. I've worked hard. I've given up my baseball games to work for you, but you haven't kept your word, and you haven't taught me anything. You are a crook like everyone in town thinks you are. You're greedy. You want all the money and don't take care of your employees. You made me wait and don't show me any respect. I'm only a little boy, but I deserve to be treated better."

Rich dad rocked back in his swivel chair, hands up to his chin, and stared at me.

"Not bad," he said. "In less than a month, you sound like most of my employees."

"What?" I asked. Not understanding what he was saying, I continued with my grievance. "I thought you were going to keep your end of the bargain and teach me. Instead you want to torture me? That's cruel. That's really cruel."

"I am teaching you," rich dad said quietly.

"What have you taught me? Nothing!" I said angrily. "You haven't even talked to me once since I agreed to work for peanuts. Ten cents an hour. Hah! I should notify the government about you. We have child labor laws, you know. My dad works for the government, you know."

"Wow!" said rich dad. "Now you sound just like most of the people who used to work for me—people I've either fired or who have quit."

"So what do you have to say?" I demanded, feeling pretty brave for a little kid. "You lied to me. I've worked for you, and you have not kept your word. You haven't taught me anything."

"How do you know that I've not taught you anything?" asked rich dad calmly.

"Well, you've never talked to me. I've worked for three weeks and you have not taught me anything," I said with a pout.

"Does teaching mean talking or a lecture?" rich dad asked.

"Well, yes," I replied.

"That's how they teach you in school," he said, smiling. "But that is not how life teaches you, and I would say that life is the best teacher of all. Most of the time, life does not talk to you. It just sort of pushes you around. Each push is life saying, 'Wake up. There's something I want you to learn.'"

20 YEARS AGO TODAY...
THE CONE OF LEARNING

Edgar Dale gets credit for helping us to understand that we learn best through action— doing the real thing or a simulation. Sometimes it's called experiential learning. Dale and his Cone of Learning tell us that reading and lecture are the least effective ways to learn. And yet we all know how most schools teach: reading and lecture.

What is this man talking about? I asked myself. *Life pushing me around was life talking to me?* Now I knew I had to quit my job. I was talking to someone who needed to be locked up.

Cone of Learning

After 2 weeks we tend to remember		Nature of Involvement
	Doing the Real Thing	
90% of what we say and do	Simulating the Real Experience	
	Doing a Dramatic Presentation	Active
70% of what we say	Giving a Talk	
	Participating in a Discussion	
	Seeing it Done on Location	
	Watching a Demonstration	
50% of what we hear and see	Looking at an Exhibit Watching a Demonstration	Passive
	Watching a Movie	
30% of what we see	Looking at Pictures	
20% of what we hear	Hearing Words (Lecture)	
10% of what we read	Reading	

Source: Cone of Learning adapted from Dale, (1969)

"If you learn life's lessons, you will do well. If not, life will just continue to push you around. People do two things. Some just let life push them around. Others get angry and push back. But they push back against their boss, or their job, or their husband or wife. They do not know it's life that's pushing."

I had no idea what he was talking about.

"Life pushes all of us around. Some people give up and others fight. A few learn the lesson and move on. They welcome life pushing them around. To these few people, it means they need and want to learn something. They learn and move on. Most quit, and a few like you fight."

Rich dad stood and shut the creaky old wooden window that needed repair. "If you learn this lesson, you will grow into a wise, wealthy, and happy young man. If you don't, you will spend your life blaming a job, low pay, or your boss for your problems. You'll live life always hoping for that big break that will solve all your money problems."

Rich dad looked over at me to see if I was still listening. His eyes met mine. We stared at each other, communicating through our eyes. Finally, I looked away once I had absorbed his message. I knew he was right. I was blaming him, and I did ask to learn. I was fighting.

Rich dad continued, "Or if you're the kind of person who has no guts, you just give up every time life pushes you. If you're that kind of person, you'll live all your life playing it safe, doing the right things, saving yourself for some event that never happens. Then you die a boring old man. You'll have lots of

20 YEARS AGO TODAY...
LIFE AS A TEACHER

Today's millennials are learning the hard facts of life. Jobs are harder to find. Robots are replacing workers by the millions. Learning by making mistakes through trial and error is more and more important. Book learning is proving to be less valuable in the real world. No longer does a college education guarantee a job.

friends who really like you because you were such a nice hardworking guy. But the truth is that you let life push you into submission. Deep down you were terrified of taking risks. You really wanted to win, but the fear of losing was greater than the excitement of winning.

Deep inside, you and only you will know you didn't go for it. You chose to play it safe."

Our eyes met again.

"You've been pushing me around?" I asked.

"Some people might say that," smiled rich dad. "I would say that I just gave you a taste of life."

"What taste of life?" I asked, still angry, but now curious and ready to learn.

"You boys are the first people who have ever asked me to teach them how to make money. I have more than 150 employees, and not one of them has asked me what I know about money. They ask me for a job and a paycheck, but never to teach them about money. So most will spend the best years of their lives working for money, not really understanding what it is they are working for."

I sat there listening intently.

"So when Mike told me you wanted to learn how to make money, I decided to design a course that mirrored real life. I could talk until I was blue in the face, but you wouldn't hear a thing. So I decided to let life push you around a bit so you could hear me. That's why I only paid you 10 cents."

"So what is the lesson I learned from working for only 10 cents an hour?" I asked. "That you're cheap and exploit your workers?"

Rich dad rocked back and laughed heartily. Finally he

20 YEARS AGO TODAY...
CHANGE WHAT YOU CAN

I've learned the truth and wisdom in rich dad's words. So much of life is out of our control.
I've learned to focus on what I do have control over: myself.
And if things must change, first I must change.

said, "You'd best change your point of view. Stop blaming me and thinking I'm the problem. If you think I'm the problem, then you have to change me. If you realize that you're the problem, then you can change yourself, learn something, and grow wiser. Most people want everyone else in the world to change but themselves. Let me tell you, it's easier to change yourself than everyone else."

"I don't understand," I said.

"Don't blame me for your problems," rich dad said, growing impatient.

"But you only pay me 10 cents."

"So what are you learning?" rich dad asked, smiling.

"That you're cheap," I said with a sly grin.

"See, you think I'm the problem," said rich dad.

"But you are."

"Well, keep that attitude and you'll learn nothing. Keep the attitude that I'm the problem and what choices do you have?"

"Well, if you don't pay me more or show me more respect and teach me, I'll quit."

"Well put," rich dad said. "And that's exactly what most people do. They quit and go looking for another job, a better opportunity, and higher pay, actually thinking that this will solve the problem. In most cases, it won't."

"So what should I do?" I asked. "Just take this measly 10 cents an hour and smile?"

Rich dad smiled. "That's what the other people do. But that's all they do, waiting for a raise thinking that more money will solve their problems. Most just accept it, and some take a second job working harder, but again accepting a small paycheck."

I sat staring at the floor, beginning to understand the lesson rich dad was presenting. I could sense it was a taste of life. Finally, I looked up and asked, "So what will solve the problem?"

"This," he said, leaning forward in his chair and tapping me gently on the head. "This stuff between your ears."

It was at that moment that rich dad shared the pivotal point of view that separated him from his employees and my poor dad—and led him to eventually become one of the richest men in Hawaii, while my highly educated but poor dad struggled financially all his life. It was a singular point of view that made all the difference over a lifetime.

Rich dad explained this point of view over and over, which I call lesson number one: *The poor and the middle class work for money. The rich have money work for them.*

On that bright Saturday morning, I learned a completely different point of view from what I had been taught by my poor dad. At the age of nine, I understood that both dads wanted me to learn. Both dads encouraged me to study, but not the same things.

My highly educated dad recommended that I do what he did. "Son, I want you to study hard, get good grades, so you can find a safe, secure job with a big company. And make sure it has excellent benefits." My rich dad wanted me to learn how money works so I could make it work for me.

20 YEARS AGO TODAY...
ASSETS OVER INCOME
Buying or building assets that deliver cash flow is putting your money to work for you. High-paying jobs mean two things: you're working for money and the taxes you pay will probably increase. I've learned to put my money to work for me and enjoy the tax benefits of generating income that doesn't come from a paycheck.

These lessons I would learn through life with his guidance, not because of a classroom.

My rich dad continued my first lesson, "I'm glad you got angry about working for 10 cents an hour. If you hadn't got angry and had simply accepted it, I would have to tell you that I could not teach you. You see, true learning takes energy, passion, and a burning desire. Anger is a big part of that formula, for passion is anger and love combined. When it comes to money, most people want to play it safe and feel secure. So passion does not direct them. Fear does."

"So is that why they'll take jobs with low pay?" I asked.

"Yes," said rich dad. "Some people say I exploit people because I don't pay as much as the sugar plantation or the government. I say the people exploit themselves. It's their fear, not mine."

"But don't you feel you should pay them more?" I asked.

"I don't have to. And besides, more money will not solve their problems. Just look at your dad. He makes a lot of money, and he still can't pay his bills. Most people, given more money, only get into more debt."

"So that's why the 10 cents an hour," I said, smiling. "It's a part of the lesson."

"That's right," smiled rich dad. "You see, your dad went to school and got an excellent education, so he could get a high-paying job. But he still has money problems because he never learned anything about money in school. On top of that, he believes in working for money."

"And you don't?" I asked.

"No, not really," said rich dad. "If you want to learn to work for money, then stay in school. That is a great place to learn to do that. But if you want to learn how to have money work for you, then I will teach you that. But only if you want to learn."

20 YEARS AGO TODAY...
GO TO SCHOOL?

While I am a huge supporter of education and life-long learning, "going to school"—especially college—has become a financial nightmare. Student loan debt is at record highs with 44 million Americans owing nearly $1.3 trillion. Again: that's trillion... with a T.

"Wouldn't everyone want to learn that?" I asked.

"No," said rich dad, "simply because it's easier to learn to work for money, especially if fear is your primary emotion when the subject of money is discussed."

"I don't understand," I said with a frown.

"Don't worry about that for now. Just know that it's fear that keeps most people working at a job: the fear of not paying their bills, the fear of being fired, the fear of not having enough money, and the fear of starting over. That's the price of studying to learn a profession or trade, and then working for money. Most people become a slave to money— and then get angry at their boss."

"Learning to have money work for you is a completely different course of study?" I asked.

"Absolutely," rich dad answered. "Absolutely."

We sat in silence on that beautiful Hawaiian Saturday morning. My friends had just started their Little League baseball game, but for some reason I was now thankful I had decided to work for 10 cents an hour. I sensed that I was about to learn something my friends wouldn't learn in school.

"Ready to learn?" asked rich dad.

"Absolutely," I said with a grin.

"I have kept my promise. I've been teaching you from afar," my rich dad said. "At nine years old, you've gotten a taste of what it feels like to work for money. Just multiply your last month by fifty years and you will have an idea of what most people spend their life doing."

"I don't understand," I said.

"How did you feel waiting in line to see me, once to get hired and once to ask for more money?"

"Terrible," I said.

"If you choose to work for money, that is what life will be like," said rich dad.

"And how did you feel when Mrs. Martin dropped three dimes in your hand for three hours of work?"

"I felt like it wasn't enough. It seemed like nothing. I was disappointed," I said.

"And that is how most employees feel when they look at their paychecks—especially after all the tax and other deductions are taken out. At least you got 100 percent."

"You mean most workers don't get paid everything?" I asked with amazement.

"Heavens no!" said rich dad. "The government always takes its share first."

"How do they do that?" I asked.

"Taxes," said rich dad. "You're taxed when you earn.

You're taxed when you spend. You're taxed when you save. You're taxed when you die."

"Why do people let the government do that to them?"

"The rich don't," said rich dad with a smile. "The poor and the middle class do. I'll bet you that I earn more than your dad, yet he pays more in taxes."

"How can that be?" I asked. At my age, that made no sense to me.

"Why would someone let the government do that to them?"

Rich dad rocked slowly and silently in his chair, just looking at me.

"Ready to learn?" he asked.

---

20 YEARS AGO TODAY...

TAXES... TAXES... TAXES

As governments expand and need more and more money, the only place to get it is the middle class. That means the workers. Every government now favors the professional investor and business owners. Workers pay tax; investors and business owners pay very little tax, if they use the tax law as intended—as a tool to build the economy.

I nodded my head slowly.

"As I said, there is a lot to learn. Learning how to have money work for you is a lifetime study. Most people go to college for four years, and their education ends. I already know that my study of money will continue over my lifetime, simply because the more I find out, the more I find out I need to know. Most people never study the subject. They go to work, get their paycheck, balance their checkbooks, and that's it. Then they wonder why they have money problems. They think that more money will solve the problem and don't realize that it's their lack of financial education that is the problem."

"So my dad has tax problems because he doesn't understand money?" I asked, confused.

"Look," said rich dad, "taxes are just one small section on learning how to have money work for you. Today, I just wanted to find out if you still have the passion to learn about money. Most people don't.

They want to go to school, learn a profession, have fun at their work, and earn lots of money. One day they wake up with big money problems, and then they can't stop working. That's the price of only knowing how to work for money instead of studying how to have money work for you. So do you still have the passion to learn?" asked rich dad.

I nodded my head.

"Good," said rich dad. "Now get back to work. This time, I will pay you nothing."

"What?" I asked in amazement.

"You heard me. Nothing. You will work the same three hours every Saturday, but this time you will not be paid 10 cents per hour. You said you wanted to learn to not work for money, so I'm not going to pay you anything."

I couldn't believe what I was hearing.

"I've already had this conversation with Mike and he's already working, dusting and stacking canned goods for free. You'd better hurry and get back there."

"That's not fair," I shouted. "You've got to pay something!"

"You said you wanted to learn. If you don't learn this now, you'll grow up to be like the two women and the older man sitting in my living room, working for money and hoping I don't fire them. Or like your dad, earning lots of money only to be in debt up to his eyeballs, hoping more money will solve the problem. If that's what you want, I'll go back to our original deal of 10 cents an hour. Or you can do what most adults do: Complain that there is not enough pay, quit, and go looking for another job."

"But what do I do?" I asked.

Rich dad tapped me on the head. "Use this," he said. "If you use it well, you will soon thank me for giving you an opportunity and you will grow into a rich man."

I stood there, still not believing what a raw deal I was handed. I came to ask for a raise, and somehow I was instead working for nothing.

Rich dad tapped me on the head again and said, "Use this. Now get out of here and get back to work."

Lesson #1: The Rich Don't Work for Money

I didn't tell my poor dad I wasn't being paid. He wouldn't have understood, and I didn't want to try to explain something I didn't understand myself.

For three more weeks, Mike and I worked three hours every Saturday for nothing. The work didn't bother me, and the routine got easier, but it was the missed baseball games and not being able to afford to buy a few comic books that got to me.

Rich dad stopped by at noon on the third week. We heard his truck pull up in the parking lot and sputter when the engine was turned off. He entered the store and greeted Mrs. Martin with a hug. After finding out how things were going in the store, he reached into the ice-cream freezer, pulled out two bars, paid for them, and signaled to Mike and me.

"Let's go for a walk, boys."

We crossed the street, dodging a few cars, and walked across a large grassy field where a few adults were playing softball. Sitting down at a lone picnic table, he handed Mike and me the treats.

"How's it going, boys?"

"Okay," Mike said.

I nodded in agreement.

"Learn anything yet?" rich dad asked.

Mike and I looked at each other, shrugged our shoulders, and shook our heads in unison.

Avoiding One of Life's Biggest Traps

"Well, you boys had better start thinking. You're staring at one of life's biggest lessons. If you learn it, you'll enjoy a life of great freedom and security. If you don't, you'll wind up like Mrs. Martin and most of the people playing softball in this park. They work very hard for little money, clinging to the illusion of job security and looking forward to a three-week vacation each year and maybe a skimpy pension after forty-five years of service. If that excites you, I'll give you a raise to 25 cents an hour."

"But these are good hardworking people. Are you making fun of them?" I demanded.

A smile came over rich dad's face.

"Mrs. Martin is like a mother to me. I would never be that cruel. I may sound unkind because I'm doing my best to point something out to the two of you. I want to expand your point of view so you can see something most people never have the benefit of seeing because their vision is too narrow. Most people never see the trap they are in."

Mike and I sat there, uncertain of his message. He sounded cruel, yet we could sense he was trying to drive home a point.

With a smile, rich dad said, "Doesn't that 25 cents an hour sound good? Doesn't it make your heart beat a little faster?"

I shook my head no, but it really did. Twenty-five cents an hour would be big bucks to me.

"Okay, I'll pay you a dollar an hour," rich dad said, with a sly grin.

Now my heart started to race. My brain was screaming, "Take it. Take it." I could not believe what I was hearing. Still, I said nothing.

"Okay, two dollars an hour."

My little brain and heart nearly exploded. After all, it was 1956 and being paid $2 an hour would have made me the richest kid in the world. I couldn't imagine earning that kind of money. I wanted to say yes. I wanted the deal. I could picture a new bicycle, new baseball glove, and the adoration of my friends when I flashed some cash. On top of that, Jimmy and his rich friends could never call me poor again. But somehow my mouth stayed shut.

The ice cream had melted and was running down my hand. Rich dad was looking at two boys staring back at him, eyes wide open and brains empty. He was testing us, and he knew there was a part of our emotions that wanted to take the deal. He understood that every person has a weak and needy part of their soul that can be bought, and he knew that every individual also had a part of their soul that was resilient and could never be bought. It was only a question of which one was stronger.

"Okay, five dollars an hour."

Suddenly I was silent. Something had changed. The offer was too big and ridiculous. Not many grown-ups in 1956 made more than that, but quickly my temptation disappeared, and calm set in. Slowly,

> *People's lives are forever controlled by two emotions: fear and greed.*

I turned to my left to look at Mike. He looked back at me. The part of my soul that was weak and needy was silenced. The part of me that had no price took over. I knew Mike had gotten to that point too.

"Good," rich dad said softly. "Most people have a price. And they have a price because of human emotions named fear and greed. First, the fear of being without money motivates us to work hard, and then once we get that paycheck, greed or desire starts us thinking about all the wonderful things money can buy. The pattern is then set."

"What pattern?" I asked.

"The pattern of get up, go to work, pay bills; get up, go to work, pay bills. People's lives are forever controlled by two emotions: fear and greed. Offer them more money and they continue the cycle by increasing their spending. This is what I call the Rat Race."

"There is another way?" Mike asked.

"Yes," said rich dad slowly. "But only a few people find it."

"And what is that way?" Mike asked.

"That's what I hope you boys will learn as you work and study with me. That is why I took away all forms of pay."

"Any hints?" Mike asked. "We're kind of tired of working hard, especially for nothing."

"Well, the first step is telling the truth," said rich dad.

"We haven't been lying," I said.

"I did not say you were lying. I said to tell the truth," rich dad retorted.

"The truth about what?" I asked.

"How you're feeling," rich dad said. "You don't have to say it to anyone else. Just admit it to yourself."

"You mean the people in this park, the people who work for you, Mrs. Martin, they don't do that?" I asked.

"I doubt it," said rich dad. "Instead, they feel the fear of not having money. They don't confront it logically. They react emotionally instead of using their heads," rich dad said. "Then, they get a few bucks in their hands and again, the emotions of joy, desire, and greed take over. And again they react, instead of think."

"So their emotions control their brain," Mike said.

"That's correct," said rich dad. "Instead of admitting the truth about how they feel, they react to their feelings and fail to think. They feel the fear so they go to work, hoping that money will soothe the fear, but it doesn't. It continues to haunt them and they return to work, hoping again that money will calm their fears, and again it

20 Years Ago Today...
THE #1 FEAR

As the world population ages and more and more people move toward retirement, it's been reported that the #1 fear is tied to money. Nearly 50% of those surveyed fear that they will outlive their money... running out of money in their "golden years."

doesn't. Fear keeps them in this trap of working, earning money, working, earning money, hoping the fear will go away. But every day they get up, and that old fear wakes up with them. For millions of people that old fear keeps them awake all night, causing a night of turmoil and worry. So they get up and go to work, hoping that a paycheck will kill that fear gnawing at their soul. Money is running their lives, and they refuse to tell the truth about that. Money is in control of their emotions and their souls."

Rich dad sat quietly, letting his words sink in. Mike and I heard what he said but didn't understand fully what he was talking about. I just knew that I often wondered why grown-ups hurried off to work. It did not seem like much fun, and they never looked that happy, but something kept them going.

Realizing we had absorbed as much as possible of what he was talking about, rich dad said, "I want you boys to avoid that trap. That is really what I want to teach you. Not just to be rich, because being rich does not solve the problem."

"It doesn't?" I asked, surprised.

"No, it doesn't. Let me explain the other emotion: desire. Some call it greed, but I prefer desire. It's perfectly normal to desire something better, prettier, more fun, or exciting. So people also work for money because of desire. They desire money for the joy they think it can buy. But the joy that money brings is often short-lived, and they soon need more money for more joy, more pleasure, more comfort, and more security. So they keep working, thinking money will soothe their souls that are troubled by fear and desire. But money can't do that."

"Even rich people do this?" Mike asked.

"Rich people included," said rich dad. "In fact, the reason many rich people are rich isn't because of desire, but because of fear. They believe that money can eliminate the fear of being poor, so they amass tons of it, only to find the fear gets worse. Now they fear losing the money. I have friends who keep working even though they have plenty. I know people who have millions who are more afraid now than when they were poor. They're terrified of losing it all. The fears that drove them to get rich got worse. That weak and needy part of their soul is actually screaming louder. They don't want to lose the big houses, the cars and the high life money has bought them. They worry about what their friends would say if they lost all their money. Many are emotionally desperate and neurotic, although they look rich and have more money."

"So is a poor man happier?" I asked.

"No, I don't think so," replied rich dad. "The avoidance of money is just as psychotic as being attached to money."

AN EXCERPT FROM

SECOND CHANCE

FOR YOUR MONEY, YOUR LIFE AND OUR WORLD

ROBERT T. KIYOSAKI

Author of the International Bestseller *Rich Dad Poor Dad*

Chapter Three

WHAT CAN I DO?

---

*"I just invent, then wait until man comes around
to needing what I've invented."*
— R. Buckminster Fuller

It took me awhile to realize that Bucky Fuller's ability to predict the future had nothing to do with picking stocks, timing markets, betting on horses, or predicting who will win the World Series. His vision of the future had to do with god's view of the future.

Bucky was hesitant to use the word *god* because, for many people, that word carried a lot of "religious dogma," emotion, and controversy. Fuller did not think god was a white guy, a Jew, an Arab, or an Asian. Rather than use the word *god*, he preferred the Native American term, *the Great Spirit*. The Great Spirit is the invisible energy that binds all things in "universe," not just heaven and earth.

Whenever I use the term *god* in this book, please know I am not making religious references. I respect a person's right to choose—to believe in god, or not to believe in god or follow any religion. Simply said, I believe in religious freedom and the freedom to choose whether or not they believe in god.

The same is true for politics. I am not a Republican or Democrat. I have no dog in that fight. In fact, I like my dog more than I like most politicians.

Human Evolution

Fuller was not a futurist in the arena of money. He was a futurist on the Great Spirit's wishes for humanity's evolution. He believed humans were god's long-term experiment, placed here on "spaceship earth" to see if humans could evolve... if they could, or would, turn planet earth into a heaven on earth, or hell on earth.

Fuller believed Great Spirit wanted all humans to be rich. He often said, "There are six billion billionaires on earth." (That was in the 1980s. Today he would say "seven billion billionaires.") In the 1980s there were fewer than 50 documented billionaires. A far cry from the "six billion" that Bucky cited. By 2008 there were 1,150. Today that figure's projected at 1,645.

Fuller predicted that humanity had reached a critical evolutionary point. If humans did not evolve from greed and selfishness to generosity and abundance, humans—as an experiment on earth—would end. He often referred to the rich and powerful who hoarded "god's abundance" only for themselves as "blood clots." He believed that if humans did not "evolve" we would not only kill ourselves, but also kill the ecology of planet earth.

The reason Fuller sought to identify the Generalized Principles is because they are the invisible forces that run the universe. In other words, the Generalized Principles were the operating principles of the Great Spirit, and the Great Spirit wanted all humans and all life on planet earth to thrive. Fuller believed there were 200 to 300 Generalized Principles. At the time of his death he had discovered about 50. I am aware of and use about five of them.

In his writing and talks, he was critical of a few greedy, powerful people who used humans and the resources of planet earth only for their personal wealth. He believed that if humans did not shift from *greed* to *generosity*—humans working for a planet that worked for everyone and everything—humans would be "evicted" from "spaceship earth." The Great Spirit's experiment would be set back a few million years. He also said that god was patient and willing to wait for humans to evolve. Unfortunately, you and I do not have the luxury of waiting another million years for our fellow humans to "get the message."

Serving More People

As stated in the previous chapter, one of the Great Spirit's Generalized Principles that Fuller identified was:

"The more people I serve, the more effective I become."

As part of my own second chance, I do my best to follow this Generalized Principle when making business decisions. Rather than just work to make myself richer, I began to condition myself to think about how to enrich *others* while I was enriching myself.

That Generalized Principle was instrumental in our decision to sell the seminar business that Kim and I founded to our partner. Although that seminar business was successful, it was limited in terms of the number of people it could serve.

In 1994, it was difficult for us to sell that seminar business, a business we loved, were successful in building and making profitable. Yet, intuitively, we knew it was time to move on. It was time to seek ways to serve more people.

In 1994, we were financially free. That freedom came not from Bucky Fuller's lessons, but from following rich dad's lessons. Financial freedom gave us the time to develop our next business. In 1996, the first commercial version of our *CASHFLOW®* game was played in Las Vegas and, one week later, in Singapore. The next step was to develop a marketing plan to sell that game.

The *CASHFLOW* game had two inherent problems that made it difficult to sell. The first problem was that it was too complex. A game expert we hired advised us to "dumb it down" or it would not sell. We decided against that recommendation. The *CASHFLOW* game was designed to be an educational game, not a game for entertainment.

The second problem with the game was that it was very expensive to produce. The same game consultant told us the game should retail for $29.95. At $29.95 retail, our cost of manufacturing had to be no more than $7.00 per game. Our problem was that the first production run of the game cost over $50 per game to produce in China, landed, and warehoused in the United States. Against the advice of the game expert, we set the *CASHFLOW* game's retail price at $195, making it one of the most expensive board games on the market.

But adversity leads to innovation. To sell the game at $195, Kim and I had to be innovative. We went to our past seminar clients and offered a $500, one-day seminar featuring our game. During the seminar, the participants played our new game twice. The first time was to get familiar with the game. The second time was to get into the game. The one-day seminar worked. Participants were excited, most claiming they learned more about money in one day than they had learned in a lifetime. When we announced the "used" games were for sale for $150, they were gone instantly. In fact there was a fight for used games, even though there were new games available for $195.

The business model worked and the "CASHFLOW Club" concept was born. In 2004, *The New York Times* ran an article, "The Rising Value of Play Money," on CASHFLOW Clubs and told us that they had identified over 3,500 clubs—all over the world. Many clubs are still in existence today, teaching and serving more people than Kim and I could ever do on our own.

Q: *If you want to serve more people, why didn't you offer the game for free?*

A: We considered using government grants to fund the manufacturing of the games, but that would have been following my poor dad's mindset, rather than my rich dad's entrepreneurial way of thinking.

Also, giving people things for free often keeps them poor. It encourages the "entitlement mentality" that destroys initiative and personal responsibility.

In spite of the high initial cost of the game, the online game is free to millions of people. One game can and has taught hundreds of people… for free, through CASHFLOW Clubs. Many CASHFLOW Club leaders around the world support the mission of Rich Dad, which is *to elevate the financial well being of humanity,* and teach the game to others. For them, not only is teaching spiritual, but the more they teach, the more they learn.

Most CASHFLOW Club leaders I have talked with report getting back far more than they give. They follow the religious principle of "give and you shall receive."

Unfortunately, there are clubs that only present the game to sell other products or business opportunities. If you encounter one of those clubs, just know that while I support free enterprise, I do not support people using my games as marketing tools.

Other Points of View

For about six months, I sat in the quaint, artist's town of Bisbee, Arizona… in an old jail that had been converted into an apartment. At one time, John Wayne owned that old jail, as a rental property. He loved Bisbee—and Southern Arizona, where he owned a large ranch.

During the day, I was working on my small ranch, converting an old stagecoach depot (a stopping point between Bisbee and the infamous town of Tombstone, where the gunfight at the OK Corral took place) into a one-bedroom home. At night I would sit in the jail, writing a book. It was a painful process. There were many starts and stops, fits and starts. Finally, late one night, exhausted from working on my property and tired of struggling with a book concept, my fingers began typing the opening lines of a new book. It began with the words "I had a rich dad and I had a poor dad."

And that's how the book, *Rich Dad Poor Dad,* was born. Most people don't know that *Rich Dad Poor Dad,* the book that started the Rich Dad series, was written as a "brochure" to market the *CASHFLOW* game.

On April 8, 1997, my 50th birthday, *Rich Dad Poor Dad* was launched and The Rich Dad Company was born.

Rich Dad Poor Dad floated around in the world of self-published books until early in the year 2000. It was selling virally, by word of mouth and one day it made *The New York Times* bestsellers list. It was the only self-published book on that prestigious list.

Soon after that, a producer from Oprah Winfrey's TV show called. But before she would book me for *Oprah*, she wanted to talk with rich dad's son. As soon as she verified the story of rich dad and poor dad, my guest appearance on *Oprah* was confirmed.

I was in Australia when the invitation came. It was a tough decision: should I stay in Australia, or fly to Chicago for the interview. Again the principle of "The more people I serve, the more effective I am" kicked in. Cutting my trip short, I flew directly from Australia to Chicago. I still remember walking onto Oprah's stage, sitting next to her for an hour, and talking about the need for financial education.

In that hour, my life changed completely. In one hour I went from an unknown to a world famous voice for financial education. It had taken only 55 years, years of many successes and failures and many second chances, to become an overnight success.

I tell you this story, not to brag or pat myself on my back, but as an example of the power of following Bucky Fuller's Generalized Principles and my rich dad's lessons on money.

The Rich Are Generous

A reporter once asked me if *Oprah* made me rich. I replied that I was already rich the day I stepped on her stage. I was rich financially because I had spent my life gaining knowledge, knowledge not taught in schools. All I was doing was sharing, being generous with what I knew.

My comment on being generous disturbed the reporter. His view was that a person had to be greedy to be rich. When I attempted to explain, the generalized principle of *unity is plural and, at minimum two*—that a person could be rich by being greedy *and* that a person could be rich by being generous—his eyes glazed over. His brain was rigidly locked around the idea that the only way to become rich was by being greedy. In his mind, it is not possible to become rich by being generous. In his mind, there is only one kind of rich person: a greedy rich person.

Q: *What happened after you became famous? Was it smooth sailing after that?*

A: No. Far from it. Fame and money made life harder, not easier. Many friends became jealous. Partners became greedy and began to steal. And many people came around to see how they could "help." It was tough trying to determine if people were coming to truly help with the mission or only to "help themselves" to what we had created.

The good news is that over the years many great people have come into our lives. Again: *Unity is plural* and we had to learn to take the good with the bad.

Bucky's Last Words

As I've said, Fuller died on July 1 in 1983. His wife Anne died 36 hours later. Both were 87 years old. Even in death, his life was supernatural.

He was speaking at an event, which would be his last, when he abruptly stopped and sat quietly for a moment. I was not at that event, but I did listen to an audiotape of his final words from that event. I will paraphrase his final words.

Bucky said he was cutting his talk short because his wife was gravely ill. He mentioned he'd had a premonition a few days earlier. His premonition was that he and his wife were to die together. Realizing death was near for both of them, he said "There is something mysterious going on." He encouraged everyone to continue on with the work, ending his talk with his usual parting words, "Thank you, darling people."

I later learned that he and his wife had made a pact that neither of them would ever see the other die. They kept their pact. Rushing to see her, Bucky sat at her bedside, where she was in a coma. As if on cue, he put his head down next to her, and silently passed on. She followed, 36 hours later, keeping their pact to never see the other die. He was a futurist who predicted how he and his wife would die. I guess he could hear the Great Spirit calling them home.

I was driving on a freeway in Honolulu when the news of their deaths came over the radio. The news so overwhelmed me that I pulled over on the side of the highway and cried. Looking back, it's clear to me that, as I was sitting on the side of the highway that emotional day, one phase of my life had ended and another had begun. I was given a new second chance. I was no longer to be an entrepreneur in manufacturing. I was about to become an entrepreneur in education.

Grunch of Giants

A few months later, Bucky's final book, *Grunch of Giants,* was released posthumously. As I've mentioned, GRUNCH stands for **Gr**oss **Un**iversal **C**ash **H**eist and refers to how the rich and powerful steal our wealth via our money, government, and banking system.

As I read this tiny, yet potent book, many pieces of the puzzle began to fall in place. My mind drifted back in time… when I was nine years old, in the fourth grade, and I raising my hand to ask my teacher, "When will we learn about money?" and "Why are some people rich and most people poor?"

In reading *Grunch*, the answers slowly seeped into my head. Fuller was very critical of the educational system, not only because of what it was teaching, but *how* it taught children to learn. He had this to say about every child and his or her special genius:

> *"Every child is born a genius, but is swiftly degeniused by unwitting humans and/or physically unfavorable environmental factors."*

And…

"I observe that every child demonstrates a comprehensive curiosity. Children are interested in everything and are forever embarrassing their specialized parents by the wholeness of their interests. Children demonstrate right from the beginning that their genes are organized to help them to apprehend, comprehend, coordinate, and employ—in all directions."

Fuller recommended that students take control of their education process. In essence: do what Steve Jobs did at Reed College in

Portland, Oregon. Steve Jobs dropped out of school so he could drop back in, studying only subjects that interested him. Steve never went back to school.

Q: *Did Bucky Fuller say everyone has a genius?*

A: Yes.

Q: *But I don't feel very smart. I don't think I have a genius. Why is that?*

A: As Bucky says, schools and parents often *degenius* children. Fuller used the metaphor of school being a diamond mine. Teachers dig into the mine looking for "diamonds"—the kids they think are geniuses. The "tailings," or the dirt and rubble that were tossed to the wayside, are the students the teachers believe have no genius potential. That is why so many students leave school feeling that they're not smart, not bright, not special… even angry at school and the school system.

Q: *So how does a person find their genius?*

A: There are many ways. One way is by changing their environment.

Q: *What does environment have to do with my genius?*

A: Let me give you some examples. Many students feel stupid in the environment of a classroom, yet their genius comes alive on a football field. Tiger Woods' genius comes alive on the golf course. The Beatles' genius came alive, with guitars and drums, in a recording studio. Steve Jobs dropped out of school, yet his genius came alive in his garage, where he and Steve Wozniak developed the first Apple computer.

Q: *So why don't I feel smart? Why can't I find my genius?*

A: Because most people go from home to school to work, environments that are not always the right environment for their genius to bloom. Many spend their lives feeling unfulfilled, untested, unappreciated, simply because they did not find the environment in which their genius could blossom.

Think of genius as three words, *genie-in-us*… the magician in us. The words genius, magician, and inspire are all related. Do you know someone who is a magician in the kitchen, someone who can take ordinary ingredients and create gourmet meals?

Q: *Yes.*

A: Do you know someone who has a "green thumb?" Someone who can take dirt, water, and seeds and create a magical garden?

Q: *Sure.*

A: Have you ever watched the Special Olympics, an event for physically-challenged children, and been inspired—spiritually touched—when they compete with all their hearts, undaunted and in spite of their disabilities and challenges?

Q: *I have.*

A: Those are examples of "genie-in-us," when the magician in us inspires others. We feel inspired when the spirit in someone else touches the spirit in us.

That is what genius is. When someone inspires us, we're reminded of the "genie-in-us."

Q: *So why don't most people find their genius?*

A: Because being a genius is not easy. For example, someone could be the next Tiger Woods, but if that person does not dedicate their life to developing their genius, their talents, their genie will never show its magic.

More Questions than Answers

For me, reading *Grunch* only raised more questions. And for the first time in my life, I wanted to be a student again. I wanted to go back to the fourth grade and find the answers to the flurry of questions I kept asking my teacher about money. I was hungry to learn, and I wanted answers to my questions: "Why is money not a subject taught in school?" and "What makes rich people rich?"

As I finished reading *Grunch* and went on to read Fuller's other books on education, I realized my questions in the fourth grade were caused by my natural curiosity. Money and why the rich are rich were my subjects of study. And, in my opinion, it's not by accident that the subject of money had been "sanitized" from academic study.

In 1983, the student in me came alive again and I did exactly as Fuller described. The student in me got back to my studies.

Over the years, my own studies verified Fuller's findings that the monetary system was designed to steal our wealth, making the rich richer, but not making you and I rich. This enslavement of others and theft of another's wealth has been going on ever since the first humans walked the earth. Fuller believed that intense greed and desire to enslave fellow humans was humanity's evolutionary test, a test to see if we could use our hearts and minds to create heaven on earth or if we would turn earth into a living hell and environmental wasteland.

In *Grunch of Giants*, Fuller described how the rich and powerful used money, banks, government, politicians, military leaders, and the educational system to implement their plans. Simply said, money is designed to keep people slaves to money and slaves to those who control the monetary system.

Ironically, and although Bucky Fuller and my rich dad would be polar opposites on the subject of money, they both would have agreed on the concept of money enslaving people. And their polarity supports and validates the generalized principle of *unity is plural*, both men disagreeing on substance, but agreeing in principle.

The Power of Knowledge

Soon after I appeared on *Oprah*, a mutual fund company offered me $4 million to endorse their mutual fund. While I like money as much as the next guy, accepting their money would have been selling out to GRUNCH. One of the great things about financial education is it gives people the power to choose… and to never need to sell their soul for money.

What Can You Do?

You and I both knew this was coming…

Q: *So what can I do?*

A: The answer is there are many things you can do. The world is filled with problems. A better question might be: What problem do you want to solve? What problem do you think god gave you unique gifts to solve? You can do it by yourself or you can join a group or an organization in solving the problem that causes you concern.

When you look at the world from the point of view of problems to solve, you will see that there is a lot to do and a lot *you* can do.

A more important question is: Are you willing to work on solving the problem? Or are you willing to work only if someone will pay you money?

In the next chapter, you will learn what I learned while looking for the answer of how our wealth is stolen via our money system and why there is no financial education in our schools.

By creating the *CASHFLOW* board game and writing *Rich Dad Poor Dad*, our wealth, income, and recognition went up exponentially. I mention this for those of you who are wondering when I will get around to what you can do for *your* second chance in life.

For those of you considering a second chance with your money and your life, you may want to ask yourself:

"How can I serve more people?"

rather than:

"How can I make more money?"

If you ask yourself how you can serve more people—rather than simply make more money—you are following one of the Generalized Principles of god.

Kim Kiyosaki

Personal Background and Entrepreneur Profile

Name   Kim Kiyosaki
Date of Birth   January 26, 1957
Place of Birth   Summit, New Jersey

Traditional Education
University of Hawaii
Degree: BS in Business and Marketing

Professional Education
On-going life-long learning

Grade Point Averages
High school: Somewhere between 3.0 and 1.0—a B & a D
College: Same as high school

Value of traditional education... relative to becoming an entrepreneur
I learned that it's more important to get something out there,
then to spend too much time making it perfect. I can waste
time on "perfect." In grade school I worked hours and hours
on a project about the leaves of different trees. It was beautiful.
Absolutely perfect. I got an A. Grant, my classmate, got an A,
too. His was nothing close to perfect or beautiful. I learned that
perfection isn't all it's cracked up to be.

Subject I liked most in school
Current Events. I loved learning about what was happening all
over the world. I loved PE, too. Sports let me vent my frustrations
about all the stuff I didn't like about being cooped up in a
classroom all day.

Subject I hated most in school

Geometry. Why? Because my high school Geometry teacher actually told me that I was a bad student and would never grasp this subject. (Setting the stage for my future as an entrepreneur...)

First entrepreneurial project

When I was young, my family would vacation in the summer at the Jersey shore. On Sunday afternoons there was always a traffic jam: vacationers headed home at the end of the weekend. At about age eight, my friends and I would sell water (this is when water was free everywhere) to drivers whose cars had overheated. Most drivers thought we should provide the water for free, however, they were not in a position to negotiate.

The key entrepreneurial skill I was *not* taught in school

How to use mistakes to accelerate my learning and growing, not avoid or fear them.

Why and when I became an entrepreneur and my first major venture

Why... My dad lost his job when he was in his early 50s when he lost the contest to be company president.

He was an honest, loyal, and hard-working man. I was angry at what seemed to be very unfair and just plain wrong. I remember thinking to myself, when we were at his office collecting his things, that I would never put myself in a situation where someone else controls my life. I didn't realize it at the time, but that's when the first seeds were planted in becoming an entrepreneur.

When... After being fired—not once, but twice—from my first job out of college (because I really *do* hate being told what to do.) It was my sign to start my first business.

My first business venture was designing a 'win/win' logo—when it was a new idea and not a cliché—and embroidered it on shirts, sweaters, and jackets. We sold them at business conferences throughout the United States.

Best lesson from first business

Learning to include everyone working with you in the entire picture and have them understand the value of the role they play. For example, when my embroiderer told me he could not have the shirts to me by the first conference, I sat down with him and showed him a chart of how getting the shirts done on time affects all the other pieces of the business puzzle. He wasn't just doing a job, he was getting a start-up business off the ground. He delivered on time, on schedule.

What I learned about myself from my Kolbe Index

KIM KIYOSAKI
Kolbe A™ Index Result

CONGRATULATIONS KIM
You Got a Perfect Score on the Kolbe A™ Index

You are uniquely able to take on future-oriented challenges. You lead the way to visionary possibilities and create what others said couldn't be done. You'll say "Yes" before you even know the end of the question – then turn it into a productive adventure.

Kolbe Action Modes®

©1907-2017 Kathy Kolbe. All rights reserved.

Reprinted with permission from Kolbe Corp.

Don't fight your natural tendencies. For many, many years I read books on getting organized. I attended seminars. I bought all the newest day planners on the market. Nothing worked. My office was always a disaster. When I did the Kolbe Index, Kathy Kolbe asked me, "Kim, have you always struggled with being organized?" "Yes!" I said, with frustration. She told me, "Kim, you will never be organized. It's not your nature. I suggest your hire someone who will organize things for you." And that's exactly what I did, I've lived happily ever after since that day.

My role in the B-1 Triangle

I am the keeper of the spirit of Rich Dad and Rich Woman. This falls under Mission. Our mission is "to elevate the financial well-being of humanity." Our company lives and breathes that mission.

Skills that are essential for entrepreneurs—but not taught in schools

1. Make a lot of mistakes, learn from them and implement that learning into your business. Mistakes are a valuable tool.

2. How to sell your vision. The entrepreneur is often selling something that doesn't even exist yet. If you cannot sell and communicate your vision then your vision isn't clear or inspiring enough.

3. Create a team, ideally of individuals who are smarter than you at what they do. A team working together can create amazing results. In school we're taught to do everything on our own. A business cannot grow if you have to do everything yourself.

My Most Important Lesson for Entrepreneurs

I have two:

1. Resiliency. When you have a setback, and as entrepreneurs we all have many, how quickly and effectively do you come back can mean the success or failure of your business. All setbacks should make you and your company stronger, not weaker.

2. Surround yourself with people who support and encourage your entrepreneurial endeavors. Find mentors, coaches, and successful entrepreneurs to guide you. The naysayers are often too afraid to make the leap to start their own business, so they'll discourage you and tell you why your idea won't work. (There is one assumption here, and that is that you do have a valid and workable business idea. Not every business idea should be pursued.)

How I learned to raise capital

Robert and I had a mentor named Frank. He took about 70 companies public. He knew how to raise money. He taught me how to present the project, ask for the money, and, most importantly, collect the money. The first time Robert and I raised money was when we launched the CASHFLOW board game in 1996. All of our investors received an annual return on their investment for several years. They then got all of their initial investment back, plus a substantial premium.

How I learned to overcome fear and failure

There is only one way that I know of: Get out there and do whatever it is you are afraid to do. I learned to overcome a lot of my fear around real estate investing by screwing up. I made a BIG mistake. I then turned that mistake into one of my best performing properties. I learned to overcome my fear of public speaking by getting up on stage again and again. There is no substitute.

My personal Strengths

My Personal Strength

1. Being happy inside. Knowing that my happiness does not come from anything outside of me.

2. Knowing that something good will come out of *every* situation.

My personal weakness

Not always saying what needs to be said.

The Entrepreneurial Skill I Teach best

I am the Queen of Cash Flow... and that's what I teach best.

The Entrepreneurial Lesson I Teach

Keys to Cash Flow: Assets over Income

Cash Flow Secrets:
Assets over Income
by Kim Kiyosaki

Kim is a rich woman, an entrepreneur, and a self-made millionaire.
She didn't get any money from her daddy—or me.
Kim is a role model for women and makes more money in a month
than most men do in a lifetime.

– RTK

I'd like you to meet Melissa. She's a bright businessperson, a
radio show producer, and, like many people, she has an investment
retirement account or IRA that she has dutifully contributed to
throughout the years. Melissa also has a financial planner, Jane, who
has been managing her IRA.

Like many people, Melissa hasn't paid much attention to her IRA.
She assumes that her financial planner is doing a good job for her.
But, since Melissa is someone who knows and understands the Rich
Dad/Rich Woman philosophy of taking control of your money, she
decides to take action by actually *opening* her investment account
statement. What do you think she discovered?

In the biggest stock market boom in history, Melissa's retirement
account had declined dramatically. Why? She had no idea. So she
took her next bold step. She met with Jane for the first time since
opening her retirement account and asked why her account was
plummeting while the stock market was at a record high. Jane had
no answers or strategies to offer. When Melissa pressed for an answer
about how she could improve her situation, Jane looked her straight
in the eye, and, in all seriousness, said, "You can always marry a rich
man." Melissa fired Jane on the spot.

What happened was that when the stock market was at all-time highs, Melissa's financial planner didn't have her invested in stocks. Instead, she put Melissa into bonds. Why? Because with little-to-no financial knowledge, some financial planners automatically move their clients out of stocks and into bonds as they get older because bonds are supposedly a "safer," lower-risk investment. However, in this instance, bond prices were falling because there was little demand for them. When the stock market is up and investors feel confident in it, they typically will choose stocks over bonds.

Trusting Strangers

As an educator, I ask, "Why are people so willing to turn their hard-earned money over to someone else—often a complete stranger—to manage? The answers I frequently hear are "I'm too busy," "it's too confusing" and "financial planners/stock brokers/asset managers are professionals." And these are only some of the reasons. Here is another theory.

The Income Trap

Those of you who are familiar with the book *Rich Dad Poor Dad*, written by my husband Robert, or my book, *Rich Woman*, know that we use simple diagrams of an income statement and a balance sheet to educate our readers.

I was raised, like I'm sure many of you were, to set my focus on the income column. I was taught to get a good job that pays well, go for that pay raise and to work my way up to president or CEO because that's where the big money is.

When I worked for an hourly wage, the advice was, "Put in a lot of hours to make more money." Or: "Work to raise your hourly rate to boost your income." Sometimes I would work for free just to learn and people would tell me, "Your time is valuable. Demand to be paid for what you do!" The fixation was always on making more money.

For most of us, we are conditioned by our parents, the school system and society to focus on acquiring more and more *income*. We are taught and driven to focus on the income column. Now, I'm not saying that's wrong or right, good or bad. There are a lot of people who do very well in the income column and make a great deal of money. But in order to *continue* to make that money, they have to *continue* to work hard. (Not to mention the huge amount of taxes they'll probably pay on that ever-increasing income.)

The bottom line is that most of us are taught from a very early age, as I was, to focus on our salary, wages, paychecks, professional fees and bonuses—the *income column.*

A Change of Focus

In 1989, Robert and I lived in Portland, Oregon. It was at that time that he began to explain his rich dad's philosophy on money and investing. The greatest distinction for me was rich dad's definition of an asset and a liability.

This is how rich dad defined assets and liabilities:

An *asset* is something that puts money in your pocket whether you work or not.
A *liability* is something that takes money out of your pocket.

Assets produce cash flow—cash flowing *into* your pocket. Liabilities produce cash flowing *out of* your pocket. Rental properties, businesses, stock dividends and commodities such as oil and gas are all examples of assets… IF they are producing positive cash flow.

In 1989, I began my focus on assets and my journey into the asset column. My first investment was a two-bedroom, one-bath rental property in Portland. Some months, it was an asset. Other months, it was a liability. We continued buying properties that we could rent… single-family homes as well as small apartment buildings. It was interesting and challenging… but at that point, I saw real estate investing only as a hobby. By 1994, our cash flow from these properties ($10,000 each month) exceeded our living expenses ($3,000 per month).

Even though we had cash flow from our investments, my attention was still on the income column. I'd ask myself, *How do we make more money so that we can acquire more assets?* I still considered our investments a hobby, something we did on the side.

In 1995, Robert and I committed to create the board game, *CASHFLOW*®. This would be the start of The Rich Dad Company. Although there were certainly no guarantees of success (or even a sure bet to break even, for that matter), I felt a sense of relief knowing that we were creating a new business that would, ideally, generate more money into our income column.

ITAC

In 1996, the *CASHFLOW* game launched. The next year, we published *Rich Dad Poor Dad*. The business—through a great deal of effort, mistakes, successes and learning—was up and running. *Income* was flowing in!

Then one day it hit me. I was hiking in the mountains of Phoenix (which is where I go when I want time to think) and, as usual, I'm thinking about how to bring more income into the company. I'm admiring the cacti and the desert flowers along the trail—with my mind chattering on about *more income, more income and more income*—when this fleeting thought crosses my mind. "It's not about the income. It's about the *assets* that we are building."

The picture I saw in my mind changed. Instead of income moving from my income column to my asset column… it was the other way around! This is what I *now* saw in my mind's eye: My *assets* were generating my income! I had it all backwards! News Flash: ITAC—It's The Asset Column!

At that moment, I shifted my focus away from the income column. It's not the income that brings wealth. It's the *asset* that creates the income that brings wealth. My focus shifted to the asset column.

"What assets are we building or acquiring?" became the question I relentlessly asked myself. The *CASHFLOW* game is an asset. The book, *Rich Dad Poor Dad,* is an asset. Today, our company builds apps for financial education. If we do a good job, then every app could become an asset. Along with our rental properties, business investments and oil and gas projects, these assets are working hard— instead of Robert and me working hard.

And life got simpler. Shifting my mindset off of the income column and onto the asset column has made a world of difference for me financially.

Most of us have been conditioned since we made our first dollar to focus on income, with little-to-no attention on the asset column. We are taught plenty about how to acquire income. We're taught very little about how to acquire assets.

So, instead of turning your money over to a financial advisor, why not turn it over to your asset column? The questions you may want to start asking yourself are: *"What asset am I building?"* And *"What asset am I acquiring?"* And, of course, *"How will these assets be working for me?"*

The income column is important, but the asset column is where *real wealth* is created.

About Kim Kiyosaki

Kim Kiyosaki, a woman dedicated to life-long learning, has learned what it takes to be successful—in life and in business. Drawing on a lifetime of experience in business, real estate, and investing to support her mission of financial education for women, Kim is a successful entrepreneur and investor, an acclaimed author, and sought-after speaker.

In 1979 Kim graduated from the University of Hawaii with a degree in Business. Her first job was in the media department of the second largest advertising agency in Hawaii where she gained an appreciation of media (and its power) that would serve her well as her business life unfolded.

Jobs with *Aloha Magazine* and *Honolulu Club* magazine, a business publication, followed and gave Kim an opportunity to test her business management skills. It wasn't long before the lure of 'owning her own business' drove her to launch a company, the first of many business ventures, that designed, manufactured and sold logoed apparel and merchandise across the United States.

The following year, 1985, she started a business seminar company that would grow, over the next decade, to span the globe with 11 offices in seven countries. It was during that time that Kim began her real estate investing career with the purchase of a small, 2-bedroom/1 bath rental property in Portland, Oregon. Today Kim's real estate company buys, sells, and manages millions of dollars in property.

In 1995 Kim and her husband Robert Kiyosaki, author of the international best-seller *Rich Dad Poor Dad*, founded The Rich Dad Company, a financial education company. Most people don't know that the book *Rich Dad Poor Dad*—a book published in 1997 that has become the #1 Personal Finance book of all time—was written as a "brochure" for the *CASHFLOW*® 101 board game, an educational game created and produced by Kim and Robert. *Rich Dad Poor Dad* has been translated into 53 languages and is sold in 109 countries around the world. The mission of The Rich Dad Company is to elevate the financial well-being of humanity.

As Kim and Robert traveled the world, sharing their mission and message, Kim became aware of the overwhelming need for tools and resources for women who wanted to take control of their financial futures. In 2006 Kim launched the Rich Woman brand, with a book by that title, and it wasn't long before that brand—powered by her personal story and her ability to connect with women in every corner of the world—grew into a worldwide movement and powerful international brand. Her second book, released in 2011, is titled *It's Rising Time!*

A self-made millionaire, Kim is a happily married (but fiercely independent!) woman who lives in Phoenix, Arizona and Honolulu, Hawaii. She loves golf, her puppy Cutie, and her husband of 30 years. The Kiyosakis host The Rich Dad Radio Show, an hour-long weekly show that airs on stations across the country and is available via podcast downloads.

Kim is a passionate advocate for personal development and the power of financial education and, in sharing her story with the world, has seen, first hand, the positive impact that education and decisive action can have upon women, families, and our world.

Books by Kim Kiyosaki

Rich Woman
Because I Hate Being Told What to Do

It's Rising Time!
What It Really Takes for the Reward of Financial Freedom

AN EXCERPT FROM

AUTHOR OF THE BESTSELLER, *RICH WOMAN*

IT'S RISING TIME!

A CALL FOR WOMEN

WHAT IT *REALLY* TAKES
FOR THE REWARD OF
FINANCIAL FREEDOM

KIM KIYOSAKI

CHAPTER 2

SEEING THE INVISIBLE

To rise beyond what's visible to you takes...

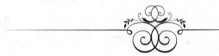

Y ou have your left brain—the logical, analytical, practical side of your world. And you have your right brain—the creative, innovative, intuitive part of your world. And then you have the physical, the spiritual, and everything in between. Rising to meet your financial dreams takes all of it. It takes all of you.

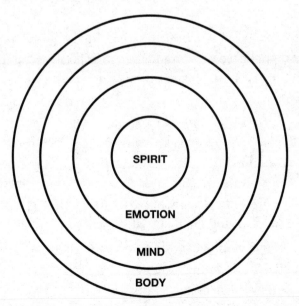

Body

We obviously need our body to get anything done in this physical world we live in. It doesn't have to operate perfectly, but it's an important tool for our financial journey.

Your body will give you signals. Have you ever had a moment when you had a physical sensation in your heart that something was wrong? Or you suddenly felt queasy in your stomach when you were around someone you didn't trust? This is your body giving you clues. Trust those signals. Your body is the physical conduit of your thoughts, emotions, and spirit.

Mind

The brain, a critical part of the body, collects, stores, organizes, and recalls the facts, figures, stories, and information that we need to make sound decisions. Your physical brain is a mass encased in your skull, but have you ever seen a mind or a thought? Your thoughts are part of your invisible world, but they are ever so powerful. They are a driving force in determining the results you have in your life. The tricky part is that some of our thoughts are conscious thoughts, while other thoughts are subconscious and lie hidden under the surface. These hidden thoughts have as much, if not more, power than the thoughts we are aware of.

For example, when you hear the word "investing," what immediate thoughts come to mind? Are they positive thoughts? Negative thoughts? Does the idea of investing excite you, or put you to sleep?

When you hear the words "financially independent," what thoughts do you have? Do you say to yourself, "Yes! I can do this! This journey will be fun!"? Or are you saying, "I'd rather be happy than rich. This sounds too hard. I don't want to lose money."? It's the "I-can't-do-it" or "I-don't-know-how" thoughts in your mind that will prevent you from having the financial success you want.

Janet, a friend of mine, and I were talking about what kind of car she should buy. She is young, bright, single, and attractive. I asked her, "Have you ever test-driven a Porsche?"

She immediately got flustered and irritated. She snapped at me, "I don't want a Porsche!" I was taken back by her instant emotion around this.

"Why?" I asked.

"Because I'm not that kind of woman!" she said quickly.

I had to do my best to keep my cool because—I had a Porsche! I kept calm and curiously asked, "What kind of woman?"

She looked at me like I should know the answer, "The kind that is flashy, loose, flaunts her sex, has no brains, and wants to be seen."

"Wow!" I thought to myself. "How in the world does she associate Porsche with all that?" That thought made no logical sense at all to me, but somewhere in Janet's subconscious, the idea that a female Porsche driver equaled a stupid sex bimbo made perfect sense to her. I decided to skip the psychoanalysis and stop talking cars with her altogether.

The Power of Your Thoughts

One of my favorite books of all time is *As a Man Thinketh* by James Allen, written in 1902. He explains that the purpose of the book is "to stimulate men and women to the discovery and perception of the truth that—*They themselves are makers of themselves.*" He goes on to say, "A man is literally *what he thinks*, his character being the complete sum of all his thoughts." He puts this concept into a poem:

> Mind is the Master-power that moulds and makes.
> And Man is Mind, and evermore he takes
> The Tool of Thought, and, shaping what he wills,
> Brings forth a thousand joys, a thousand ills;—
> He thinks in secret, and it comes to pass:
> Environment is but his looking-glass.

We Hear What We Want to Hear

According to Allen, your thoughts create your world. Your thoughts also determine how you process the information you take in.

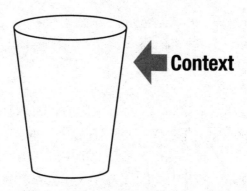

Let's talk about this in relation to money. Imagine that the glass in the diagram represents your thoughts, beliefs, opinions, and judgments—in other words, the foundation or context of your viewpoint on money.

The water being poured into the glass represents information and data you are learning on the subject of money. Let's say we are talking about "financial independence." If your secretly embedded thought is that "I will never become financially independent," then it's quite simple. You will not. If your thought is, "I don't have the time," then you will not have the time.

No matter what information is poured into your glass, it has to pass through your context, or your filter, around money and financial independence. Like brewing coffee, the flow of information is filtered first through your thoughts, opinions, and beliefs before it lands in your glass. The information that does not match up with your core thoughts and beliefs around money will either be rejected or filtered out so that the information can be made to fit your context.

Your context, how you think about money and investing, is often more important than the actual content of investing information. All the data in the world will be of little value to you if your filters, your invisible thoughts, are at odds with your stated goals. When you change your context or thoughts to be supportive and aligned with your goals, then the invisible becomes visible.

How Do You Make the Invisible Visible?

It's not difficult. The first thing is to begin to watch your thoughts. Listen to that little voice in your head. In 1985, a friend challenged me to "spend the next hour catching glimpses of your thoughts." I did, and it changed my life. I had no idea how many self-defeating thoughts were floating around in that head of mine. I challenge you to do the same.

You may also want to write down your thoughts in a journal. When fear sets in, ask yourself, "What am I afraid of?" and just start writing. Don't think about what you're writing. Don't edit it. Don't judge it. Just write. Write until you come to an aha, or realization. You'll be amazed at how much clarity will come through.

Emotion

Your emotions are typically driven by your thoughts. For example, if someone says something very mean and hurtful to you, you will probably get upset because your thought may be that you would never speak so rudely to anyone. What if, on the other hand, you grew up in a society (or family) where really rude remarks were a sign of affection? If that were the case, instead of getting upset, you might actually feel loved. It all depends on your context, which is created by your thoughts.

The primary emotion that comes up for women around money is fear—fear of making a mistake, fear of losing money, fear of what other people might think. One of women's greatest fears today is running out of money during retirement. It's a bit of a Catch-22: One fear is the fear of not having the money to support us as we get older. The other fear is the fear of actually doing what we need to do so that we have that money as we get older. The thing we need to learn is that fear, and then breaking through that fear, is a tremendous catalyst for our own personal development.

I do not know of one woman investor who did not have some, or a lot of, fear in the early stages of her investing life. Even today, given how volatile and uncertain the economy is, I get nervous venturing into new areas of business and investing. It's natural. The problem arises when the fear paralyzes you to the point that you do nothing because you are frozen in your tracks. Or you turn your financial responsibilities over to someone else because you fear making a mistake or losing money. Shelby Kearney of New York City learned that lesson the hard way.

I read Rich Dad Poor Dad *and believed every word, but fear had me paralyzed from taking any action. However, a couple of years later, my boyfriend, who was a realtor, encouraged me to buy a duplex and a triplex. I felt he knew a lot about rental properties, and I was less fearful investing with someone I knew. He also offered to manage the properties for me so I turned over all management responsibilities to him and paid no attention to it.*

Needless to say, both properties went into foreclosure because of mismanagement. I was able to sell one property, but lost the other. After that devastation, I knew I had to educate myself and not rely on anyone else's judgment of a good deal or good management.

In the last few years, I have attended several seminars and read many books on real estate. I tried purchasing several four-plex properties in the Atlanta area, but either got out-bid by other buyers or discovered something unappealing during my due diligence. I figured it was a sign from God and turned my focus to Pennsylvania, which is much closer to where I live in New York City.

Earlier this year, I closed on a single-family property and a duplex in Harrisburg, Pennsylvania. It's been a long time coming, but I'm on my way and it feels soooo good!

Shelby got her lesson. Her solution to reducing her fear came from getting financially educated, trial and error, and then securing her two current properties. There will be no stopping her now.

Spirit

In times of pressure and emergency, you often see a woman's spirit rise to the occasion. When there is a crisis in the family, such as a job loss or a home foreclosure, it is frequently the woman who will step up and do what needs to be done. Her natural instinct is to protect herself and her children. It is her spirit, not her mind, that takes over.

Our spirit also shows us that we are capable of achieving more than we would ever believe. It gives us strength, energy, and focus. There will be times throughout your financial journey when you will call upon your spirit to provide the courage and willpower to take that next step.

Here is a compelling poem about the power of spirit.

Will

You will be what you will to be;
Let failure find its false content
In that poor word, "environment,"
But spirit scorns it, and is free.

It masters time, it conquers space;
It cows that boastful trickster, Chance,
And bids the tyrant Circumstance,
Uncrown, and fill a servant's place.

The human Will, that force unseen,
The offspring of a deathless Soul,
Can hew a way to any goal,
Though walls of granite intervene.

Be not impatient in delay,
But wait as one who understands;
When spirit rises and commands,
The gods are ready to obey.

The river seeking for the sea
Confronts the dam and precipice,
Yet knows it cannot fail or miss;
You will be what you will to be!

— *Ella Wheeler Wilcox*

"The human Will, that force unseen" is the invisible power within you that emerges when you are tested at critical times.

"Can hew a way to any goal, though walls of granite intervene." Your spirit can do whatever it takes, even though it may seem impossible. This is the magic that emerges for something of great importance and meaning to you.

It is when your "spirit rises and commands" that the invisible becomes visible. And it is brilliant.

It Takes All of You

Pursuing and attaining your financial vision will take all of you: body, mind, emotions, and spirit. Achieving your financial dreams is a process. It is an incredibly enlightening, frustrating, eye-opening, and honest process of self-discovery and personal development. There is so much to learn. But in the learning come the growth, the confidence, the fun, and that special freedom.

Ken McElroy

Rich Dad Advisor on Debt, Real Estate and Raising Capital

Personal Background and Entrepreneur Profile

Name   Ken McElroy
Date of Birth   1961
Place of Birth Everett, Washington

Traditional Education
Pacific Lutheran University
Degree: Business

Professional Education
Various Real Estate courses, Entrepreneurs Organization,
Young Presidents Organization, Trade organizations

Grade Point Averages
High school: 3.0
College: 3.0

Value of traditional education... relative to becoming an entrepreneur
I learned accountability and discipline.

Subject I liked most in school:
Field Trips

Subjects I hated most in school:
Math and English

First entrepreneurial Project
A paper route... when I was 12 years old

The key entrepreneurial skill I was *not* taught in school:
How to build strategic relationships

Why and when I became an entrepreneur and my first major venture
I wanted financial freedom and started a property management
company.

Best lesson from first business
Accounting—and how to follow the cash.

What I learned about myself from my Kolbe Index

KEN MCELROY
Kolbe A™ Index Result

CONGRATULATIONS KEN
You Got a Perfect Score on the Kolbe A™ Index

You are uniquely able to take on future-oriented challenges. You lead the way to visionary
possibilities and create what others said couldn't be done. You'll say "Yes" before you even
know the end of the question – then turn it into a productive adventure.

Kolbe Action Modes®

©1997-2017 Kathy Kolbe All rights reserved.

Reprinted with permission from Kolbe Corp.

I learned that I need a team to be successful.

My Role in the B-1 Triangle
Sticking to the company mission

Skills that are essential for entrepreneurs—but not taught in schools
How to sell, how to build teams, how to motivate others

My Most Important Lesson for Entrepreneurs
Hire the best people you can and follow the cash.

How I learned to Raise Capital:
Out of necessity: I ran out of money. The deals got so big that I
had to learn how to raise capital.

How I learned to overcome fear and failure
Trial and error. I sincerely believe that being an average student
helped a lot. I was used to failing on things I attempted,
which helped me become resilient. Over time, worrying about
something failing becomes less of an issue than trying something.

My Personal Strength
Humor

My Personal Weakness
I can be impatient.

The Entrepreneurial Skills I Teach best
How to use debt
How to manage teams.

The Entrepreneurial Lesson I Teach:
Leveraging Debt Can Make You Rich

OPM:
How Leveraging Debt Can Make You Rich
by Ken McElroy

Debt makes the rich richer.
Ken proves that you don't need money to get rich.
And, like President Donald Trump, he's a king of debt.

– RTK

In the words of Ben Franklin: "The money that money earns, earns money."

When most employees get their paychecks they typically deposit them into some kind of savings institution, like a bank. To the bank, these deposits are OPM (Other People's Money) and an expense or a liability of the bank, because it's not the banks money and they owe the depositors interest. At this point, the banks are in "debt" to all the depositors.

This is the beginning of the use of debt—as your hard-earned deposits become a bank's most important source of potential revenue. Banks need your money to lend money. Not only do most checking, demand, NOW, and savings deposits yield low- or no-interest rates, which means the bank is paying almost nothing for the use of this money, but they are often a stable and growing financing base.

Basically, a bank holds OPM (Other People's Money) from depositors, creditors, and other banks at low interest rates, and it lends these deposits, in the form of debt at a higher interest rate to real estate developers, homeowners, and small businesses. This is why banks are referred to as *spread lenders*.

So a bank uses your deposits (their liabilities) to buy assets, which earn income for the bank. By using liabilities, such as deposits or borrowings, to finance assets—such as loans to individuals or businesses, or to buy interest earning securities—the owners of the bank can leverage their bank capital to earn much more than would otherwise be possible using only the bank's capital.

You can use that same strategy and this exact system to get rich—and it is how the rich become richer.

Loans are the major asset for most banks. They earn the banks more interest than they have to pay on deposits, and, thus, are a major source of revenue for a bank.

So the bank uses debt, in this case your deposits, to make loans that enable the bank to exist.

We all need to think like a bank. I'm sure everyone has heard this directive related to money: "Save your money, don't get into debt." Sounds like good financial planning, doesn't it? After all, how can a person get rich if they're up to their eyeballs in debt? Well, I'm here to tell you that that advice is the *worst* piece of financial advice ever given. I just showed you how your savings is used for lending to others, in the form of debt. So why in the world would you save money—if that money (your deposits) is going to be used for the benefit of others? You should be borrowing other people's deposits!

To get ahead you must be heavily leveraged in good debt, just like the banking example above. The key is to have the right *kind* of debt. If you use debt to earn income, just like the banks do, then you are on the right track.

The problem is most people have bad debt. And lots of it.

The strategy is to avoid debt that doesn't pay you. Make it a rule that you never use debt that won't make you money. Rich people use debt to leverage investments and grow cash flow. Poor people use debt to buy things that make rich people richer.

Most advice these days is that your money is safest in the bank. Not exactly. And certainly not always. Money market accounts, savings bonds, your retirement accounts, and index funds may all be alternatives. Obviously, you must do your research or talk to your financial advisor. True, if your money is in the bank, it's safe because it isn't going anywhere and banks' checking and savings accounts are also typically insured.

But if you have a lot of cash sitting in a savings account, you're technically losing money with interest rates so low these days. And while you might have the comfort of seeing a stable account balance, you're also guaranteeing that your buying power will decrease due to inflation.

Currently, inflation is reported at about 3 percent, some people believe it is much higher. Unfortunately, the average savings account today yields about 0.05 percent, so you're still losing money. People are losing about 2.5 percent of their asset's value because their yield on savings isn't keeping up with inflation.

One of the only ways to get ahead is to "invest" in assets that produce returns above the rate of inflation. The quickest way to the highest returns is by using OPM (Other People's Money) in either the form of debt or equity. The system is set up to lend, so use it wisely.

Lastly, compounding your money is the secret to getting ahead much faster. Albert Einstein called compounding "the greatest mathematical discovery of all time."

For those regularly carrying hefty debt on their monthly credit card bill, Einstein's law of financial physics is not good news. But for the savvy investor, the principles of compound interest can be used to make a substantial amount of money over time.

To tap into the money-making magic of compound interest, it's crucial to first understand what compound interest is and how it works. That's when I refer to the "The rule of 72."

As interest compounds, things get bigger. Often it's useful to know how long it will be until the original principal has doubled. It goes like this. Let's say you have an investment with an annual interest rate of 6%. How long would it take for your initial investment to double in value? To estimate this, simply divide 72 by 6. The answer is 12. So, with an interest rate of 6%, it will take approximately a dozen years to double your initial investment.

At 4% interest, it would take 72 divided 4 —or 18 years, approximately, for your investment to double. The rule also works the other way around: What interest rate would you need to receive to double your investment in 5 years? The answer: approximately 14.4%

The best part about this Rule of 72 is that the returns get even greater when you use debt, or OPM. Yes, you can actually get really rich without even using your own money! The long-debated secret of the wealthy.

So the next time you're faced with a big financial decision, do your homework rather than making a snap decision based on what you've heard your entire life. And remember, it costs money to borrow money so be mindful of the interest rate on your loans and focus on cash flow versus capital gains.

This is a long term strategy will allow you to live a lifestyle that you love.

About Ken McElroy

Ken McElroy is the epitome of the word entrepreneur. For over two decades, Ken McElroy has experienced massive success in the real estate world–from investment analysis and property management to acquisitions and property development. With over $700 million investment dollars in real estate, Ken offers a unique perspective on how to get the biggest return on investments.

Ken is the author of the best-selling books *The ABCs of Real Estate Investing*, *The Advanced Guide to Real Estate Investing*, *The ABCs of Property Management*, and most recently his book on entrepreneurship: *The Sleeping Giant*.

As the Real Estate Advisor to Robert Kiyosaki of The Rich Dad Company, Ken and Robert have co-authored several audio programs including How to Increase the Income from your Real Estate Investments, How to Get your Banker to Say "Yes!" and How to Find and Keep Good Tenants. Ken is also a chapter contributor in the newly re-released, *The Real Book of Real Estate*.

A champion and advocate for entrepreneurs and real estate investors, Ken has spoken worldwide at top industry events and does numerous television and radio interviews.

Never taking life for granted, Ken is active in the community and has served as chair two years in a row for the Autism Speaks Walk in Arizona. Ken has also served on advisory boards for Childhelp, and AZ Food Banks where he conducted the largest food drive in the state of Arizona. Ken and his family reside in Scottsdale, Arizona.

Books by Ken McElroy

Rich Dad Advisor Series Books

The ABCs of Real Estate Investing
The Secrets of Finding Hidden Profits Most Investors Miss

The Advanced Guide to Real Estate Investing
How to Identify the Hottest Markets and Secure the Best Deals

The ABCs of Property Management
What You Need to Know to Maximize Your Money Now

... in Spanish

El ABC de la Inversion en Bienes Raices

El ABC de la Administracion de Propiedades

KyleKade Press Books

The Sleeping Giant
The Awakening of the Self-Employed Entrepreneur

AN EXCERPT FROM

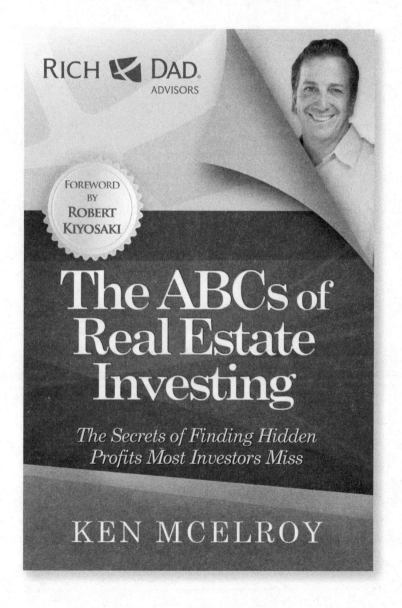

RICH DAD. ADVISORS

FOREWORD BY ROBERT KIYOSAKI

The ABCs of Real Estate Investing

The Secrets of Finding Hidden Profits Most Investors Miss

KEN MCELROY

Chapter One

The Myths
and the Magic

In every business and every industry there are people who just seem to drip with success. They seem to know all the right people, make all the right decisions, be in all the right places at exactly the right time. They seem destined for success whether they even try or not. Real estate investing is no different. In every city or town, there seem to be real estate tycoons that struck it rich through real estate.

These are the people who just make success look easy. They appear confident, knowledgeable, savvy, and seem to see opportunities where others don't. It's easy for onlookers to think the achievements of these golden few are the result of luck or some sort of magic. But magic and luck have absolutely nothing to do with it.

Over twenty years ago, I decided I was going to be one of the people I just described. I was going to make my own success, be my own boss, and achieve financial freedom. And I chose property management as my route. Call it instinct, call it impatience, call it burning desire. I wasn't about to wait for a lucky break or a magic charm. I set out to make my dream happen, and I did it through action.

In the early days of my first property management and real estate deals, there was a lot of trial and error and I made my share of mistakes. But for every one mistake I made, I learned ten lessons and got smarter every day. I started to see patterns, discover formulas and systems, and develop a network of people I could count on. It took time and it took work, but the more I pursued my dream, the luckier I felt and the more often magical opportunities presented themselves to me.

Maybe there is a bit of luck and magic in success. But it's luck and magic that comes from working hard and being prepared. At the Rich Dad Seminars, where I often speak, I see people all the time who are taking the first steps toward future success, much like I did nearly two decades ago. Many have what it takes: the drive and desire that will help them overcome obstacles and be prepared.

Unfortunately, I also see at the seminars some who lack what it takes. They are the ones looking to get rich quick and have little or no idea of the commitment required to achieve business success. Others have a lot of desire, but lack the technical skill and the knowledge that can only come from experience. I wrote this book for them. This is not a get-rich-quick book. It is not a book written to motivate, although I hope you'll be inspired to follow your real estate investment dreams. Instead, it is a book that will disclose proven methods, remove the unknowns, and shorten the learning curve for anyone who chooses investment real estate as his or her path to financial freedom.

Before we get too deep into the how to's of finding, buying, and managing investment property, let's take some time to drive out a few myths, myths that if you buy into them, will only hold you back. I think you'll find the following list familiar. Have you or others said these very things? Are any of these statements echoing in your head and preventing you from moving forward? Are these untruths paralyzing you with fear? Let's get rid of them right up front. It's time to dump the baggage!

Myth #1: You Have to Already Be Wealthy to Invest in Real Estate

People think they need to have a large lump sum of money to invest in real estate. They think it is like saving for their first home or that it's something they can only do once they have made their fortune elsewhere. Both of these thoughts couldn't be further from the truth. You don't need hundreds of thousands of dollars in the bank to invest in real estate and you certainly don't need millions. All you need is a good real estate deal that makes sense—one that has profit potential and is based on solid financials.

My partner and I have been working this way for years. My very first investment deal was a condo that I bought furnished and rented out. It was a two-bedroom unit that I put into a rental program. People who wanted to get away from it all could call up and rent my condo or one of a hundred others for a weekend getaway. A cool $116,000 was what I paid and I put down $20,000 out of my own pocket. You're probably thinking, "See, I knew you had to have some cash to get started in this business."

Well, I did that deal before I knew better. Contrast that with a more recent acquisition of a 182-unit apartment complex in Sun City, Arizona. The total cost was $9 million. Before you close the book and say, this is out of my league, let me finish the story. The down payment was $2 million, which we raised from other investors. My out-of-pocket was zip. I gave the majority of the ownership to the people who lent me the down payment; in essence, I formed a partnership with them. My salesmanship had nothing to do with it. The deal was the hero; it was so good that people wanted to be a part of it. What I've come to know is that there are a lot of people looking for good real estate deals.

Some people are partner-averse, but I think partners are valuable. They help you spread your risk by allowing you to own smaller positions in a number of properties rather than a big position in just one. And it's a fact that teams accomplish more. As for the return? Which deal would you rather do, the $116,000 property that cost you $20,000? Or the one that cost you nothing and yielded you 10 percent of a $9 million deal? For the record, that's $900,000 and I'd choose the latter any day of the week.

Once you have located a real estate opportunity, the task is finding investors who are looking to earn a good return on their money. The first deal you do, granted, is the most difficult, because you are an unproven entity. But trust me: It gets easier and easier with every successful deal you put together.

All things are difficult before they are easy.

Today, my partner and I have people literally standing in line who want to invest in our next real estate venture. Not because we're anything special. But because we are thorough. We look at a lot of deals and choose only the ones that are financially viable like the one above. We also communicate with our investors and treat them fairly. They make money when we make money.

You may be surprised to learn that there are plenty of people interested in investing in real estate, particularly when other investment vehicles like the stock market and bonds are flat or declining. Just look around at a Rich Dad Seminar. There are thousands of people in every city in which we speak who are looking for real estate investment deals that make sense. One of the people in a Rich Dad Seminar could be your first investment partner.

Myth #2: You Need to Start Small-Big Deals Are Too Risky

There is nothing wrong with starting small. Perhaps you're thinking about buying a $250,000 single-family home and making it a rental property. Or even a $320,000 duplex. But why rule out a $2 million, fifty-unit building? Believe it or not, any of these properties are within your reach.

Of course right now you're thinking, "No way! I can't afford a $2 million mortgage!" And to that I say, you may be right, but you don't have to be able to afford it. Here's why. Mortgages on smaller properties like single-family homes are almost always guaranteed through the buyer's own personal earning potential and wealth. You may be surprised to learn that larger investment property loans are secured by the asset itself. In other words, instead of the *$2* million building riding on your own wealth, it is riding on its own valuation. This already is less risk to you.

Let's look at the previous example. The condo I purchased for $116,000 with a $20,000 out-of-pocket down payment was 100 percent my responsibility from mortgage to management. The $9 million project that I owned 10 percent of and no out-of-pocket cost was actually less risky because I had no cash invested and the property was professionally managed. The other property was mine, all mine—for better and for worse. Five years later, I sold the condo for $121,000, a gain of $5,000. Recently we refinanced the 182-unit building, which we had owned less than a year. Its newly appraised value was $11.3 million, more than $2 million above what we paid for it. And since I own 10 percent of the project, I made over $200,000 in less than a year. A testament to the power of buying and managing right and managing well.

This example also demonstrates risk related to valuation. When you buy a house or condo and rent it out, appreciation of the property rests solely on the appreciation of the surrounding neighborhood. You better have bought in the right neighborhood, because there is little you can do to increase the value of your property. By contrast, appreciation in commercial property, like apartment buildings, is based on the cash flow of the property itself. The more money it makes, the more money it is worth. Now you're in control! When cash flow increases so does the value of the property. Manage your property right and you'll increase the value. Don't manage it right, and the value will stay the same or go down.

Another way larger properties are less risky relates to occupancy. When a single-family home is rented, it's 100 percent occupied. When it is empty, it is 100 percent vacant, and you are covering the mortgage out of your own pocket in its entirety. In a larger property, even an eight-unit building, if one resident leaves, you still have seven residents paying rent. Your exposure related to occupancy is greatly reduced the more residents you have.

Myth #3: You Can "Flip" Your Way to Success or Get Rich Quick with No Money Down

Many people think that flipping property, in other words buying it and quickly turning around and selling it for more than you paid for it, is the way to grow wealth. The people who believe strongly in this have been lucky enough to make money this way. But in my opinion, this is like day trading in the stock market. It isn't easy, and it is very risky.

No money down is another way of saying that the property is 100 percent financed. That means a much larger part, if not all, of your cash flow is going toward the monthly payment. In no-money-down deals, you'll be paying higher interest rates because there is greater risk to the lender, have higher loan costs, and have virtually no money to improve the property or even repair it should something break. With this model, you are banking on the property appreciating to make money rather than improving the operations of the property and making money through cash flow. Let's hope the market is high-flying and that you time it perfectly because you'll be banking on external factors being just right. Appreciation, as you'll see in great detail later, is only in your control when you've improved cash flow. In this scenario you have none!

As you might have guessed, I don't believe in zero dollars down, and I don't believe in flipping property. Even in the example where I personally put no cash down on the $9 million apartment building in Sun City, we as an investment team put $2 million down. I believe that buying and holding income-generating assets like rental properties is how you build wealth. You may say, "But I need the capital gain—the additional equity I've made on this property—to buy a second bigger rental property with more units. That means I have to sell the first one." In my experience this just isn't true. What you need is a second investment deal that makes sense that you can bring to investors. They will help you raise the down payment on the second property and you will reward them as the investment makes money.

In 2004, we finished construction of a 208-unit property located in Goodyear, Arizona, which cost us $13.8 million to build. Upon completion it appraised for $16.3 million. We have received numerous offers to sell this property and brokers were standing in line for the listing. As tempting as it was to walk away after two years' work with $2.5 million in cash, we did not sell it. The problem is one of taxation. Had we taken the $2.5 million gain, we would have been forced to place that money back in the market to avoid a pretty hefty tax bill. Sure we had appreciation, but we also had what is known as a "taxable event." Imagine the tax bill of 30 percent on a $2.5 million gain. That's an unnecessary $750,000 tax payment.

If you want the money out, you don't need to sell. You refinance the property and pull out what equity you can. There is no taxable event, and you are not forced to put the money into another investment. In the case of the 208-unit property, we will refinance and we will use the equity that we pulled out of the property to pay back our investors with interest. It's a great system and best of all you still own the property, you continue to receive cash flow from the building in the form of rent, and as the building appreciates, you can refinance and take the gain—tax-free—again. That's the money that you can use for other deals and it's what I do every day.

Property 95 percent of the time is going to become more valuable, not less valuable as the years pass. Especially if you follow the methods in this book that teach you to buy property right so you can afford the necessary improvements that will revitalize the neighborhood and make it a better home for residents. All that adds value and it makes sense to ride the wave of appreciation long term.

Myth #4: Some People Just Have the Midas Touch

It is easy to think that people who are successful investing in real estate have some sort of Midas Touch. But there is no such thing. They are just people who see opportunities and know how to make them real and profitable.

Take any ten-acre piece of land. Let's say this parcel is flanked by significant retail presence on all sides and most of the big retail chains are represented in adjacent centers. There's also a large microchip manufacturer nearby that employs 1,000 people.

Ask a tract home builder and he'll see forty single-family homes on that ten acres. Ask a custom builder, and he'll see ten luxury estates. Ask a retail commercial developer and she'll see a new shopping center anchored by two large retailers, with specialty stores and restaurants as fill-in. Ask a multifamily developer and she'll see a 150-unit apartment community with clubhouse, pool, and workout facility. Another commercial developer who specializes in office space may see a three-story office building. In other words, everyone sees the property differently, and each vision will deliver a different level of payout—some better than others.

The important part of recognizing opportunities is common sense. People who seem to have the Midas Touch use their common sense when looking at property and opportunities. In the example here, common sense tells me that building custom homes would be a tough sell on a ten-acre parcel flanked by heavily trafficked retail. Single-family tract homes may be just as challenging. Additional retail may be viable if the developer can lure high-quality anchor tenants to the location. But they may already be operating in other nearby centers. By far in this example, either multi-unit housing or office space are the most viable options. Why? Because of the nearby employment base, the absence of apartments in the area, the proximity to retail, and the lack of office rentals. The developer in this instance who builds offices or apartments will have the best chance of success and will appear to have the Midas Touch. There's no magic, just common sense.

How do you know you're relying on your common sense? It's easy. If everyone you talk with is having difficulty seeing your vision for a property it can be either one of two things: A revolutionary idea that will prove everyone wrong. Or a bad idea that everyone recognizes as a bad idea, except you. In 99 percent of the cases, the latter proves to be true. Remember, if you have to hard-sell your vision for a property to everyone you share it with, it is likely your project when completed will be a hard sell, too! And that will cost you money.

Myth #5: You Need a Great Deal of Confidence

Not true. People underestimate themselves all the time. They listen to that little voice of self-doubt that whispers and sometimes shouts in their brain telling them all the reasons why they can't do something, why they shouldn't even try. I believe there are two voices: the voice of reason, and the voice of self-doubt. The voice of reason is common sense; the voice of self-doubt is your past leading your future.

I made a conscious decision not to let my past dictate my future. I grew up in an average middle-class home. There's nothing wrong with that. In fact, in my estimation, there's everything right with that. I worked for what I got. I learned solid values. A good deal of that came from my parents. My father was not particularly entrepreneurial until later in his career. Hardworking, yes, but not entrepreneurial. He worked for the same company for most of his career and earned a stable living that supported our middle-class lifestyle. It was a good life for me, my brother, and two sisters.

When I got out of college I followed in my dad's footsteps and got a job. But while in that job, I began to meet people—people who showed me their entrepreneurial ways. They became my mentors, and from them I became entrepreneurial. Then I combined the innate values I received from my parents and my own newfound entrepreneurial spirit and I became whole.

Nothing in my upbringing would have prepared me for what I'm doing now. And yet everything did. I believe it is up to each of us to let go of the memories and the scars of unsupportive fathers, ultra-critical mothers, ridiculing friends, and teachers who labeled us from the first day of school. Everybody has had negative influences in their lives and every one of us will have lots more. Look at Hollywood. What's a celebrity profile on E! without the struggles, without the strife? Everyone must rise from challenging situations—that's what successful people do. They decide to get beyond their past, whatever it may be. I've chosen to accept my past, learn from it, copy what was good, and realize the bad stuff only makes me stronger.

Real estate investing is a business where you will need to draw on your strength. My advice is not only to look for strength in all that is good in your life, but also to use the hard times for what they are: character-building experiences. And contrary to what most people think, we can never have enough character. That's my soapbox on confidence and character. The rest of this book is dedicated to building your property investment business.

Myth #6: You Want to Do It but Don't Really Have the Time

This really comes down to choices and priorities. There is always time to do the things we need to do like go to work every day, mow the lawn, feed the dog. Often there isn't time to do the things we really want to do. Learn to speak a second language, build a bookcase, or volunteer in the community. There is a difference between need and want. We'll often do what we need and put off what we want. Unfortunately our wants are what truly enrich our lives.

The investment real estate business is something you should want to do and may even need to do. It's work. To be truly successful, especially in the beginning, you will be involved in the day-today activities of finding and evaluating property, negotiating deals, overseeing contract repair work, possibly even managing the property once it's yours. I can honestly say, I find the business rewarding, fun, and because of that, it is profitable.

I fell victim to the myth of not having enough time myself, and I take full blame. Robert Kiyosaki asked me to write this book several years ago. Finally I embraced the idea and actually started wanting to get it done. But wanting was not enough. What got me going was a do-it-or-else deadline.

That got my attention and made me realize I needed to get disciplined and write the book. That's what got the book done.

If you don't have the time to begin your real estate investment business, maybe in your mind, you don't really *need* to do it. Maybe you simply *want* to do it, and "want" alone may not be enough to get you started. After all, if you work during the week at another job, you will have to search for and evaluate property on the weekends. You'll need to make phone calls when you can during the week or in the evenings. There's always a way to make your dreams come true...as long as they are truly your dreams.

Myth #7: You Have to Know Somebody to Get Going in This Business

While knowing a few key people such as a real estate agent, an attorney, or a banker may save you some time, you don't need to know anyone even remotely connected with investment real estate to get started. In this book, you'll discover the key people you need to have on your team. And you'll find that the goals you set for yourself will actually define the team. People you know today may or may not be the ideal people for your team once you determine what you want to gain from your real estate investment business.

Just get started and you'll be surprised how many people you'll get to know and how much they will teach you. You'll have "friends in the business" before you know it. Here's what I mean. We're doing a deal in Portland, Oregon. I live and work in Arizona. I hadn't been to Portland in over ten years. Anyone I had once known there was long since gone. Neither I nor anyone else in my company knew a soul in Portland. What we did know was that the city was situated on two rivers and that unemployment was high. The latter meant that the people who owned property were probably not doing so well. And to me that spelled buying opportunity. We had one big problem: We knew *about* the city, but we didn't know a single person *in* the city. We figured the market conditions were at least worth a plane trip and a few days in Portland.

Before our trip, we made our minds up to find our team, at least the start of it. So we went on the Internet and looked up property managers, city officials, brokers, and so on in preparation for our trip. We were not about to travel that far and not meet with anyone who could educate us about the market. As a result, we had ten or twelve meetings over a period of two days. It cost us a few lunches and dinners, but we had the beginnings of our team.

Myth #8: You Have to Be a Seasoned Negotiator and Businessperson

Again, this is just not true. Experience in business may make that first walk into an investor's office more comfortable, but that's all it will do. Your true power and confidence won't come from your past experience. Instead, it will come from the solid deal you assemble that is a win-win for everyone involved. This book will show you how to find and evaluate property with the ultimate goal of establishing a realistic purchase price that maximizes your monthly income and appreciates the asset. Find a deal like that and everyone will want a piece of the action.

Over the years, I've walked away from a lot of deals, and negotiation had nothing to do with it. One of those deals was a 205-unit building in Glendale, Arizona. The listing price was $7.9 million and the broker told me there were other offers—the highest one being $7.2 million. We did our homework on the property and by my estimation, $7.2 million was fair based on the operations of the property. The seller declined every offer and pulled the listing. Six months later, the seller relisted the building for $8.1 million. If I had still been interested in the property I would have made an offer based on operations. It would have been the same $7.2 million offer I made before. The seller would probably kick me out, along with everyone else who made him an offer based on operations. Are you surprised to learn that he still owns the building today?

With the method in this book, you'll find out that the listing price is meaningless. There is no point negotiating based on this number, and actually doing so is a recipe for disaster. That's because in most cases, the listing price is the seller's opinion of what the property is worth. It is not founded on the actual operations of the property. What most people consider negotiation meetings are for me more accurately described as presentation meetings. That's when I present the numbers, and they are pretty much take-it-or-leave-it deals. When I get kicked out, and in truth, usually it is a mutual parting of the ways, it's because the numbers don't work. Walking away is a good thing.

Myth #9: You Have to Know a Lot About Real Estate

This myth holds people back every single day. They feel they have to already be experts in a field in order to be successful, whether it is real estate or stock investing or dry cleaning! First of all, success is a journey, it's not a destination, and all successful people start at the same place. One day they wake up, they throw their legs over the side of the bed, they yawn—and they begin.

Only by beginning and by continuing day after day do we ever become experts. We gain expertise through experience. By reading this book, you'll get a solid framework from which to begin. And you'll gain enough knowledge to sound really smart at cocktail parties and backyard barbecues, but more importantly you'll learn tons more from your first deal. And more still from your second and third. And even more from your fourth.

I learn something new with every venture. Some of the buildings we had bought in Portland were built on an old wooden pier constructed in the 1930s. Who would have guessed when I embarked in this business that I would have to learn everything about the structural integrity of seventy-year-old piers? Not me, but we needed to find out everything about the condition of that pier before we went forward and purchased the property. I live in the desert. So you can imagine how foreign it was for me to hire divers and a boat and structural engineers to do the inspections. It was a real learning experience. I'm always encountering something new. That's part of what keeps it all interesting.

The only way you'll know a lot about real estate is to begin in real estate. Once you do that, you'll meet people, learn your market, see the patterns, and understand the trends. You'll encounter your own seventy-year-old wooden piers, but that will keep it fun. And before you know it, you'll be wowing people at cocktail parties and barbecues with experiences you've lived rather than just read about.

Myth #10 You Can't Be Afraid of Failing

Show me an entrepreneur who says he or she isn't afraid of failing and I'll show you a liar! A bold statement, absolutely, but a true one. Everyone is afraid of failing. The difference is that some of us let that fear of failure hold us back. Sometimes fear stops us from beginning altogether and that's unfortunate. If that's the case, make the decision now to just begin putting one foot in front of the other, making one phone call at a time, visiting one property, and then another. It's not hard, but it can seem so if we focus on the end result instead of the tiny—and very doable—steps in between.

Sometimes fear of failure occurs when it comes time to "pull the trigger" on a property. I call it analysis paralysis and people fall into it all the time. They overanalyze an opportunity and are never quite able to sign on the dotted line. This book will prove especially helpful to people with this sort of fear because it will show you exactly what you need to know to analyze an investment property. When the numbers add up, no further analysis is necessary. Frozen in fear will be a thing of the past.

Another way fear of failure presents itself is through regret. In other words, we've pulled the trigger, but then when difficulties occur—and they will occur, they always do—we regret the decision and waste energy by asking "Why did we do this?" instead of "What can we do to get past the hurdle?" This form of fear can turn an otherwise great opportunity into a bad investment. In my life, I don't regret decisions. I just consider the place where I'm at as the starting line and go for the gold every day.

I admit when I was just starting out I had an acute fear of failing. The difference is I knew that if I did nothing and remained frozen in fear, I would fail. I felt I had a better chance of success by just going forward one step at a time to make some opportunities pay off. That's the thing about fear of failure, if you don't use it to your advantage as a motivator, it becomes a self-fulfilling prophecy.

Myth #11: You Have to Know the Tricks of the Trade

There are no tricks of the trade in the purest sense of the term. But there are secrets to success in life. And as long as you know those, you'll be successful at anything. First, you have to set goals. Goals will be the foundation of the roadmap for your success. They will also tell you when you have arrived, so you can pat yourself on the back. Everyone needs that reinforcement. Not coincidentally the next chapter is all about goal setting.

Second, you have to persevere. Quitting when things get tough doesn't produce winners. In fifteen years, I could have quit a hundred times. I've had plenty of tough problems. Financing that falls through, employee problems, and downright frightening resident issues. But successful people work through difficulties and they come out on the other side stronger, more confident, and better prepared for the next challenge. And trust me, there will be more challenges.

Finally, you have to understand the process. That's what this book will do. It will take you from beginning to end and every step in between. From setting goals to setting up your team, to finding property, to evaluating it, to determining a purchase price, to managing it, I'll let you in on fifteen years' worth of experience. I hope this book will become your handbook for success.

CHAPTER ONE ACTION STEPS

- Understand the myths in this chapter.

- Ask yourself if there are any others.

- Identify the ones you believe to be true.

- Determine which myths have been responsible for hindering your success.

- Make the commitment to abandon these unproductive myths.

- Make the commitment to learn techniques and preparedness so magical things happen.

Blair Singer

Rich Dad Advisor on Sales and Teams

Personal Background and Entrepreneur Profile

Name   Blair Singer
Date of Birth February 20, 1953
Place of Birth Canton, Ohio

Traditional Education:
Ohio State University, Columbus Ohio
Degree: Bachelor of Arts
Major: Political Science

Professional Education
Professional Selling System, Burroughs Corporation

Grade Point Averages
High School: 3.3
College: 3.0

Value of traditional education... relative to becoming an entrepreneur
Traditional education was actually a huge handicap—as I started into business completely risk averse and terrified I'd screw up.

Subject I liked most in school
Political Science in college... and the study of how to get people to do things they would not normally do. How to make change on a global scale.

I also liked being a manager for the OSU football team and travelling the country learning the lessons of leadership and team.

Subject I hated most in school

Organic Chemistry and Genetics —I started school in Pre-Med!

First entrepreneurial project

Cutting grass and shoveling snow in Ohio. I "owned" two city blocks, which I thought was a big deal at the time. Later I was part of an ill-fated surf and sail shop in Waikiki in which we made no money, had a lot of fun, and got introduced to personal development—which set the direction for the rest of my life.

The key entrepreneurial skill I was *not* taught in school

How to make mistakes and learn how to learn from them instead of being embarrassed and avoiding them all together. I was also not taught how to be accountable and responsible for myself. It took moving half way around the world and being totally on my own to finally get it.

Why and when I became an entrepreneur and my first major venture

My first real entrepreneurial endeavor was something that "seemed like a good idea at the time." It was in 1981. I was a top sales rep for the Burroughs corporation at the time and bored as... you know what. Because I was a competitive sailboat racer and because I was new to Hawaii, and had just gone through a painful divorce, I was looking for a way to become part of something bigger. A friend of mine convinced me to invest $10,000 into a business he had just taken over. It was a surf shop and Prindle catamaran dealership. The one thing we could both do well was sell. What we could not do was run a business.

When it came to inventory, purchasing, retailing, accounting, and cash management we were like a couple of children. However it was some of the best fun of my life. I would never take it back. The friends I made were all crazy entrepreneurs and I found out in a short period of time I had a TON to learn. Ever since I had been a little kid, I loved to learn new stuff…. and this was a world with endless possibilities and certainly endless learning opportunities. I had always revolted against people telling me things I could NOT do—parents, teachers in school, employers... As an entrepreneur the freedom was instantly infectious. I also learned that freedom would sometimes come at great cost, I also learned it was ALWAYS worth it.

Best Lesson from first business:

The best lessons I learned from my first business were how little I knew about business!! I had always figured that there was no problem in business that more sales couldn't solve. Boy was I wrong. I learned that little omissions or small inadequacies become super big when you add more sales to them. Bad accounting, questionable partners, no cash flow management... all set us up for lots of drama and countless fire drills.

It was not until my second major entrepreneurial endeavor that I REALLY got the lessons. In the first case, I was convinced that most of our problems were my partners' fault. I had yet to truly learn my lesson about being 100% responsible for my actions, in business and in my life.

Years later, in Los Angeles, I took over a failing air-freight trucking operation with hopes of becoming a multimillionaire instantly. Another rude awakening. It was there that I learned powerful secrets of great organizations. From the brink of numerous disasters in that business, it was our Code of Honor or internal rules that pulled us through time and time again. I learned how to take ordinary, sometimes uneducated and even skeptical people and turn them into a championship team. I learned that success was a function of business skills, like the ability to sell, recruit, and run a team, teach others how to sell, accountability to numbers and to a Code of Honor. It also required a ton of personal development training for myself and my team. I realized that the biggest problem with my business in Hawaii and my business in LA was ME!! I realized that the more I worked on getting my head right, the more the business flowed. It was all my well-intended conditioning from growing up on a farm in Ohio, going to school, being good and not making mistakes, not trusting anybody that had put the brakes on my success.

Best lesson: I learned that I really love to lead, teach, and inspire teams.

What I learned about myself from my Kolbe Index

CONGRATULATIONS BLAIR
You Got a Perfect Score on the Kolbe A™ Index

You are uniquely able to take on future-oriented challenges. You lead the way to visionary possibilities and create what others said couldn't be done. You'll say "Yes" before you even know the end of the question – then turn it into a productive adventure.

Kolbe Action Modes®

©1997-2017 Kathy Kolbe All rights reserved.

Reprinted with permission from Kolbe Corp.

The biggest lesson from my Kolbe is that there are really no weaknesses… just a series of specific strengths. I had always beat myself up for not planning well. But from the Kolbe I discovered that it was an apparent weakness that was covering my ability to be incredibly creative under pressure and at a moment's notice. Planning actually squashed my creativity.

My Role in the B-I Triangle

My role in the B-I Triangle is clearly communication. Aligning teams, establishing and communicating mission and purpose, and of course sales and marketing.

Skills that are essential for entrepreneurs—but not taught in schools

1. I agree that the willingness to make mistakes is by far the most important skill of all. Learning to embrace them as learning experiences rather than indictments. To eliminate the shame, the denial and the justification that goes with them. Most of those responses, by the way, are actually taught in school as a matter of survival.

    Learning how to embrace mistakes and the lessons they hold is as critical as learning not to fear making them in the first place. Once you make a mistake, you end up having to deal with it one way or another. However the fear of making one has at times paralyzed me from making any decision at all. That fear causes stress, confusion, worry, self-doubt, and a host of other ailments that simply rob you of your dreams.

2. The most important business skill by far is the ability to SELL. Sales = Income. From that ability comes the ability to generate income, allocate resources, recruit great partners and team players, negotiate, and the ability to get others to buy into your goals and dreams. There are many who consider sales to be a "dirty" word. Something they would choose to avoid. Why? Probably because of their fear of rejection or embarrassment.

    I have NEVER seen a successful entrepreneur that could not sell. It is the life-blood of any business, but it is also key to getting anything you want from life. I have worked with hundreds of thousands of individuals over the last 25 years and thousands of businesses and any time I see a person or business with a cash flow problem it is because that person or someone key in that business doesn't know how to sell, doesn't like to sell, or doesn't think its important.

Every person on a business team must sell!

3. The second most important skill is the ability to recruit and build a championship team. Unless you played sports in school, you never learned team. Trying to cooperate in school was considered cheating. Yet in business, cooperation is essential. We are trained to work hard and do things on our own. I was actually taught that asking for help is a sign of weakness! It was no wonder that I had such a rough road early in my business career. Simply learning how to establish and implement a simple Code of Honor, or set of team rules, will radically improve any group of individuals working toward a common set of goals.

4. As an entrepreneur, I learned that you have to learn how to "teach." Why? Because the skills of business are not well taught in school. Therefore you have to teach your teams how to sell, how to cooperate, how to succeed. I consider this to be one of the most underplayed skills in business. Those leaders who are great teachers build incredible teams and organizations.

5. I would say that learning how to "win the war between your ears" is critical in this day and age. Learning how to manage your own emotions, psychology, and personal development is not an option—it's mandatory. As things get more complex, emotions tend to rise and intelligence can drop. Continually working on myself and on my emotional responses—my doubts and my fears—has paid me back millions of times over.

My Most Important Lesson for Entrepreneurs

Bad partnerships have led to finding great partners… and powerful lessons.

It is true that you cannot do a good deal with a bad partner, but I know that I have had a series of dubious partners who have led me to the greatest partnerships and friends of my life. My first partner in the surf shop was a hustler, but it was through him that I got started into the world of personal development. Once in that world, I partnered with my teacher and mentor who was brilliant and changed my life, but was a financial disaster. But through him, Robert, Kim and I became true friends and partners.

In my life, partners have always been there to show me the next big lesson I needed to learn. Even in the trucking business, the shady dealings of my partners taught me the true meaning of accountability and taking 100% ownership. My ex-partner in our global sales franchise taught me the importance of having alignment of values and how powerful it can be when an organization is lined up with them—as well as how destructive it can be when it's not. He got me clear on my own values and direction and cured me of my lack of confidence in myself.

How I learned to raise capital

I first learned to raise capital under major duress. When my trucking company was upside down $750,000, due to the loss of a lot of money to a factoring company, we had no money for payroll (for our 30+ staff) or operating expenses. I had to literally BEG the bank to cover our payroll for a few weeks until I could go to all my customers and BEG *them* to pay us in advance for services we had not even rendered yet, and BEG suppliers to keep working with us until I could pay them. At the time it didn't seem like raising capital, it seemed more like lots of passionate selling. That was a tough nine-month period, but it taught me how to ask for money.

It was not until very recently that I actually took the time to learn to raise capital in an organized, legitimate way to fund a business and real estate project.

How I learned to overcome fear and failure

I don't know if I ever fully learned how to overcome fear. I still have fear and I certainly still fail from time to time. I guess I have learned how to manage it. I have learned to change my response from fight or flight to inquisitiveness and curiosity. I continually seek counseling, coaching, and mentorship in the areas that scare me the most or consistently. Whenever there is something that I am afraid of, I've found that I have this built-in response that forces me to want to do it anyway—simply conquer the fear.

I have helped thousands of people make billions of dollars over the years. I have done well for myself, too, but actually raising capital from investors for my own deal was something I had never done until recently. I was afraid that if I failed in my endeavor, I would take others down with me. Because of past business experiences, it was a legitimate fear. Yet I was determined to overcome that fear and, under the amazing mentorship of Ken McElroy and other Rich Dad Advisors, I successfully did it. The whole exercise was as much about overcoming my fear and learning something I had always wanted to learn as it was about doing the deal itself.

I also learned that when failure or mistakes do happen, assemble your team or advisors to help you work through it rather than suffering alone and trying to figure your way out of it by yourself. Soooooooo much easier and so much more successful. Big improvement for a guy who didn't trust anybody and had to prove to the world I could do life on my own.

My personal strength

My strength is definitely my energy and my endurance. I believe that highest energy wins… physically, mentally, emotionally and spiritually. I was a distance runner in high school and I built an inner thought that I can out last just about anyone (for the right reasons of course). It has kept me in the fight longer than most and allowed me to learn the most. I do not give up easy, am very disciplined about some things and very willing to be a student or even an apprentice in the areas I want to grow in.

My personal weakness

My personal weakness is still my concern about what others think about me. It has held me back more than once. As I have learned to accept myself with all the good, the bad and the ugly… my ability to be real and not worry about what others think fades away.

The Entrepreneurial Skills I Teach best

Team-building and Communication

The Entrepreneurial Lesson I Teach

Sales = Income

Sales = Income
by Blair Singer

If you want more money,
learn how to sell.

– RTK

It's not unusual for people to remember their "firsts"… and I'm no exception. Like most people, I've had a lot of firsts. Here's one that taught me a lot of things.

My First Sales Presentation

It was a bitter cold February morning in the rural farmlands of northeastern Ohio. I remember the details because my Mom had bundled me up in a blue snowsuit that made me look like the Michelin tire guy and was so stuffed that I could only waddle. It was around my 5th birthday and I was bumping along the dirt roads sitting next to my grandfather in his cattle truck. The cold didn't matter to me because there was a lot on the line.

In the back of the truck was Sam. Sam was my lamb that my grandfather had "loaned" to me about a year earlier. (He got the lamb as part of one of the many livestock deals and trades that were part of how he made his living.) It was part of a lesson he was determined to teach me very early. The deal was this: He loaned me Sam and I had to take care of him and beef him up for the purposes of selling him. Why? Because for my last birthday I wanted an electric train set, but my parents (hard working dairy farmers at the time) said they could not afford it. My grandfather however told me if I wanted the train, I would have to earn it. That's how I learned… that if I want to buy something, I must first SELL something.

So as we pulled into the parking lot at the livestock auction, I was still practicing the sales presentation that I was going to give. They unloaded Sam and we walked inside to the auction arena. There were probably 75 to 100 farmers there, mostly Amish, waiting to either watch their stock get sold or buy stock they needed for their herds. My grandfather was well known in the community and I had been there with him many times. But this time it was different.

Almost immediately there was a pause in the furious auctioning and bidding. A big handler came over, lifted me over the brass railing and hoisted me waaaay up onto the auctioneer's podium. The whole place went silent. Everyone was looking at me. Sam was led into the ring and, with a huge smile, the auctioneer pushed the big microphone over to me and nodded his head. I saw my grandfather sitting there grinning from ear to ear. IT WAS SHOW TIME!

All these year later, I thank my grandfather for his wisdom to teach me so much with so little effort. At age five, he gave me a gift that ensured that I would always be able to make money—anytime, any place, and in any economy. He taught me that sales is the ticket to having whatever I wanted. He taught me the value of exchange. That I had to somehow add value to other people's lives or businesses and that if I learned how to ask for it, I could always make money. He taught me the freedom of having my own money and the idea that my lifestyle could determine my income. Not the other way around.

That is why when I met Robert and Kim we became such great friends. We shared the same philosophy: "Let your lifestyle and your dreams determine your income… not your income determining your lifestyle."

That's only possible, however, if you know how to SELL. Robert had gone to work for Xerox after his tour in Vietnam because his rich dad told him that sales was the Number 1 skill a person had to master to be a successful entrepreneur. I went to work for the Burroughs Corporation for the same reason. At the time, those companies were world-renowned for having the best sales training programs in the world.

In the 30 years that I have worked with entrepreneurs, big and small businesses and aspiring individuals, any time I have seen cash flow struggles it is because that person—or that business or certain people in the business—either don't like to sell, don't think it's important to sell, think their products will sell themselves (crazy!), or think they already know how to sell when they don't.

YOU know the stats: 95% of businesses fail in the first three years, not because they do not have great products or services or because the business owners don't work hard. They work their you-know-whats off. Businesses fail because the owners, manager, or sales teams cannot sell. They fail because they run out of money and can't raise capital… same (sales!) problem. Or they work alone and cannot recruit a team… same problem.

By the way, I still remember part of my well-rehearsed presentation that day at the auction. "This is Sam. He is my lamb. I got him at an early age and fed him with a bottle. I am using the money I make from selling Sam to buy an electric train." I remember they all chuckled. I didn't know if that was good or bad. All I know is that, as usual, the bidding was fast and furious. I am sure the audience of buyers was amused and simply trying to get this one over with so they could get on with their other business. I actually think I got the sympathy vote that day.

My grandfather collected the money. I don't know how much I made at the end of the day, but I do know that on my 5th birthday, I had a brand new HO-gauge electric train set. More importantly, I was now in control of the rest of my life.

So the lesson here is clear. You must know how to sell. Because sales = income. It is what separates the rich entrepreneurs from struggling and poor ones. So why is it so elusive for so many? In some of my programs that I conduct throughout the world, I have my audiences do a free word association on the word *salesman*. I hear people shout out words like *pushy, slimy, no integrity, used cars, annoying, pest, manipulator* and many others. For many, the word *sales* is a dirty word. It brings up negative images and disdain. And the easiest way to avoid all of that is to convince yourself that you are not a selling-type-of-person and don't sell. But then you're broke!

If you are going to be a rich entrepreneur, learn to master the three parts of sales. This is true whether you are selling person-to-person, on social media, via digital marketing, or business-to-business.

First Part of Sales

The **first part** is the obvious. Learn how to find out what people want and give it to them. That's it!! Really simple. How do you do that?

Here are the steps:

- **Find people with money and a need**... don't waste your time with those who cannot exchange with you. In social media this is critical. Identifying a very specific niche and catering to their needs is far better than a shotgun approach.

- Approach and **contact** them... learn the art of building **rapport**. Ask questions, be interested, go into their world first.

- **Identify their problems** and challenges, both technical and emotional.

- Learn to be able to **present** your solutions based upon what they tell you.

- Give the **benefits** of your solutions. Take the time to explain the **value** of your solutions based upon their problems. This is the most important part. If the person objects to "price," it is because you have not articulated enough value.

- Turn their **objections—a No into a Yes—**through lots of questions and digging out the truth.

- Make a compelling **offer and close** the deal by learning how to ASK. Because if you don't ask, the answer is already NO.

- Return to get great **testimonials**. These are clearly great for marketing, but also force you to make sure that you delivered on the promise you made during the sale.

We could spend a long time on any one of these steps, but in the brief time I have with you here, just know that with lots of practice, you will master these pieces. Much of this is covered my Rich Dad Advisor series book *SalesDogs—You Don't Have to Be an Attack Dog to Explode Your Income.*

Toughest Sale of All

The **second part** of sales is the toughest sale of all. It is the part that truly draws the line between rich or poor as an entrepreneur. The toughest sale of all is… YOU.

That's right. You selling to yourself. Getting yourself to do what you know you should do, but for one reason or another you don't. Making sales calls, eliminating procrastination, stopping the incessant self-abuse that goes with being overly critical of yourself. I call that argument going on in your head your "Little Voice." You know the one I am talking about? The one that just said, "What Little Voice?" That's the one.

The second part of mastering sales is learning to master that Little Voice so it stops shooting you in the foot and sabotaging your best-laid plans.

I remember in my first real business, I was struggling. I think it was Robert, back in 1982, who suggested I go to a personal development program. It was my first. Somewhere in the middle of that program, I realized that the one thing in common with all the successes and failures in my life, both in business and in relationships (I had just gone through a very painful one-year marriage and divorce) was… ME!! At that time in my life, that was a massive revelation.

All I know is that for the several months after that program, my sales shot through the roof. I was on fire. I went from almost getting fired to becoming number one in sales within the next 18 months. I stopped arguing with myself. I stopped hiding at the Flamingo Café drinking coffee instead of making sales calls. I stopped quitting early when I had "made my quota" of sales calls. I stopped talking myself out of doing what needed to be done. My confidence level was sky high. My close ratios were amazing.

Sales is an emotional contact sport. Every day is a personal development program in which you get a chance to get better as a person. The more you train yourself to deal with the Little Voice, the more you will win.

Most important, I had learned to master the number one Little Voice issue that stops sales dead in their tracks. It's the one issue that sends dreams to the grave with their creators. It is what buries genius, snuffs out leadership, and creates life-long struggle and misery. You want to know what it is?

It's your concern about what other people think or might think about you!

That's it.

Robert and I and about a dozen others used to lock ourselves in a room every Thursday night for months practicing our presentations, practicing handling the most nightmarish objections we could dream up. Why? In order to de-sensitize that killer Little Voice that undermines your plans and goals.

So here is the list of Little Voice issues that could be blocking your income and shutting down sales:

- Lack of **discipline**…
- As my coach Mack Newton defines it: "Doing what you are supposed to be doing, when you are supposed to be doing it, whether you like it or not!"

- Low **self confidence**
- When two people come together in a selling situation, the person with the highest energy wins.
- **Fear**… of humiliation, looking stupid, rejection….you name it.
- **Procrastination**
- Being "**Not** _____ **enough**" (You fill in the blank…)
- Trying to be somebody you are not…

And while we're on that subject…

There are some who would tell you that you have to be like someone else in order to succeed. In my opinion after working with hundreds of thousands of people, not only does that not work and hurt your income, it will crush your spirit.

In *SalesDogs* you will discover your selling genius because there are at least five different sales personalities. You do not have to be the Pitbull attack dog. Perhaps you are the charming and always-looking-good Poodle, the filled-with-irrefutable-evidence Chihuahua, the do-anything-for-you Retriever who operates by the Law of Reciprocity or even the look-you-in-the-eye-super-connected Bassett hound. The key is to be your authentic self and play to your strengths.

The Numbers

The **third part** of mastering sales is also the key to mastering any business. It's called **accountability**. I have been asked my opinion of the most powerful sales motivation tool. I usually say it was the "Monday morning sales meeting" where everyone would have to put their numbers up on the board and be accountable. Number of calls, number of appointments, proposals, closes, etc.

Numbers do not improve unless you measure them. You have to keep track of and be accountable to your activities. If you are only focusing on the sales at the end, you are too late. Selling is a process and you have to master each step of the process before you can master the whole process. That is why you measure each step so you know how and where to improve.

Numbers do not lie. And they tell a story. A story of behaviors and attitudes and efforts. The absence of numbers also tells a story. To lose weight you have to get on the scale. To improve your financial health you have to pull a financial statement.

I find that companies leave millions of dollars sitting on the table because they do not use numbers to train, coach, or improve the way they could. A couple of our trainers worked with a small massage clinic not too far from my home in Phoenix. They simply worked on **one** number in their selling cycle and within six weeks they had improved annual sales from $300,000 to over $700,000. Originally that business owner had said he wanted more leads. They did not need more leads. They simply needed better conversion of the leads they had.

It's clear you have a dream—or you wouldn't be reading this book. But if you can't sell that dream to others, they will not support you. You may sell products and services, but if you are going to be a rich entrepreneur you need to sell more than that.

When I had my little trucking company at LAX in the 1980s, we went upside down over $750,000 in the first nine months. I had 30-plus people on staff, and lots of demanding customers. I begged the bank to cover our payrolls when I had no money, pleaded with customers to pay us in advance for services we had not yet rendered, sweet-talked our suppliers and carriers to continue to work with us even though I could not pay them. It saved our business at the time. It was my first experience raising capital. Yet it terrified me to think that I might not be able to pay it all back.

Many years later it came time for me to expand and build my current business. *My* dream. But I knew that the only way it would happen was for me to raise capital. The memory of those difficult times in the trucking business still haunted me. But I knew it was a Little Voice issue. With great mentorship and lots of Little

Voice coaching, I slowly learned each step of the process of raising capital… from the best in the business. It seemed that once I got my LV—that's Little Voice—out of the way, and healed my past, money started coming in until our first private placement offering was fully subscribed.

Bill Gates SELLS shares in Microsoft. We buy them. Big difference in wealth and income.

Whether it is capital, resources, support, or even love… you must be able to successfully *ask* for what you want and be willing to *exchange* something in the present or the future to make that happen.

At the end of the day you are asking people to trust you. The question is: Are you good for it?

Be awesome.

About Blair Singer

For nearly three decades, Blair Singer has empowered people around the world to go beyond their ordinary selves and reach peak performance rightfully earning him a worldwide reputation as an expert in sales, business and personal growth.

He is a facilitator of personal and organizational change, a trainer and a dynamic public speaker. Blair's approach is one of high energy, intense and precise personal development, and inspiration. His unique ability to get entire groups of people and organizations to shake up the status quo, change behaviors quickly and achieve peak performance levels, in a very short period of time, is due to his high-impact approach.

Blair's clients span 20 countries on five continents and range from Fortune 100 companies to small business owners, entrepreneurs, sales teams and just regular folks. Blair's programs and his teams of world class coaches and trainers touch hundreds of thousands of people globally each year. He applies the same tried-and-true principals that work for big corporations and successful entrepreneurs to the Business of Everyday Living, helping individuals hungry for greater success.

As one of Robert Kiyosaki's original Rich Dad Advisors, Blair imparts two of the most critical skills and elements for success in business (and in life): being able to sell your idea, dream or concept and building a great team to deliver it. His unique slant, however, is that the road to success is paved through a powerful combination of both business development and personal development and knowing how to overcome the limitations and obstacles that arise both personally and within groups.

Blair is the author of three best-selling books. *SalesDogs—You Don't Have to be an Attack Dog to Explode your Income and The Team Code of Honor* are Rich Dad Advisor series books. His latest book, *Little Voice Mastery: How to Win the War Between Your Ears in 30 seconds or Less—and Have an Extraordinary Life!* has led to the creation of several personal development programs that Blair facilitates in cities around the world.

With the creation of SalesDogs®, a methodology that offers life-changing sales and communication success, he and his global team of trainers and coaches have helped thousands increase their income worldwide. This unique process identifies and magnifies the natural strengths of an individual or team and converts them into positive results, personal satisfaction and income.

Blair is considered the "teacher of teachers" in the arena of personal development training and business education. Using his unique brand of high impact teaching, he has taught thousands of individuals and leaders how to be world-class trainers, presenters and spokespeople for their brands and messages.

For the past twenty-seven years, Blair has conducted thousands of public and private seminars with audiences ranging in size from three to three hundred to over 10,000. His clients typically experience sales and income growth of 34% to 260% in a matter of a few short months. His work spans across 20 countries and five continents. Overseas, he works extensively in Singapore, Hong Kong, South East Asia, Australia, South Africa, and around the Pacific Rim.

Books by Blair Singer

Rich Dad Advisor Series Books

SalesDogs
You Don't Have to Be an Attack Dog to Explode Your Income

Team Code of Honor
The Secrets of Champions in Business and in Life

... in Spanish

Vendedores Perros
El codigo de honor de un equip de negocios exitoso

XCEL Press Books

Little Voice Mastery
How to Win the War Between Your Ears in 30 Seconds or Less
and Have an Extraordinary Life!

... in Spanish

La Vocecita

AN EXCERPT FROM

RICH DAD™ ADVISORS

FOREWORD BY ROBERT KIYOSAKI

SalesDogs

You Don't Have to Be an
Attack Dog to Explode Your Income

BLAIR SINGER

Chapter Ten

Dogged Belief
Four Mindsets of Champion SalesDogs

Humans seem to think that they have a complex brain. We have cortexes, limbic systems, reptilian brains and all sorts of other stuff! A big brain is handy for doing your taxes, remembering your anniversary or reading this book. But in sales, sometimes too much gray matter can get in the way.

Dogs, on the other hand, are very simple creatures with rather small brains. They usually react positively to whatever goes on around them because they do not overanalyze, over-theorize or overcriticize themselves. They live for the moment. They respond directly to simplicities of pain, pleasure, love and respect.

The Golden Retriever chasing after a Frisbee is entirely focused on success. He probably doesn't worry about all the times he's dropped the disk in the past. He probably doesn't lie awake at night panicking about whether he is going to be able to catch the Frisbee tomorrow. He just knows he wants to catch it now and nothing else matters!

If that were a human, by the time he got to the park he would be stressed to the max and worrying about what others would say if he dropped it. He'd wonder who he would be letting down if he dropped it and would be already thinking of excuses! The human brain has an amazing gift for linking totally unrelated events in order to come up with weird and wonderful belief systems, superstitions and rituals.

We sometimes come to complex conclusions whenever something out of the ordinary occurs—either good or bad. For example, you make a sales call and it goes particularly badly, you make a total mess of the presentation and the prospect is really rude.

Because our brain is ultimately a pleasure-seeking/pain-avoiding mechanism, it will search the environment for something unique that it can attribute these events to. The conclusion could be as ridiculous as "I washed my hair with new shampoo today." And if you have another painful experience (of any kind) *and* you used that same shampoo in the morning, you suddenly have a belief system that links pain to that shampoo—you will probably suddenly "go off" that shampoo. This is a very simplistic description, but the point is that we often tend to find correlations between totally unrelated items or events. It could take the form of an "unlucky" suit, the way you started your day or the last conversation with your boss.

The quality of your decisions determines the quality of the result. If your decisions are based on a faulty belief system then the results will be warped.

So remember, the next time you get knocked back, or asked to perform a difficult task, or you have to face a fear—see it for what it is in that moment. Just catch the Frisbee—be a dog!

Have you ever noticed that there are some people who seem to have the "magic touch"? It seems that no matter what they attempt, they achieve success. In more than twenty years of personal development, I have always wondered how that happens. I now believe that it is because they instinctively think like dogs.

SalesDogs have four basic mindset disciplines that, once integrated, can dramatically change the results in all areas of life. With these disciplines, you too can have that "magic touch."

Are you interested?

The first and critical question is "Are you willing to truly think like a dog?" If your ego can handle it, I am sure that your bank account will appreciate it, because these mindsets are the reasons some dogs can hunt—sell—and others never will.

These mindsets are all about how you mentally deal with four critical areas everyone encounters every day:

1. Taking on challenges or adversity: Face the challenge.
2. Responding to a negative experience: Trap negative dialogue.
3. Responding to a successful endeavor: Celebrate all wins.
4. Viewing yourself and others on your team: Project the power of your personal intention.

The success formula for all four points above takes only minutes to learn and seconds to apply and is guaranteed to positively affect all areas of your life. Enjoy more sales, more money, better health, peace of mind and happiness. This is a proven formula, one I've been using for more than fifteen years to help organizations make millions of dollars by coaching million-dollar SalesDogs, building Championship SalesDog sled teams, high-performance players and inspirational leaders.

Using these mindsets on a systematic basis has proven to improve sales by 30 to 80 percent. And it's even possible to test some of these mindsets in advance to predict and affect future performance.

1. Face the Challenge

Taking on a challenge or facing adversity can be intimidating and is often loaded with anxiety. Most high-performance dogs are able to take on very challenging tasks because of their conditioning and training. For inspiration, they rely on very simple memory banks that tell them that reward follows successful completion of their task. They don't remember the times they failed, unless these moments were linked to punishment or pain.

The Golden Retriever probably doesn't poison her mind with visions of failure. You can tell by her eager expression of pure excitement and enthusiasm that she fully anticipates success—she's going to get that stick. All she can see is the stroke, treat or cuddle that lies ahead. She relies on the successes of the past, while allowing the failures to slip on by. From her past, there are a series of memories of success that can be leveraged to give strength in the present and courage in the future.

When basketball legend Michael Jordan talks about how he handles the pressure of always having the ball in his hands at the end of any close game, he says, "I do not try to visualize it or hype myself into it."

Instead, he recalls in vivid detail the drama-filled closing seconds of the 1982 NCAA National Championship Finals when he made a twenty-two-footer from near the baseline to win the championship for North Carolina. He says that when a challenge is imminent, he pictures that moment in 1982, says to himself, "Okay, I have been here before," calms down and waits for something positive to emerge (from *Sacred Hoops,* by Phil Jackson).

Even when you haven't succeeded in exactly this situation, search for a similar experience from your past so that you can draw confidence and assurance from that event to assist you in the present moment.

SUMMARY

The present can create high emotion, which can yield low intelligence and as a result sometimes low resourcefulness. Strength can come from the past. You must learn to capture those successes and use them in the present.

---

2. Trap Negative Dialogue

The most phenomenal discipline you can implement is learning **how to trap the mental dialogue that occurs during adversity.**

Have you ever seen a dog get depressed about missing the Frisbee in front of the other dogs? Have you ever seen a dog give up after one try? Have you ever seen a dog sulk off and sit in the corner and tell himself how stupid he is for dropping the tennis ball? For that matter, have you ever seen a dog catch a cat? They have been chasing them for thousands of years and I doubt if any dog has ever caught the cat. Do they lie on the floor, with paws over their head, crying about how their life doesn't work? Or do they just find another cat!

DOG-ESTEEM IN BAD SHAPE

Adversity is part of life. Getting knocked back is part of the natural testing and feedback process of life. You may burn your tongue on the soup a couple of times until you discover it is the right temperature to eat. It's testing!

You don't give up eating soup or eat only cold soup for the rest of your life.

Dogs keep their energy high and keep bouncing back until they get the response that they want. They don't need a formula, because it's in their blood.

SalesDogs, on the other hand, need the formula for winning in order to keep their brain from going into meltdown. Here are some keys to keeping your brain in check and concentrating on sales success.

First, contrary to many traditional New Age personal development programs, it is critical to know how to *externalize* the event. That means it is important to attribute the cause of the problem to circumstances *outside* your total control. In other words, shift the blame AWAY from you.

For example:

- Prospect having a bad day
- Bad timing
- Bad hair day

- Information that was unavailable to you
- Someone else's personal issues

Basically, it's important that you keep your mental house clean of any damaging trash. You can't allow a negative moment to be a reflection of any other part of your life, your business or your sales cycle. That one prospect rejected your cold call doesn't mean that your whole week is going to be bad. It doesn't mean that your sales cycle is inherently flawed or that you're not cut out to be a salesperson. And it doesn't mean that you'll never get your finances in order. That is all crazy big-brain thinking. A dog would never dream of making such wild and random correlations.

Being responsible does NOT mean that everything bad that happens to you is caused by you!

Making the assumption that you yourself are the sole cause of all negative experiences can be incredibly damaging to you. This doesn't mean that you don't learn from your mistakes. It just means that you don't allow your mistakes to ruin your mental well being. This ability to deal with and explain adversity can be found in the mindset of every great salesperson, sports player, team, coach and investor.

You *are* responsible for how you respond, what your next action will be or how you interpret the experience . . . but not necessarily the *cause of the experience itself.*

It does not even matter if your conclusion or interpretation is true! Your mind does not know the difference. If you interpret the cause to be you, your energy goes down. If you externalize it, your energy goes up. Remember that sales is a pure energy business, so as long as you keep the energy high, you will recover faster and sell more.

Second, tell yourself that the rejection is a specific occurrence and do not let your brain interpret it as having any long-lasting or extended significance. Take it for what it is—that a particular person does not have a particular need for your particular product or service at this particular time.

Here is the formula for dealing with a negative situation.

MEMORIZE THIS!

1. First, a problem occurs. It must be actually happening, like leaving your suit coat at the airport and realizing that you've forgotten it only after the plane has taken off! Or perhaps a prospect tells you that he no longer has a need for your product.

2. As soon as you discover the problem, you'll experience a flash of some sort of emotion. This must act as your alarm bell, telling you to be aware of what comes next.

3. The dialogue in your brain begins.

4. Within seconds of the dialogue starting, you must override it by asking yourself, ***"What am I saying to myself right now?"*** This question forces your brain to answer and you then step outside yourself and observe the internal dialogue.

5. You must first identify the REAL emotion—anger, frustration, disappointment and so forth. Ask, **"What is it that I am feeling right now?"** Once you have identified the emotion, say the word out loud. ***"Ah ha—it's frustration!"*** You can shout this out or whisper it depending on where you are and how you feel! Have fun with it... for example, say it in an Inspector Clouseau accent!

6. Within about ten seconds you can usually recognize that you are using a "universal" descriptive word, such as "always," "never," "every time," "all," or "every." For example: "This *always* happens to me" or "I'm *never* going to get this."

7. Upon recognizing the universal word, you should pause, put it in check, smile and say ***"There it is!"*** Spotting the word(s) is 95 percent of the battle to ward instant recovery. The smile lightens the load and raises your energy level.

8. You must then mentally correct the universal words with something specific like "this time," "it just so happens that," "it turns out that," or "in this case it didn't work."

9. You should then spot the internal directive. "I," "me," "my fault," "what is it about me," "why me" and so forth.

10. Smile again and say ***"There it is!"*** Then find some way to lay blame, justify it or blow it off to logical circumstances. This part can be fun and humorous to do! "That guy was in a bad mood today." "With a toupee like that it's no wonder he's having a bad day!" "The competition was lucky this time—hey, there's room for all of us!"

11. Then, based upon whatever you told yourself, quickly create a stack of facts and evidence to justify what you told yourself. "I was tired from twenty-four hours of traveling and a bit burned out when I set down my jacket somewhere in that airport," or, "That guy was nice every other time I talked to him, it was just today that he was a jerk."

12. **Most important step:** Ask yourself this question: "How do I REALLY want to *feel* right now?" (optimistic, happy, excited, strong, confident and so forth). Ask the question to yourself and then try to actually get that feeling inside. If you cannot, think of an experience, vision or episode that will bring a small smile to your face. Once you do that, then hold the feeling for as long as you can (seconds, minutes, hours!?). This will shift the energy all around you. This is the magic part. Do not ask me why it works, just DO IT! I have found that once my emotions or feelings begin to change, everything else does too. **Example:** I say to myself, *"I would really rather feel happy right now."* I picture a scene of Benjamin scoring his first goal at soccer camp and his two little fists raised into the air as he explodes with joy. A smile is on my face. I hold it for a few seconds, anticipating my next present-time action, and the process is complete.

©EINSTEIN

GETTING IN TOUCH

13. After all of this you should tell yourself to expect a good thing to happen soon. And then it does! The phone rings and someone from LAX security will tell you they found your jacket, or you will get a call from a long-lost prospect who wants to see you.

This whole process takes about one minute maximum! To sum up, if something negative happens, you have to know how to tune in to your internal dialogue, how to trap the "little voice" in your head and steer it toward award-winning conversation. This technique is CRITICAL for generating sales at any level of business. It is critical to have a winning attitude about life! Have fun with adversity.

3. Celebrate All Wins

Responding to success when the wins start happening, or when anything positive happens, is an important two-step process. First, you have to get to CELEBRATE THE WIN! A physical "anchoring" of the win with a high-five, handshake, clenched fist or verbal "YEESSSSSS!" are all methods that most of us are familiar with. As a SalesDog, I suggest you at least give yourself a pat on the head or release a big howl at the moon.

These methods drive the moment deep into your mind, your spirit and your body for permanent strength. The cementing of that moment builds momentum for the next task. Over the years I have seen the most phenomenal shifts in people, organizations and performance as a result of continual acknowledgment and celebration of wins.

If you have ever watched sports on TV or even played yourself, you will know and accept that celebration is part of the game. Every time a player scores a point, gains a few yards, does something well, gets a hit or makes a catch, instinctively the rest of the players give him a high-five, a pat on the back, a head butt (not recommended) or something to acknowledge his contribution. There is no way a player in the NBA can score a basket without getting a high-five. That is why they are so achievement-oriented. Of all the techniques, this is probably the most powerful, yet least used by adults, because adults get embarrassed and think it's childish or unprofessional.

Several years ago, I worked with an overseas hotel. It was a good company with several hundred people on staff. Working with the heads of the departments, I coached them into the habit of always celebrating wins— not only their wins, but also the wins of their staff. This was not easy because the culture of many Asian regions does NOT include this kind of celebration. Yet over the months, the new habits began to sink in.

This hotel slowly but surely began to see the results as the entire staff overcame their reserved natural habits. The organization became a money-making sales machine. Their combined energy was so high that during the last Asian economic downturn, when most other hotels in the region were

CELEBRATE ALL WINS!

operating at 40 to 50 percent occupancy, this hotel was 90 percent plus. They banded together and decided that *everyone* in the hotel was responsible for sales. In fact, the largest account was actually landed by members of the housekeeping department! The successful turnaround was a direct result of the constant acknowledgment and active celebrating of the wins, not to mention the increased morale and general happiness throughout the hotel.

You see, we all know how to do this. We did it when we were young and we do it when we play. As kids we are born with a natural instinct to persist, to ask and to have fun doing whatever it is we do.

I think we are all born as perfect SalesDogs. But then we get told things like "it's rude to ask" or "stop being silly" or "stop annoying others" or "sit down and be quiet." All of the things that we do instinctively—like speaking to strangers and shouting at the top of our voices just because we feel like it—are conditioned out of us.

I recently met a woman who told me that at her last parent-teacher conference for her five-year-old daughter she was told that her daughter was fine in school, but that she had "a little bit too much self-esteem." Can you imagine?

As we get scolded, punished, ridiculed or ignored, we get pushed back into a system of "seriousness"—especially when it comes to business.

Dogs will abandon their bones, their food and all their playthings for a good scratch behind the ears. They get super-excited the more you acknowledge them. Little kids do this too. Nothing has changed just because we are adults. Our brains and spirits are still the same.

This technique of celebration is foreign to most people, but second nature to high achievers. It also has to do with trapping the "little voice" and steering the dialogue in the right direction. And remember, it doesn't matter if what you are saying to yourself is true or not! Your body and mind do not care! Part of this dialogue has to do with how to make the event filter into all areas of your being and own it for yourself.

Handling success is the absolute opposite of handling setbacks. If something good happens, such as a prospect agreeing to an appointment or receiving any positive sign from the client, not only should you celebrate it as I mentioned, but to *really* build momentum you have to use it to become a Legend in your own Lunchtime!

Tell yourself that because of this success your whole week is going to be great. You can see how everything in your life is going to be successful just because of this tiny event.

Finally, it is important to internalize it by telling yourself that the success happened because of YOU. You earned it, you worked for it, you are smart and you know this stuff! Get the picture? Your energy and momentum will soar, and all SalesDogs know that the greater the energy the greater the next success.

You may not be aware of it, but you already know how to do this, because you did it with your kids, with your pets and with yourself in other areas of your life. When your kids were little, didn't you make a big deal and celebrate all of their new accomplishments? If your kid managed to stand, even for a split second, didn't you picture future Olympic glory? If you ever played golf, you've done this. Just as your frustration hits its peak and you're ready to toss your Pings into the lake, you knock a nine iron stiff, within three feet of the cup, or nail a forty-foot putt for birdie. What do you do? You clench your fist and give it the ol' Tiger Woods thrust and the frustration evaporates.

Imagine if you treated your whole life that way! Your energy and your results would be incredible. The problem is some people, even when they get a win, want to cut it off at the knees. They sink the putt and say to themselves, "Lucky that time." They make a successful call and say, "Too bad they aren't all like that." That is the dialogue that drives a spike into the heart of your spirit, your energy and your results. From now on, Be a Legend.

Bone for managers: Your pack of SalesDogs needs to celebrate their wins too! As a matter of fact, the smarter the breed and the more aggressive the dog, the more you have to bury them in lavish praise to ensure good performance. If neglected, or if only scolded for poor behavior, SalesDogs can get mean and nasty and may even turn on you one day. You must celebrate wins early and often to make them great hunters and companions.

For some reason, when we get older, go to work and take on careers, celebration become childish.

We are actually taught NOT to sell. We are taught NOT to ask. We are taught to work hard, be good, color within the lines and hope that someone will recognize us for our efforts and throw us some scraps. We are told that "all good things will come to those that wait." We are taught to accept, not object, to give, not to ask, and to accept our lot in life. We are manipulated and contorted to fit snuggly into a ready-made box where we are expected to live quietly until we die. We are judged by our ability to answer questions, not ask them, and God forbid we should ever make a mistake!

I believe that everyone has the natural talent to sell. Every child can sell. You can sell. We are all born to sell. Some need more skills than others do. Some need a new attitude about it. Some are already hot on the hunt. The next time your kid pesters you for something, rather than telling him to knock it off, ask him to present you with at least three good reasons why you should act on his request. When you see those little eyes glance skyward in the search for solutions, smile to yourself and know that your training in this moment will be preparing him for a life of joy, love and wealth. And that is his birthright and destiny.

So celebrate, celebrate and celebrate some more. And by the way, a dog doesn't need a party or a raise to feel acknowledged or celebrated. A simple clap, pat, stroke or scratch of the neck will do.

SUMMARY

Wins are the most precious commodity you have. Most people have a natural mindset that minimizes them, but that is a killer of enthusiasm and energy! It is critical to learn how to spot the wins, trap them, own them, leverage them and save them for the next big event!

---

4. Project the Power of Your Personal Intention

The mastery of this technique is critical to forming a high-power sales team or organization. It is also the secret to reducing stress in the job, creating inspirational leadership and, most important, obtaining personal wealth. Learning how to project your intention of yourself and others can be the difference between frustration and riches.

Let me explain in dog terms. When a dog takes off after a squirrel, a cat or a ball, it fully intends to GET IT! There is no "trying" involved, it is just doing. When they go up to you with their tongue hanging out and drool dripping on your shoes they fully intend for you to pet them. No question about it. That is their intention. If you, as a SalesDog, think that you are going to charm everyone you meet, you probably will do better than you think. However, if you think that you are going to be a nuisance to the prospect or that you are going to be boring— you probably will be! That is intention.

Learning how to project your intentions and expectations can be the difference between wealth and frustration. In other words, What do you expect the response to be from your next presentation? Will they think you are a rookie? Will they think that you are truly there to help them find new solutions? Will they like you, hate you, think you are a nuisance? What do you think that they will think? What is your intention?

Research shows us that whatever you believe the response is going to be will help to predetermine what the real response is! If you think that you are going to be a pest by making a sales call, you may very well be right. If, however, you think that you are going to be a welcome messenger of critical information, you may be right as well. Your mindset helps to predetermine the results.

Not too long ago, my son Benjamin (then aged four) had a dilemma. We were in Singapore during one of our overseas trips and we were staying in a serviced apartment complex in the city. We have stayed there many times because it has a great location and a big pool and there are always lots of kids for Ben to play with.

This place also has a game room with a pool table. Ben loves to play pool by rolling the balls without using the stick. The pool table requires two one-dollar Singapore coins. Ben knows this. On this day he had earned his two dollars by setting and clearing the table and was excited about playing pool later.

Before going to the poolroom we went down to the swimming pool to catch some sun and a little exercise. In typical SalesDog style, Ben spotted the soda machine and went for it and bought a Sprite and a Coke. Happy with his purchases he came back to Eileen and me with his goods. We explained to him that he had just spent his pool-table money on the drinks. After a convoluted discussion that only a parent can understand, he was faced with the dilemma of two drinks that were now not nearly as desirable as his beloved pool table. A few moments later I heard a loud pounding sound. It was Ben trying to shove the cans of drink back into the machine in the hope of getting his money back!

After calming him down a bit, we made him realize that his only option was to somehow exchange the drinks for money. The light went on and you could see his little blue eyes survey his territory with laserlike precision—young couple, poolside, lock and load!

They had no chance! I do not know to this day if they even spoke English! He raced over to them, set the cans down and began his pitch. I could not hear anything, as he was too far away, but I watched in amazement. They obviously understood that he was offering the cans and that he wanted money in exchange. And judging from his gestures I think he was also explaining why he needed the money. At first they shook their heads, but his intention to sell those drinks was undeniable.

From the outset, there was no fear, no hesitation, no fear of looking foolish, only the pure intention to get them sold. I watched from a distance and laughed to myself. What a SalesDog! Ben had the mindset that he would not be denied. Finally, I watched in proud disbelief as they handed over the cherished coins. Ben even offered to open the cans for them so they could enjoy the drinks immediately (showing traces of the Retriever).

With coins in hand, he happily skipped back to us to tell us with delight of his accomplishment, leaving two refreshed customers in his wake.

That is intention!

He had no doubt that he would sell those things. Months later, he is still that way. He will persist and persist and never give up because he KNOWS that sooner or later he will find a chink in our armor and we will agree to his requests. All kids are SalesDogs.

BONES FOR MANAGERS REGARDING EXPECTATIONS AND INTENTIONS OF OTHERS

What is your expectation of your kennel? Whether you ever communicate it or not, that expectation will show itself somehow or other. Your intention or expectation of the performance ability of others will also partly predetermine their results. If you were to rank each of your SalesPups with a number from one to ten in terms of their potential for success, what would those numbers be? If you ranked someone with a three or four, you have already, in part, predisposed him or her to that level. It will show up in your management style and attitude and in their performance results.

Unfortunately, this also happened in school for many of us. Teachers hung invisible numbers on our foreheads. What numbers were hung on you? Did you believe them? What number have you hung on yourself? Is it helping or hurting you now? It is a rare SalesDog that overachieves what its master expects. Be careful of your intentions and expectations.

I had a salesman working for me in the airfreight business whom most other vendors and associates historically considered to be a pain in the butt. He and I had a great relationship though, and within a short period he doubled our volume in one of our toughest and most competitive cities. I kept telling him that I knew he could succeed, even when he was whining and whimpering. After a while the sulking began to dissipate and was replaced by howling and celebratory yipping as one small win led to another and another.

This is a simple example of the effect a good Dog Trainer can have on a SalesDog—an example of a person who, because of his mannerisms, alienated lots of people. Every job that he held had produced mediocre results. He had drifted from job to job. He was a stray.

When I took him in, I started his training all over again. We identified him as a yipping Chihuahua that drove everyone nuts. We then trained him in the skills of the Retriever and the Basset Hound. His incredible Chihuahua mental quickness coupled with softness of tone and commitment to service made him one of the wealthiest salespeople in the territory. We celebrated wins, I acknowledged his efforts, and I told him

I KNEW that he could make a ton of money. In other words, I believed in him even though others had taken the newspaper to him. The results spoke for themselves.

SUMMARY BONE FOR MANAGERS

Just as your intention affects your sales, your intention for your SalesDogs can limit them, or urge them to achieve extraordinary success. There is a number that ranks your expectations of others, yourself and your actions. If it is an expectation of others, it dangles right on that person's forehead and plays a large part in determining the level of performance that is achieved. It is most important that as a Dog Trainer, you shouldn't be prejudiced by limitations put on your SalesDogs by previous managers. Some of the scroungiest mutts make the best hunters, because their new master/trainer gave them a whole new expectation and perception of themselves. If you see them as champions, they will invariably rise to meet your expectations and become champions.

AN EXCERPT FROM

RICH DAD ADVISORS

FOREWORD BY ROBERT KIYOSAKI

Team Code of Honor

The Secrets of Champions in Business and in Life

BLAIR SINGER

Chapter One

Why Do You Need a Code of Honor?

In the absence of rules, people make up their own rules. And some of the biggest collisions in finance, business and relationships occur because well-meaning people are simply playing by different sets of rules. By the same token, the most miraculous results come from "like-minded" folks who band together under some invisible bond to achieve greatness.

By experience and default, we all formulate our own sets of guidelines, rules and assumptions. That's natural. But when we start coming together with other people, organizations and cultures, we sometimes have a tough time figuring out why "those guys" don't understand, or how they could so blatantly turn their back on our feelings, our way of doing things and our rules. In most respects, "those guys" feel the same way about us. Why? Because we assume that certain basic rules are the same. Bad assumption.

This book is about revealing the process for eliminating one of the biggest causes for financial loss, frustration and heartbreak. It is about surrounding yourself with folks who subscribe to the same sets of rules and how to establish them so that you can ensure peak performance, fun and incredible results in all you do.

For about twelve years now, I've actively studied teams; looking at what makes them successful and how they are able to operate at peak performance. And after all this time, I can tell you this: You cannot have a championship team, in any facet of your life, without a Code of Honor.

Team Tip:

Sometimes the easiest way to avoid upset, collisions and disharmony in any group is to take the time to make sure that everyone is playing by the same rules.

If you are interested in building a great relationship, whether it's with your business, your community, your family or even yourself, there have to be rules and standards for the behavior that will ultimately achieve your goals. A Code of Honor is the physical manifestation of the team's values; extended into behavior. It's not enough to *have* values, because we all do. What's so crucial is knowing how to put physical behavior into practice to reflect those values.

Let me illustrate what I mean. When I was in high school in Ohio, I was on the cross-country running team. Typically, any human being of the male sex living in the state of Ohio was expected to play football. But if you could see my size, you'd realize that I was just not built to go up against a two-hundred-pound linebacker, even though I love the game. Cross-country was more my style.

What a lot of people don't know about cross-country is that there are typically about five to seven runners per team racing at the same time. Usually there are several other teams running at the same time. The only way your team can win is if the whole team finishes relatively close together close to the front of the pack of runners. In other words, having a superstar who runs ahead of the pack and places first doesn't do the team any good if everyone else is all spread out across the field. Cross-country is a low-scoring sport, meaning that first place receives a point, second receives two points, and so on. The idea is to get the whole team to finish near the front; so your team gets the lowest score possible. If we could get fourth-, sixth-, seventh- and ninth-place finishes, then even if another team got a first, second, twelfth and eighteenth, we would still win the meet.

So for the entire two-and-a-half-mile race each of us would push the others on, encouraging, threatening, supporting, and yelling with each gasping breath for air. With muscles burning and body strength faltering, it was as much a race of emotional endurance as it was physical. We pushed each other both on and off the course. If someone was slacking, you can rest assured the rest of the team would be on him quickly to pick it up. It took ALL that each of us had for us to win. Whatever it took for us to cross that finish line close together, that's what we did. In other words, part of our code was to do whatever it took to support everyone to win.

We won most of our cross-country meets, or placed very high, even though we had very few superstar runners. We were a championship team. It was my first experience with teams, at the most basic, physical, gut-wrenching level, but the lessons it taught me remain the same today. I have always surrounded myself with people who would push me that way and who would allow me to push as well. It serves them and it serves me. As a result, I have always been blessed with incredibly great friendships, success and wealth. I have also observed that it is in times of pressure, when the stakes are high, that people are transformed. I've NEVER seen a great team that didn't come together without some type of pressure. It could be from competition, from outside influences, or it could be self-induced. We knew in those cross-country meets that every person, every second, every step counted toward a win for our team, and it bound us together. We knew that the success of the team took precedence over our individual goals. No one wanted to let the others down. It drove you as hard as the desire to win. We had a code that said we stuck together no matter what. And in those really important moments, we came together and did what we needed to do to be successful.

Team Tip:

A Code of Honor brings out the best in every person who subscribes to it.

But when pressure increases, sometimes so do emotions. When that happens, intelligence has a tendency to drop. People revert to their base instincts in times of stress, and that's when their true colors come out. Sometimes that's not such a pretty sight. Have you ever said something to someone when you were upset that you wished you had not said a few minutes later? I thought so. That's what I mean about high emotion and low intelligence.

I've seen teams that work well together day to day, but when things get tough, they revert to "every man for himself." A crisis came along and everyone ran for cover, because there was no set of rules to help them see their way through it. Judgments based upon heightened emotions became their guide, which may not turn out to be the best choice for all concerned.

For example, more than half of all marriages end in divorce. In times of stress, the people involved are unable to negotiate their differences. No common code of honor or set of rules holds them together. It is the same issue in the case of a business partnership dispute that has no rules or guidelines. Both situations can get nasty.

It isn't that people don't *want* to work out their differences. The problem is that without rules and expectations mutually agreed upon up front, they act on instinct, particularly when emotions are running high. Each does what he or she thinks is best based upon his or her feelings at the time. Decisions made in that kind of setting may not be the best ones.

Now I know *you've* never been under any kind of stress, right?

Of course you have. You know that when you're upset, when you're under a deadline, when you're angry at a family member or a coworker, it is *impossible* to try to negotiate terms. Why? Because you aren't in your right mind! THAT'S why you need a Code of Honor.

You must create, in a *sane* moment, a set of rules for your team that tell everyone how to operate when the heat is really on. That way, in those moments of high stress, the rules legislate the behavior, rather than the emotions. The Code is NOT just a set of guidelines to be used only when it's convenient. These are rules that must be "called" when breached.

The needs, tasks and problems of a team determine how rigid its code is. The Marine Corps has a code that holds its teams together under fire.

When bullets are flying, life and death may have to take second place to logic and team play. Repetition of their code and its rules conditions the team to come together as a cohesive, trusting unit rather than just running for individual survival.

Having a Code of Honor doesn't mean that everyone on the team is happy 100 percent of the time. Sometimes things get messy. A code can cause upset, create confrontation and even put people on the spot. But ultimately, it protects every member of the team from abuse, neglect and breaches of ethics. A Code of Honor brings out the best in every person who subscribes to it.

You can NEVER assume that people know the code on their own. It isn't something that's necessarily intuitive. You learn it from others—parents, coaches, leaders or friends. Someone has to "show" it to you. And everyone involved must agree to it. This is true for any relationship, be it with your business, your family or yourself—any relationship with an interest in its own happiness and success.

Currently about 50 percent of the gross domestic product of the United States comes from small businesses, and of that, about half of those businesses are sole proprietorships or home-based businesses. I tell you this to emphasize a point: The average person has much more power than you think. The way you conduct your business affects the lives of many others.

Team Tip:

Your code is a reflection of you and will attract those who aspire to the same standards.

Your reputation, your income and your longevity depend upon your consistency of behavior internally and externally. The future of the country is in the hands of those who drive the economy, the markets, our businesses and our families. That's you! Your significance may seem minuscule, but never doubt your influence on others. Your code is a reflection of you and will attract those who aspire to the same standards. How you conduct your business may have a bigger impact than the service you provide.

Decide here and now that you will create a Code of Honor for yourself and for the teams you're a part of. What do you stand for? What code do you publicize to the world? How tight is your team? How happy do you want to be?

My purpose here is to give you steps, motivation and insights to building a great team that will give you and those you touch the wealth, satisfaction and joy that you all deserve. So let's talk about who's on your team.

Team Drill:

1. Discuss great teams that you have been on. What was it like? What were the rules? How did it feel?

2. What would be the benefits to having a code for your business? Your finances? Your health? Your family?

Garrett Sutton, Esq.

Rich Dad Advisor on Business Entities and Asset Protection

Personal Background and Entrepreneur Profile

Name	Garrett Sutton
Date of Birth	April 15, 1953
Place of Birth	Oakland, California

Traditional Education:
Colorado College, Colorado Springs, CO 1971-1973
University of California, Berkeley, CA 1973-1975
Degree: B.S. – Business Administration

Professional Education:
Hastings College of the Law, San Francisco, CA 1975-1978
Degree: Juris Doctor

Grade Point Averages
High school: 3.4
College: 3.3

Value of traditional education... relative to becoming an entrepreneur
Two classes: Marketing at Cal and Corporations at Hastings were very useful.

Subject I liked most in school:
English/Journalism (followed by History)

Subject I hated most in school:
Calculus – two quarters of hell. I still don't know what it tries to measure.

First entrepreneurial Project:

Collecting stray golf balls at Lake Tahoe and selling them back to golfers

The key entrepreneurial skill I was *not* taught in school:

The importance of raising money

Why and when I became an entrepreneur and my first major venture

I became an entrepreneur because it seemed like the greatest challenge and because I don't like being told what to do.

My first major venture was publishing an entertainment and lifestyle monthly in Santa Rosa, California called "Sonoma Monthly." The publication lasted about three years.

Best lesson from first business:

That I had no idea what I was doing. I needed more staff, more funding and more staying power. I did not know how to build a brand. I relied on a team that was not as committed as I was. The best lesson (in hindsight) was to fail fast.

What I learned about myself from my Kolbe Index

GARRETT SUTON

Kolbe A™ Index Result

CONGRATULATIONS GARRETT
You Got a Perfect Score on the Kolbe A™ Index

You're terrific when juggling rapidly changing priorities. You are known for taking risks that are grounded in practical realities. You don't mess around with what has always been done, but temper your trial-and-error approach by strategizing options.

Kolbe Action Modes®

Reprinted with permission from Kolbe Corp.

I learned that I was a Quick Start, ready to take risks. I also realized that I was not as strong on the implementation and the follow through, meaning I needed a strong team effort to accomplish goals.

My Role in the B-1 Triangle

Within the triad of team leadership and mission my role is the legal line. My job is to provide legal information on entities and their structure and develop strategies for minimizing liability and personal risk.

Skills that are essential for entrepreneurs—but not taught in schools

1. The legal system allows all of us to protect ourselves.
    Our legal system doesn't automatically and beneficially make the right choices for you. But it does allow you to make such choices to your advantage. The key is in knowing what your choices are, since the school system doesn't teach them. You can operate as a sole proprietor, with no protection. The system doesn't teach otherwise. You, like everyone else, can take an extra step and be protected with a corporation or LLC. But without any entrepreneurial education you wouldn't know to—and how to—take that step.

2. The legal system is based on fairness and justice and not on overly complicated minutia.
    The legal system seems so complicated when you talk to an attorney. But know that while some areas are indeed mind numbing (statutes written by regulators and lobbyists) others are really not. Attorneys play hide the ball. They keep their clients intentionally in the dark to justify their hours and billing. A basic course on contract law would identify that much of our system is based on the public policy of protecting private property rights. The legal system flows from that great concept. Once you understand that, much of the law makes sense (with the exception of government interference with such rights.) Entrepreneurs who perceive the big picture, which is not taught in school, can then hire attorneys to carry out the details.

3. Disputes Will Occur – Prepare for Them
    Any time two or more people come together for a business venture disputes are certain to arise. This is okay and natural. The key is not allowing such disputes to take down the company. Two 50/50 partners (or four 25% each partners) may come to a deadlock. Neither side will budge. Each side hires an attorney. And the only parties to win are the attorneys. You are better off discussing and implementing

deadlock procedures. One side can win one year and the other the next or 1/10th of 1% can be given to a neutral party to be the tie breaker. While not taught in school, deadlocks occur in business. You must be ready for them.

My Most Important Lesson for Entrepreneurs

Get your team together. I can recount several horror stories where entrepreneurs realized too late that they needed professional help. A CPA and attorney need to be on your bench so you can use them when needed.

How I learned to Raise Capital:

I learned on my clients' dime. The proper way to raise money is with a private placement memorandum (or PPM). I have prepared PPMs for numerous clients.

How I learned to Overcome Fear and Failure:

By fearing and failing several times

My Personal Strength

I am willing to put in the time to do my part if the tasks are what I enjoy doing. I enjoy being a team player on a winning team.

My Personal Weakness

I don't do well in partnerships where the others aren't pulling their weight. I need to be part of a team where certain tasks are assigned to other team members. I resent having to do all the work in a team environment.

What is the Entrepreneurial Skill That I Teach Best?

How to use entities, cover your assets, and prepare business plans.

What is the Entrepreneurial Lesson that I teach?

Cover Your Assets

Cover Your Assets
by Garrett Sutton, Esq.

You don't need to be a crook to get rich.
Crooks break the law. The laws were written
to make the rich richer.

– RTK

Like most, you probably would like to stay out of trouble. Right?

But do you worry that if you start a business or invest in real estate you could get into trouble? This is not an unreasonable worry. There are so many laws that not even the best lawyers know all of them.

I know that for a fact—because I'm a lawyer. I'm the Rich Dad Advisor for Corporations, LLCs and asset protection strategies. I am also General Counsel for several companies. We'll discuss the importance of General Counsel in a minute, but first, a little background.

I grew up in the San Francisco Bay Area. My dad was a county judge in Oakland, California and I was raised to respect the legal system. I also learned early on that some people could lose everything because they didn't take the proper steps at the start. I heard horror stories at the dinner table about sole proprietors (nameless, of course) being sued and getting wiped out, all for failing to take some simple legal steps towards protection. It left quite an impression.

When it was time to go to college I wanted to get out of state and ski. I somehow managed to get into Colorado College, an excellent small school in Colorado Springs. Their course schedule was the 'block plan' whereby you would take one course at a time every 3 ½ weeks (with half a week off to ski.) Unfortunately, I didn't take to the block plan. I needed more time for the course work to sink in. So I transferred to the University of California at Berkeley. This was when Cal was a B+ school. After years of riots and craziness parents wouldn't send their kids to Berkeley. That was the window I needed, and I was fortunate to earn a business degree from Cal. Then I crossed the bay to attend Hastings College of the Law, the University of California's law school in San Francisco. After passing the bar exam I practiced law in San Francisco and Washington, D.C. But I always liked the mountains and Lake Tahoe and skiing so I moved to Reno, Nevada. It was a great move. I have raised a family here and Nevada is a great state to set up a corporation or an LLC.

I know corporate and asset protection law. But back to our original point. Do I know every law? Of course not. There are too many of them. In a typical law library there are rows and rows of books and books filled with laws, laws and more laws. But what is more striking is that not knowing every law is no defense. You are expected to follow every law even if you don't know it exists! It is estimated that each of us unknowingly breaks over three laws every day.

How do we survive in such an over regulated system?

Well, it can be done. Look around you. There are plenty of businesses and real estate investments thriving in today's world. How do they do it?

It comes down to one word: Proper. They do business the proper way. They follow the law. They work with an attorney to be properly protected. Corporations and LLCs protect against unlimited personal liability. This is a proper first step. There may be more. In some cases you must work with an attorney who specializes in the business niche you are entering. If you are going into pay day lending you need a specialist in the ever changing laws of that field. If you are going to provide consulting services and know your specialty you may only need an attorney to help set up your LLC or corporation. Whatever your situation you want to do it the proper way.

Doing it right also includes paying your taxes. If you are going to stay small maybe you cheat the government by taking cash under the table and not reporting it. You probably know people who do this. I won't help such people on principle. Everyone should follow the law. But also, as a practical matter, I can't help cheaters grow their business.

If you don't accurately report income your business appears smaller. This doesn't help when you are trying to get a bank loan to expand your operations. You want to show higher revenues, not lower ones. It also doesn't help when you are trying to sell your business to present improperly lowered revenues. Businesses are sold on multiples of revenues. By cheating the government on taxes you are cheating yourself out of five times that amount in a business sale. Short term cheaters are usually punished in the long run.

Most importantly, the owner sets the tone for the business. When the owner cheats they tacitly permit others in the organization to cheat. Businesses lacking integrity rarely survive.

Smart entrepreneurs and investors pay their taxes, while taking advantage of proper and legal methods to reduce their taxes. But you say, I don't know all the proper and legal methods. Of course you don't. No one does at the start. They certainly do not teach this in school. To do it properly you need a team on your side. Others have succeeded before you. With the right team so can you. The tax laws can be used to your great advantage. An accountant on your team can help with that. As well, a bookkeeper can assist you to keep track of things right from the start. You need to pay any employee withholdings properly. Let your bookkeeper handle it. Given all the laws, a lawyer is a key member.

Let's talk about all those laws. They apply equally to all of us.

If you are an employee (an E, in the upper left corner of the CASHFLOW Quadrant) the laws on employment benefit you, to the detriment of Ss, Bs and Is. (Or the Small Business Owners on the lower left and the Big Business owners and Investors on the right side.) Employees will always be protected under the law. Of course, there will be cases where employees manipulate the system to their advantage. The Ss, Bs and Is will always face this issue. Their only recourse is to stay ethical and accept that a few bad apples will appear along the way.

Aside from employment laws, there is a whole other area of laws that are exciting and inspiring to Bs and Is. These are the incentives in our tax code and legal system specifically written to benefit risk takers. If you follow what the government wants you to do you can achieve great success. This is true in every country on earth.

What is stopping an E or and S from moving over to the right side of the quadrant? Do the laws force them to stay on the left side?

Of course not. The laws apply equally to everyone. As an E or an S you are free to take advantage of the same incentives offered to Bs and Is. There is no person or legal system restricting your movement into these quadrants. The only person stopping you, is you.

But once again, if you are going to operate in this quadrant you need a team. You need the services of professionals, a professional team that is on your side, and a team that will serve your best interests.

If you are going to operate in a proper manner you need to remember this chart:

Proper:
Professional Performance

To be proper—to do it right—you need professionals performing their services for you. As you grow these professionals will keep you out of trouble and will allow you to take advantage of the laws that encourage your growth. The people who are succeeding in business and real estate are doing it the proper way, using the professionals on their team to propel them forward.

Do you have to know everything too? Not at all. First of all, as we've discussed, you can't possibly know everything. No one can. Secondly, you are going to be too busy growing your business and real estate investments to bother with learning, much less knowing, everything.

There is an interesting story about Henry Ford that helps prove the point. The founder of Ford Motors did not have a formal education. He was 'new money' and some would ask Ford questions to belittle him and to make themselves feel superior. Finally Ford blew up. "I don't have time for foolish questions" he said. "Give me five minutes and I can get anything answered." Henry Ford was smarter than all the others. While he knew his limitations, he knew that a smart person draws on the strength of their team. A smart person knows when to consult with their experts. It is only the stupid person who is too proud to ask for help. Like Henry Ford, use your team.

As you move to the B and I side of the quadrant you need to be a generalist, not a specialist. You need to know who to call. Similarly, while I am a specialist in asset protection I am also a legal generalist for several companies. This attorney role is called 'General Counsel.' As the term implies, it is a lawyer who knows the general lay of the legal landscape and can provide counsel on it. As General Counsel I advise companies when to bring in a specialist. I don't deal with employment law. When a client has an employment issue I help them find a specialist in employment law.

Every team needs an attorney. But make sure your attorney is confident enough to direct you to a specialist. Some attorneys want to do all your work. But if they don't specialize in all areas (and no one does) they may be doing you a disservice by trying to handle all matters. A good attorney knows when you need a good specialist.

As well, as a business owner or real estate investor you must be a generalist. Our education system cries for everyone to be a specialist. That's fine. Now we have plenty of specialists. But you as the business owner and real estate investor need to keep your eye on the bigger picture. Wealth is gained by being a generalist and using your team of specialists, when needed.

As a generalist you want to acquire assets and grow businesses. You will generally know the incentives afforded you. At a level or two below that, the nuts and bolts of the proper maximization of incentives can be handled by your specialists.

This shift in focus will greatly benefit you. I'll leave you with a famous quote from Henry Ford: "Whether you think you can or you can't, you are right." Good luck with assembling and using your team. Together you can operate in the proper way to your great advantage.

About Garrett Sutton, Esq.

Garrett Sutton, Esq., is a Rich Dad Advisor and the bestselling author of *Start Your Own Corporation, Loopholes of Real Estate, Run Your Own Corporation, Buying & Selling a Business, The ABCs of Getting Out of Debt,* and *Writing Winning Business Plans* in the Rich Dad Advisors series. He is also the author of *How to Use Limited Liability Companies and Limited Partnerships* and *Toxic Client: Knowing and Avoiding Problem Customers.* Garrett also co-authored *Finance Your Own Business* with credit expert Gerri Detweiler. As an attorney Garrett has over 35 years' experience in assisting individuals and businesses to determine their appropriate corporate structure, limit their liability, protect their assets and advance their financial and personal goals.

Garrett is the owner and operator of Corporate Direct, Inc., which provides formation and company maintenance services in all 50 states.

Garrett attended Colorado College and the University of California at Berkeley, where he received a B.S. in Business Administration in 1975. He graduated with a J.D. in 1978 from Hastings College of Law, the University of California's law school in San Francisco.

Garrett is a member of the State Bar of Nevada, the State Bar of California, and the American Bar Association. He has been featured in *The Wall Street Journal, New York Times* and other publications.

Garrett enjoys speaking with entrepreneurs on the advantages of forming business entities and is a frequent lecturer in the Rich Dad's Advisors series.

Garrett serves on the boards of the American Baseball Foundation, located in Birmingham, Alabama, and the Reno-Nevada-based Sierra Kids Foundation and Nevada Museum of Art.

For more information on Garrett Sutton and Sutton Law Center, please visit his website at www.sutlaw.com. Additional resources are also found at www.CorporateDirect.com. For a free 15-minute consultation with an incorporating specialist please call 1-800-600-1760.

Books by Garrett Sutton, Esq.

Rich Dad Advisor Series Books

Start Your Own Corporation
Why the Rich Own their Own Companies and
Everyone Else Works for Them

Writing Winning Business Plans
How to Prepare a Business Plan that Investors Will
Want to Read–and Invest In

Buying and Selling a Business
How You Can Win in the Business Quadrant

The ABCs of Getting Out of Debt
Turn Bad Debt into Good Debt and Bad Credit into Good Credit

Run Your Own Corporation
How to Legally Operate and Properly Maintain
Your Company into the Future

The Loopholes of Real Estate
Secrets of Successful Real Estate Investing

... in Spanish

Inicie su propia corporacion

Como disenar planes de negocios exitosos

El ABC para salir de la deudas

SuccessDNA Books

How to Use LLCs and LPs
Getting the Most Out of Your Legal Structure

Finance Your Own Business
Get on the Financing Fast Track
with Gerri Detweiler

Toxic Client
Knowing and Avoiding Problem Customers

AN EXCERPT FROM

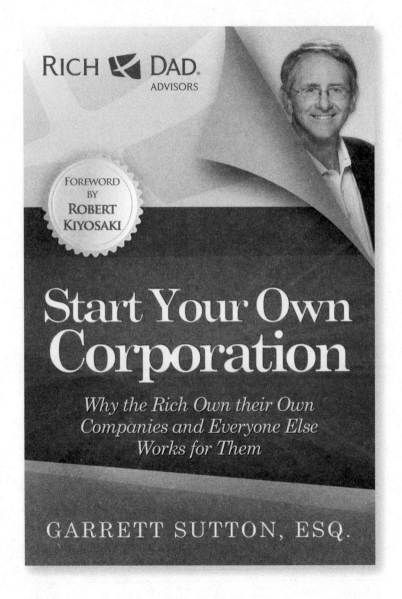

RICH DAD. ADVISORS

FOREWORD BY ROBERT KIYOSAKI

Start Your Own Corporation

Why the Rich Own their Own Companies and Everyone Else Works for Them

GARRETT SUTTON, ESQ.

Chapter Twenty-Two

Seven Steps to Achieve Limited Liability

Whether you are concerned about protecting your business, preventing business claims from affecting your personal assets, or planning for the distribution of your assets to your heirs, you need to know how to limit liability. As we have discussed throughout this book, the proper use of tools that limit liability may prevent creditors from stripping your business of its equipment, property interests, or hard-earned capital. It may prevent the obligations of your business from leaving you personally penniless. In addition, it may help to ensure the most efficient transfer of wealth from generation to generation. To protect what you have worked for and all that you have, you must know how to limit liability.

As a review in closing, here are seven key steps for ensuring limited liability:

1. *Form a Limited Liability Entity.* Before you can enjoy the benefits limited liability provides, you need to form an entity that provides limited liability. As we have discussed, various entities are available and each provides different features and limitations. Your menu of entities includes corporations, limited liability companies, and limited partnerships. If you have a business that is not operated as a limited liability entity, your personal assets and all of the assets of the business may be in jeopardy. If you haven't used limited liability entities to protect your personal assets or plan for the future, all that you have may be vulnerable. The first step you need to take involves discussing limited liability entities with an advisor and forming the entity(ies)

best suited to your needs.

2. *Use a Reliable Resident Agent.* A resident (or registered) agent is the person who receives service of process on your entity's behalf. Service of process is notice that your entity is subject to a lawsuit. It does not cost a lot to follow this very important corporate formality. Our firm charges $125 a year and the service is free for the first year you form your entity. While you can be your own registered agent in your home state, some states require you to be open daily from 8am to 5pm. You may want a firm to do this for you. Please know that many businesses provide resident agent services. If you use an unreliable resident agent who does not get notice of a lawsuit to you promptly, your entity may be subject to a court judgment without having a chance to defend itself. Do not use a resident agent that may not be in business next year or who will not inform you when they receive service of process for your entity.

3. *Perform Required Annual Filings.* While forming a limited liability entity and using a reliable resident agent are crucial steps, they will not provide any benefits if you don't maintain certain formalities and use your entity properly. After you file the Articles of Incorporation (for a corporation), Articles of Organization (for a limited liability company), or the LP-1 Certificate of Limited Partnership, you must file annual reports and pay an annual fee to your state. It is not difficult, but it is necessary to achieve limited liability.

4. *Prepare or Have an Advisor Prepare Minutes of Meetings.* By preparing minutes of meetings, you indicate that you are treating the entity as something distinct from yourself. Minutes of meetings are written records of your entity's decisions. They should be prepared when the entity is initially formed, annually to reflect the substance of annual meetings, and whenever the entity makes a substantial decision. While most states require corporations to have annual meetings of their board of directors and shareholders, annual meetings and minutes for a limited liability company or a limited partnership are advisable as well to ensure limited liability. We provided the templates back in Chapter 10. But if you are intimated by the prospect of preparing minutes

of meetings (and many of our clients are) have someone do them for you.

5. ***Put the World on Notice of Your Entity.*** Telling the world when you are operating as a limited liability entity distinguishes the entity's activity from your personal activity. If you do not distinguish between your personal activity and the entity's activity, you may lose the benefits of limited liability. So on your cards, brochures, contracts and checks you want to have Inc., LLC or LP displayed so that people know they are dealing with an entity and not you personally. This will prevent a claimant from arguing that they thought they were dealing with you personally and should be able to collect against you personally.

6. ***Maintain Separate Bank Accounts.*** In addition to telling the world that you are acting as a limited liability entity, you must distinguish your personal assets from the entity's assets and maintain separate bank accounts. Using a single bank account for yourself and the entity, taking loans from the entity, diverting entity funds to non-entity uses, or otherwise co-mingling assets or monies may deny the entity its ability to serve its purpose. Open and use a separate bank account for your entity's activities.

7. ***Prepare or Have an Advisor Prepare Separate Tax Returns.*** Limited liability entities are separate tax entities, and require separate entity tax returns. Listing revenue and/or expenses on your personal tax return that property belongs on the entity's tax return is not a good idea. Work with a good accountant and avoid any problems.

The seven steps are important to follow. Recall what happened to Roger and Donny back in Chapter 10. They failed to follow these corporate formalities and were held personally responsible for claims against their business.

You can avoid having the corporate veil pierced and protect your personal assets by following these important (but easily achieved) steps. Once again, having an attorney, accountant and other advisors by your side will be to your great benefit.

In selecting and building a group of advisors be sure to work with people you like and trust. You are going to want your attorney, accountant, graphic designer, engineers, consultants, and other professionals you bring in to be team players. There should be no room for individuals who are egocentric, abrasive, negative, or nonresponsive. Your team members should be able to work with you and the other team members to achieve a common goal—protecting and advancing your business interests. This is not that much to ask, especially since you are paying these people.

To that end, consider interviewing for your professional team. Meet with several accountants, attorneys, and other service providers to get a feel for them and their practice. Ask specific questions such as how much their fees are and what their level of experience is in certain areas. Be a comparison shopper.

And, like any coach or manager, feel free to replace members of your team if they are not performing for you. If, for example, your accountant won't return your phone calls for weeks at a time you may want to start looking for someone who's more responsive.

By building and cultivating a team of professionals that care about you and your business, you will be able both to concentrate on your core goals and succeed in the future.

Of course, your advisory team can only take you so far. The true source of your success is going to come from within you. The choices and decisions you make, the means by which you approach your business, and the ways in which you deal with people and situations will all be determinative factors in your achievement. The balance you strike between the obligations of work, family, and community will also be important.

Please also remember to focus on working smarter, not harder. As Robert Kiyosaki's rich dad taught him, by using the same strategies the rich use to your advantage you too can become wealthy.

All the strategies discussed herein—the use of corporations, LLCs, and LPs, the strategic utilization of Nevada and Wyoming entities, and maximizing the use of the tax code to your advantage—can be implemented easily and without great expense. They are all present to help you achieve your greatest dreams and goals.

Good luck.

AN EXCERPT FROM

RICH DAD ADVISORS

FOREWORD BY ROBERT KIYOSAKI

Buying & Selling a Business

*How You Can Win
in the Business Quadrant*

GARRETT SUTTON, ESQ.

Chapter One

Before You Begin

Being Your Own Boss

It sounds like paradise – being your own boss. Owning your own business, setting your own hours, answering to no one, even dressing how you like. Robert Kiyosaki's Rich Dad advocates owning businesses, ideally managed by others, for the income they generate and the freedom they can provide. But whether you are a non managing entrepreneur or a day-to-day boss, being the owner also means taking the responsibility – all the responsibility – for the business's health. The success or failure of your business (and correspondingly your personal financial success) lies squarely on your shoulders. There are no sick days, no vacation pay, no downsizing opportunities. A turn in the economy no longer means only worry over job security, but worry over utter financial ruin. There are no security blankets in the entrepreneurial world, so you'd better know from the start if you are a Linus or a Lucy. Linus was the intellectual of the Peanuts gang, but he required security. Lucy was the go-getter, schemer who never thought anything through. Somewhere between the personalities of this brother-sister duo is the ideal entrepreneur. Do you have the right entrepreneurial personality?

Before you buy a business, recognize that knowing your strengths and weaknesses going in can save you hours, possibly years, of frustration, as well as limit your financial risk. Ask yourself some questions. Here are a few with which to start:

- How does your education compare to the demands of the industry you plan to enter?

- Do you know how to track financials and plan for taxes?

- How do you feel about sales and marketing? How does your experience stack up?

- Do your skills lend themselves to running the type of business you are considering?

- Will your needs be met by your skills? If not, are these skills ones you can learn? If so, how long will it take you to get up to speed?

- On a more interior level, how do the needs of the business fit your personality? If you don't really like people, you may not enjoy retail. If you abhor math, the intense financial and money management aspects of manufacturing won't likely be to your liking.

- Some businesses live and die at the feet of a strong leader. The identity of the business may be the identity of the owner. Can you be all things to all people?

- Some businesses require travel or heavy lifting or working nights, weekends and holidays. Does your lifestyle allow for that? Are you willing to make the necessary changes? The odds of succeeding at a business you don't like, or whose demands do not naturally suit you, aren't good. Go with what you enjoy, what you know, or what you can learn.

- How do your goals measure up to what the business can realistically offer? Passion will take you far, knowledge even further, but in the end it may be the numbers that tell the tale. So don't make decisions without them. Let your passion be for your objectives, even an industry, but not a particular business. Let your heart have its say, but let your head lead the way.

- Will you be a good entrepreneur? Consider the following:

1. Do you need a lot of supervision or do you find your own way?
2. Are you trusted by others?
3. Are you responsible by choice or by force?
4. Are you a people person?
5. Are you a leader?
6. Are you willing to go the distance even if there is no immediate reward in sight?
7. Are you a decision-maker?
8. Can you put the big picture before immediate reward?
9. Do you finish what you start?

- Do you know who you are and what you want? Pull out your resume. Analyze it realistically. Write out your goals. Write out the realistic potential of the company you are considering. Imagine yourself running the company. Be specific. There is power in the specificity of written goals: Let them guide you in deciding if you are right for the business and if the business is right for you.

- How will your family adapt? Now, before any papers are signed and any obligations finalized, is the time to bring in family considerations.

1. What will the extra hours and extra worry do to your family?
2. Will family members be able or willing to help carry the load?
3. How will the decrease in financial security affect the cohesiveness of your family?
4. Is it worth giving up the concreteness of paychecks, insurance, retirement benefits, vacation and the like for the pride of ownership and the hopes of long-term payoff? In the language of Robert Kiyosaki's Cash Flow Quadrant, are you ready to go from being an E (Employee) to an S (Self-Employed Business Owner) to hopefully a B (Owner of a Business Managed by Others).
5. What is the flexibility of family members – financially, psychologically and emotionally? Make sure you know everyone's needs and consider whether this purchase will meet those needs.

6. If you don't get family support, will you be able to do it on your own? Family-run businesses don't necessarily put the whole family to work. If you expect help from a spouse, children or others, you need to get their support long before the closing.

•   Are you running from something (dead-end job, mind-numbing boredom, the boss from hell) or toward something (self-esteem, independence, creativity)? If you are running from something, no business will take you far enough. But if you are running toward something, the distance will be greatly shortened with a bit of forethought and planning.

Why Buy (vs. Start Up)

Preparation and hard work can lead to personal fulfillment, a career you control and financial independence. When you're the boss, you determine how much time you put in and how much money you take out. When success does come, it is your success. Your hours lead to your income. You are not just lining someone else's pockets.

There is much less financial risk involved with buying an existing business than with starting one up. It is that initial period from startup to breaking even that is the most deadly for a business. An existing business must be doing something right to still be in existence. The rewards of ownership and independence are the same for a startup and for an existing business, but an existing business has a past to help guide the future. A path has been cleared for new owners to tread.

History is a valuable tool in any business. There is a level of expectation – a theoretical roadmap for the future. It is this aura of predictability that makes financing a purchase easier than financing a startup. The existing business has financial statements, assets, cash flow – in short, collateral that can be used for bank loans. And if the banks prove uninterested, many a motivated seller will help out with the financing, often with better terms than a commercial lender. An owner may even stick around after the sale to help with the often complicated, always delicate transition period.

We live in a time when small businesses are not only able to exist alongside big businesses; they are able to thrive. Technology has made access nearly seamless. Your business can reach customers on the other side of the world just as easily as the other side of the street. Fax, E-mail, Internet, video conferencing, printed material – all allow a local business to reach a global market while keeping overhead low and inventory small. These avenues may not have been explored by a company's current owner and could be the difference between his or her getting by and your getting ahead.

Why Sell (vs. Hang On)

The best time to sell is when the economy and the industry are in good shape. While sellers have little or no control over these factors, they can keep their companies in prime selling condition in order to take advantage of unforeseen opportunities. A well-run business is a valuable commodity in any market. Knowing economic and industry norms and how the company stacks up against them will help a seller set the best price should he or she decide to sell.

Sometimes events completely out of a seller's sphere of influence pop up and motivate a sale. Some of these include:

- Change in the competition (such as when a large company decides to move into the arena and is looking for a company to buy)

- Death of a partner or a majority shareholder (the owner may have to sell to pay off other partners or to divide up the deceased's estate)

- The owner's own heirs don't want the company (or are not competent to run it)

- Unexpected changes in finances (such as from divorce or medical emergencies)

- Changes in the rules (such as zoning changes or new laws)

Sometimes events completely within the seller's sphere of influence are prompting the sale. Sellers must understand their motivations to avoid making a mistake.

Burnout is a common sale motivator. But burnout is seldom long-term; a sale is. Maybe the seller just needs a vacation or shorter hours. Maybe he or she needs to shake things up and bring the fun and adventure back into the business. If the owner decided to sell, that freedom (just as with short-timer's syndrome in the workaday world) might prompt him or her to make changes. Sellers, why not make those changes now?

Timing

Timing is important whether buying or selling a business. The health of the overall economy, the state of the company's specific industry, and the condition of the company all play into the decision-making process. The overall economy's health may dictate the availability of loans while also coloring the perspective of potential buyers. Good economic times breed optimistic buyers. Optimistic buyers have rosier hopes for the future, and it is this future they are purchasing. The state of the target company's industry and the health of the target business help define levels of perceived risk. Lower risk means higher prices, even if those risks are only in the eye of the beholder.

While buyers and sellers have no control over the health of economy or even the state of the industry, assessing trends and perceptions will greatly influence their ability to be in the right place at the right time. The key ingredient to good luck is good planning.

Economic slumps may be good news for buyers. If buyers have the purchasing power (or better yet, the cash), there are usually bargains to be had during a recession. Of course, the risks are higher. After all, buyers are likely buying in the hopes of the economy turning around. Eventually it will, but weathering the storm can be an expensive proposition.

Economic booms may be good news for sellers. Optimism loosens purse strings. But higher purchase prices generally mean more debt for the buyer and if optimism turns out to be unfounded, carrying a company with significant debt and insufficient valuation may require a buyer to sell. A struggling company in a struggling economy is the worst of all situations for the seller.

Either way, in good economies or bad, buyers want to be sure they have enough money on hand to cover not only the purchase but also the initial slump that generally accompanies new ownership.

Risk of No Sale

Imagine putting a company up for sale and getting no offers. Or getting only low offers. What went wrong? Maybe the asking price was too high. This would be the time for the seller to go back to the value analysis and reconsider the assumptions used in projections of future sales. Were the assumptions realistic? If the owner still wants to sell, he or she will need to consider lowering the price or taking the company off the market. If the former, the seller may need an ego check first. If the latter, damage control is warranted.

A good way to understand some of the concepts we're discussing is through the use of case studies. Our first one is instructive.

Case No. 1 – Walter, Peter and Anian

Walter owned a chain of three closet design and home organizing businesses in a large, populous state. Walter did a fair amount of advertising and so many people throughout the region knew of The Closet Admiral.

Walter had built the business up to the point where he could step away and do other things. He had brought in Peter to be the general manager of the three closet design businesses. Peter, being aggressive and confident in his abilities, insisted that he be able to acquire an ownership interest in the business over time. Walter agreed to this, but beyond an acceptance in principal, the negotiations had not yet begun and the terms for an acquisition of ownership had not even been discussed.

Shortly thereafter, Walter's plans for the business changed. An opportunity to own an even more profitable business with a much greater upside potential had landed in Walter's lap. To pull it off, he would have to sell The Closet Admiral in order to generate enough cash for the down payment he needed on the new business.

Walter decided to quietly solicit offers to purchase The Closet Admiral. He wanted to fly under the radar, so that no one would know of, or impede, his future plans. He didn't tell Peter or his banker or any of his inside circle of advisors.

Anian owned a chain of five closet design locations in the southern part of the state. She was a hard-nosed businesswoman, always interested in a deal. When Walter approached her about a quiet sale she responded with interest. On a handshake, she agreed to keep the whole matter confidential. In reality, she just wanted to see Walter's books. She wanted to know how he had been able to expand so quickly.

After reviewing the books, Anian placed two disastrous phone calls. First, she called Walter's banker to demand why she couldn't get the same favorable terms that Walter had received for equipment purchases. The banker was very angry that the confidential relationship between he and Walter had been compromised. Then, Anian called Peter to see if he would work for her. Peter learned for the first time that the business he thought he had an ownership interest in was for sale. He was furious at Walter for what he considered to be an offensive betrayal of trust.

Both Peter and the banker refused to do business with Walter again. Peter quit in a very loud and derisive manner, encouraging other employees to quit as well, many of whom did. The banker called several of Walter's promissory notes, forcing Walter to scramble to find alternative financing, and killing all of Walter's hopes for completing the other business opportunity he had sought to pursue.

The disruption caused Walter to almost lose the business. When the employees left they took some of their regular referral sources with them. Some of his best employees started working at two new, very competitive closet design firms – that Anian had opened up in the area.

Walter hung on by assuring the remaining employees that they would always have a place to work, that he was not selling the business, and that their job security was as important to him as it was to them. It took almost a year, but Walter brought the business back. And he had learned a very valuable lesson about the confidentiality needed when selling a business, and the care needed in selecting the right potential buyers.

As we have just seen, company sales affect more than just buyers and sellers. Customers, vendors and employees can all find out about the possibility of a sale, and emotional reactions are inevitable. Fear of what is to come may have some already looking for new suppliers, customers and jobs. The fallout can be far-reaching without the owner ever even knowing about it. Therefore, sellers need to be proactive from the beginning. Confidentiality agreements are a must to keep the news of a sale on a need-to-know basis. The agreement should be in writing with, if possible, a damage provision for the unauthorized release of confidential information. However, this type of contractual provision will only take the seller so far. Once the others find out, or are likely about to find out (and be assured, they WILL learn of a potential sale), the seller needs to start talking and alleviating fears. And you'd better have your story consistent and down pat, because your employees are going to want to hear something that is reasonable, reassuring and makes sense.

How to Handle a Failed Sale

If the sale does not go through and the company is taken off the market, the owner will need to talk to those involved and reassure them all that he or she is recommitted to the business and looking forward to future success. Any sense of failure projected by an owner will lead others into the cycle of uncertainty. As we all know from experience, uncertainty leads to fear. Fear leads to grasping for safety. And that search for safety can mean customers, vendors and employees finding new opportunities elsewhere and leaving the owner behind.

To allay customer fears after deciding not to sell, owners should redouble customer service efforts. It is unlikely that most customers will even know there was the potential of a sale, but the owner has no way of knowing who might or might not have heard the news. Customer service never hurts a business and making service a priority not only convinces those who did hear that you are recommitted to the business but may increase loyalty of those who never even knew anything was in the offing. For those who ask what happened, be frank but don't give away details. Customers need reassurance, not a lesson in capitalism. As Henry Ford said, "Never complain, never explain."

The fallout with vendors could have financial consequences. Most vendors have relationships with owners based on long-term rewards. They may offer good credit deals in hopes of keeping an owner's business for a long time. The news of a company being up for sale makes those long-term hopes less likely. Don't expect the news of the sale not going through to be a relief. It is likely that vendors will now see the company as a short-term investment (they will be wondering if the owner is still trying to sell, questioning his or her commitment). This is especially true with smaller, privately held businesses where relationships are more intimate. Owners may find vendors have hurt feelings about being kept in the dark. While from your perspective it is none of their business, from their viewpoint it is their business. Your business is their business. Appreciating their position will help in understanding the dynamics involved.

Employees likely will be relieved the company is no longer for sale, but they may have some of the same feelings as vendors and customers. They may still question owner loyalty. Once that happens, their own levels of loyalty are likely to decrease as they turn more toward protecting themselves. Morale is likely down. Owners might consider having a company party or perhaps a team-building retreat to reinvigorate the company.

No matter what work the owner puts in, the damage may be done. In the end, there is still the danger that not selling will cost the owner more than dropping the price would have.

Rich Dad's Tips

- Know your strengths and weaknesses before buying a business.

- Be prepared to accept complete personal responsibility for the success or failure of your business.

- As a seller of a business know and understand the consequences of a failed business sale.

Tom Wheelwright, CPA

Rich Dad Advisor on Taxes and Wealth Building Strategies

Personal Background and Entrepreneur Profile

Name   Tom Wheelwright
Date of Birth   October 26, 1957
Place of Birth   Salt Lake City, Utah

Traditional Education
University of Utah
Degree: Bachelor of Arts
University of Texas at Austin
Degree: Masters of Professional Accounting
Highest level completed: Masters

Professional Education
Certified Public Accountant
Ernst & Young National Tax Department – involved in 1986 Tax
Reform Act

Grade Point Averages
High School: 3.97
College: 3.91

Value of traditional education... relative to becoming an entrepreneur
It was required. I could not have formed my own CPA firm
without traditional education.

Subject I liked most in school
Tax – and I had a great teacher: Dr. Haney.

Subject I hated most in school

Cost Accounting – Lots of memorization and no concepts to learn.

First entrepreneurial project

We harvested seeds from dead marigold flowers in the fall, packaged them, and sold them (in the spring) back to the people who had supplied the dead marigold flowers the previous fall. (My buddy and I correctly calculated that these were the most likely buyers for marigold seeds).

The key entrepreneurial skill I was *not* taught in school:

Sales – There is no revenue without sales. Even when I went to work at Price Waterhouse, I asked for a sales course since I was expected to develop a new practice of multi-state tax clients. They agreed to send me to a brief course, but refused to send me to a full sales program. These were "educated" people who didn't understand the importance of learning how to sell.

Why and when I became an entrepreneur and my first major venture

I became an entrepreneur when I started my CPA firm in 1995. I had just been fired by Price Waterhouse and was tired of being told what to do by people who had no clue.

I had been an employee at large companies for 13 years, including four years with a Fortune 500 Company. When I was there, I discovered that an employee has a lot of risk, since they only have one customer: the company. My first responsibility when I was hired was to cut my staff by 50%. These were people who had done a good job but were being laid off because the company was cutting costs.

After Price Waterhouse fired me, I realized that if I created my own company that I would have a lot less risk, more control, and a lot more potential for reward. If one client had financial struggles and could no longer afford my services, it wouldn't be the end of the world. I would have many others that could replace that revenue.

I also knew several other CPAs with their own firms who were not nearly as knowledgeable as I was when it came to tax law—and they were driving much nicer cars than my old Mazda. I decided it was time to lower my risk and increase my potential income.

In 1995 I formed Thomas Wheelwright, CPA that later became ProVision. I started with two clients who had followed me from my Ernst & Young days. The early days were tough, as I was only able to add two more clients in the first nine months. Then I realized I could buy a CPA firm. I borrowed the money from the seller, from a friend, and from my parents since I didn't have any money of my own.

In four years, my firm grew from those first two clients to a firm with 10 employees. Since then we have grown into one of the largest firms in Arizona with clients in all 50 states and over 30 countries.

Best Lesson from first business:

After my second year in business, I was growing so much that I needed help to handle my client load—and fast. I was worried that if I didn't handle the clients then my referral sources would stop sending people to me. I didn't plan for the growth. It happened quickly and I was too busy taking care of clients to look at my business and plan for the future.

The result was that I took on a partner and gave up 50% of my company because I was desperate. This came back to haunt me big time several years later when I had to fire that partner. It set the firm back a couple of years and was very painful, personally and financially. All this could have been avoided had I hired an employee instead of taking on a partner.

It wasn't the fact of having a partner that was the problem; I have had some really good partners over the years. It was the fact that I was desperate… and didn't follow my instincts. Instead, I listened to other peoples' advice—that I needed to do whatever it took to serve the clients, even if this meant giving up half of my company.

The good partners I have had since then did not come from desperation. They came from planning. That doesn't mean I have always had good partners since then. But the good partners I have now are the result of good planning and not a knee-jerk reaction.

The best lesson was to trust my instincts and plan for growth.

What I learned about myself from my Kolbe Index

TOM WHEELRIGHT
Kolbe A™ Index Result

CONGRATULATIONS TOM
You Got a Perfect Score on the Kolbe A™ Index

You are uniquely able to take on future-oriented challenges. You lead the way to visionary possibilities and create what others said couldn't be done. You'll say "Yes" before you even know the end of the question – then turn it into a productive adventure.

Kolbe Action Modes®

Reprinted with permission from Kolbe Corp.

My Kolbe explained to me why I chose the path I did in my career and why I was never happy as an employee.

Traditional education is designed for Fact Finders and Follow Thrus.

As you can see from my chart, I am a Quick Start... which means I become bored easily. So I didn't take the normal route for a CPA which is to stay in one office doing tax returns for many years. Instead, I spent a couple of years learning the tax routine and then jumped at the chance to transfer to the National Tax Department in Washington, D.C. where I could focus on consulting and on teaching other CPAs.

I learned from my Kolbe that my "genius" is to simplify. So I was able to take the complex tax laws and simplify them for my students at Ernst & Young. Later, when I moved to Phoenix, I spent 14 years simplifying the complexity of multi-state tax laws for graduate students at Arizona State University in their Masters of Tax program.

My book, *Tax-Free Wealth*, simplifies tax strategies for entrepreneurs and investors. While most tax advisors make the tax law seem like the most difficult thing ever, I look at it as a simple road map for reducing taxes and building wealth.

Now we use Kolbe with our employees and also with every client. We use it with employees to make sure we hire employees with the right natural instincts and have them doing the right jobs. And we use Kolbe to help us understand how to manage our employees. A Quick Start like myself, for example, needs clear deadlines, while a Follow Through like my partner, Ann, never needs a deadline because she can't wait to get a project off of her desk.

We find out our clients' natural instincts and pair clients and tax professionals with similar Kolbe scores. That way we can better serve and understand our clients. We also use Kolbe to help our clients determine what their personal role should be on their business and investment teams and to determine what positions they should hire first.

My role in the B-I Triangle

My role in the Rich Dad B-I Triangle is tied to Cash Flow and how the company can keep more of the money it earns and implement sound and profitable tax strategies. My job as the CEO and leader of ProVision is to find new ways for our clients to save taxes, teach our staff how to best serve our clients, and communicate our message to the world.

Skills that are essential for entrepreneurs—but not taught in schools

That's easy: Number one is communication. We are not taught in schools how to communicate, either verbally or in writing. Instead, we are taught to regurgitate book reports, write essays, and evaluate poetry. It's not that these are bad things to learn or do; they just don't help an entrepreneur. Entrepreneurs need to know how to communicate their message to the public, to customers, to investors, to clients and to employees.

I had one terrific accounting professor who understood this. He had just left one of the big CPA firms as the partner in charge of audits worldwide. He understood that accountants need to learn how to simplify financial statements. For our major project, he had us explain in simple terms a portion of the financial statement of a public company. This was the only time I really got a good lesson on communication from a professor.

I spend most of my days communicating. I could be communicating with a client, simplifying the tax law for them or explaining a tax strategy to them. Or I could be on stage explaining how the tax law works to a group of entrepreneurs or investors. Or I will be teaching my partners and staff about how to improve our client service. Or I'm meeting with partners and staff to follow up on projects they are doing.

Everything I do as an entrepreneur involves clear and concise communication. When I fail at communicating, I fail the people I am trying to serve.

My Most Important Lesson for Entrepreneurs

Follow your instincts. Every entrepreneur instinctively knows when something is going wrong. Jim Collins in his book, *Great By Choice*, describes this as "productive paranoia." Every time I have gotten into trouble in business it has been because I have ignored my instincts.

School teaches us to follow others, especially those in authority. I have found that while I want to learn from others, I am always better off trusting my own instincts. An entrepreneur has to learn to trust his or her instincts, even if it gets them into trouble sometimes. The mistakes we make help us learn and our instincts become better and more refined.

Instincts can warn you against bad partners, bad deals, and bad employees. They can warn you when you might have challenges with a particular client you haven't spoken to in awhile. Your instincts will lead you, if you let them. It's important to have people around you who will challenge your instincts while allowing you to move forward in acting on them.

How I learned to raise capital:

My first experience raising capital came when I did my first CPA firm acquisition. (I have done three acquisitions over my career). My friend, also a CPA, heard of a CPA firm that was for sale and he knew I was looking for a book of business to acquire. It was a small CPA firm, with a hundred clients, the owner, and one employee. At the time, I was flat broke. I had spent the first nine months since leaving Price Waterhouse cold calling all of the people I could, day in and day out, with limited success. In fact, I was even considering going back into the j-o-b market.

This firm seemed like a great opportunity. I met with the owner and we worked out a price. I just had to find the money. The first person I approached was the seller. She was willing to carry 50% of the purchase price. That meant I only had to find about $60,000. The friend who told me about the firm offered to finance $30,000 for one year, provided he could take a lien on my house. I said OK. The final money came from my parents.

The revenues from the firm paid back my friend the first year. By the end of the second year I had paid back the seller. My parents wanted the cash flow from the loan and asked that, in lieu of repayment, I make monthly interest payments for the rest of their lives.

It was only later that I discovered I could have gone to a bank that would have gladly loaned me 50% or more of the money I needed to purchase the practice. My ignorance paid off in this case. The terms of the financing I got from others was much better than what I would have received from a bank. After that, I always went first to the seller for financing. This was like getting the practice for free, since the practice was going to pay back the seller.

How I learned to overcome fear and failure:

I was a Mormon missionary in France for two years right after I finished high school. I knocked on thousands of doors and approached hundreds of people in the street asking them to listen to me about my religion. The vast majority of people said no. And some of them said, "Hell, no!" I had been in France less than a month when I approached a man to discuss religion and he turned around and slugged me. Most of the doors I knocked on either didn't answer or were slammed in my face.

There's nothing like selling Mormonism to Catholics in France to teach one to overcome fear and failure. I remember one time, after I had been in France for over a year, going door-to-door through an entire apartment building without a single person inviting us in. My young companion asked me afterwards how I was able to stay so positive. I told him that if the people only knew what we knew, they would open their doors to us. They only closed them because we weren't getting the message across. It was our job to get ourselves invited into people's homes.

The lesson I learned from this was that as long as we are driven by our mission—whatever it may be—we don't ever need to fear rejection or failure. Our mission isn't about us. It is about the people we serve. Whether I am on stage in front of 10,000 people in Australia or speaking to a prospect on the phone, my thoughts are on how I can serve. When we place our focus on other people, our fear goes away.

My personal strength

I care about everyone. And I want everyone to succeed. I never lose sleep over my own challenges, but *do* lose sleep regularly over my clients, my partners, and my staff. I have an undying belief that people are good and have the potential to succeed if they are given the right tools and education.

My personal weakness

I am too suggestible. I have a tendency to take other people's advice over my own. That's why I have such a hard time trusting my own instincts.

The Entrepreneurial Skills I Teach best

How to use the incentives in the tax law to keep more of the money you make.

What is the Entrepreneurial Lesson that I teach best?

How to Use the Tax Law to Increase Your Cash Flow

How to Use the Tax Law
to Increase Your Cash Flow
by Tom Wheelwright, CPA

Taxes make the rich richer.
Unfortunately, for most people, the opposite is true.
That's why Tom is an important member of my team.
For most people, taxes are their largest single expense.

– RTK

I love the tax law. When I was an undergraduate at the University of Utah, I took my first tax class in my junior year. I loved it so much that I postponed my intermediate accounting classes until my senior year, taking, instead, every tax class that was offered. I found the tax law to be complex and creative. And it all made sense to me.

The tax law makes sense when you understand the purpose of the law. True, the tax law raises revenue for the government. But the tax law does much more than that. The tax law drives economic activity.

Many years ago governments began to recognize just how much people hate paying taxes. (Remember the Boston Tea Party?) They figured out that people will take steps to avoid paying taxes. So they began asking themselves *What activities would we like people to undertake?* That question—and its answers—led to providing tax breaks for those who did what the government wanted them to do.

The primary activity the government wanted was for people to build businesses. Businesses employ people. When people are employed, they don't rely on the government as much and they don't cause as many social problems. And they pay taxes. So if the government could find a way to encourage people to start and grow businesses… that would be good for everyone.

The primary way the government encourages businesses is through business tax breaks. These breaks are not loopholes. They are intentional incentives for starting and building a business. The more money a person invests in their business, the bigger the tax breaks.

Let's start with the biggest tax break – deductions. Any money you spend that has a business purpose and is considered typical and helpful to the business is tax deductible. That includes meals, travel, rent, automobile expenses, and supplies. Any money you earn in your business that is spent on business activities is deductible. Even money you set aside for employees for their retirement is deductible. And employees don't have to report that income that was set aside (called a qualified plan) until they get it. Because the government *wants* people to have money for retirement, there is an additional tax incentive.

There are many other tax incentives for businesses. In most countries, there are tax credits available for businesses that do research and development work. France is noted for having one of the biggest tax credits for research and development in the world. This means that not only do you get a tax deduction for spending money on research and development, you also get a credit—or direct offset to your taxes—for a percentage of the money you spend on developing new products for customers and systems to improve your business.

Another terrific tax benefit for entrepreneurs is depreciation. When you purchase a piece of equipment, or buy a building, or improve a space you are renting, you get a depreciation deduction. Every year you get a percentage of the equipment, building, or improvement as a deduction against your business income. This is true whether you paid for the asset directly or whether you borrowed money from the bank to buy or improve the asset. So the bank pays for the asset and you get the depreciation deduction.

There are hundreds of other incentives for business owners as well. There are employment credits, deductions for charitable contributions, credits for buying solar panels for your building, agricultural tax benefits for agribusiness, and special deductions for drilling oil and gas wells, timber, and coal mines. It doesn't matter what business you are in, there are tax benefits waiting for you to use them.

Entrepreneurs also can take advantage of better tax rates in different states and countries. If you are an employee, you are stuck with paying the taxes on your income in the state and country in which you live and work. When you own a business, you can set up your business to take advantage of the low tax rates of countries like Ireland, the Netherlands, and the Caribbean. If you are in the United States, you can take advantage of the zero tax rates of states like Nevada, Wyoming, and Texas. These states and countries are providing incentives for entrepreneurs like yourself to do business in their state or country.

Of course, a true entrepreneur won't stop with the business tax benefits. A real entrepreneur will take what money they cannot reinvest into the business and will invest it elsewhere into assets that produce cash flow, like real estate and oil and gas. And those assets also produce tax benefits. Governments want people to build housing and commercial projects so they give tax incentives to those who do that. In the United States, the government wants investors to build low-income housing, so in addition to the regular tax benefits for real estate (like depreciation), the U.S. government gives tax credits.

Governments want to encourage people to invest in energy as well. So there are deductions and credits for investing in solar heating, oil and gas, coal, hydroelectric power, and windmills—and even for electric vehicles.

No matter what business you choose, there are tax benefits available to you. And it doesn't even matter what country you live or work in. All countries provide tax benefits to entrepreneurs. All it takes is for you to get a basic education of how the tax law works and find a good tax advisor to work through the details. Some of the best tax incentives are in Europe, Australia, France and the U.K. There are tax incentives for businesses in Russia, China, and Japan as well.

When I plan to visit a new country, I look up the tax laws and one thing is consistent: tax laws everywhere benefit the entrepreneur. And when you are paying less in taxes, you have more money to invest in your business.

When you are an entrepreneur and use the tax laws the way they were intended to be used, taxes can truly make you rich.

About Tom Wheelwright, CPA

Tom Wheelwright, CPA, is the creative force behind ProVision, the world's premier strategic CPA firm. As the founder and CEO, Tom has been responsible for innovating new tax, business and wealth consulting and strategy services for ProVision's premium clientele for over two decades.

Tom is a leading expert and published author on partnerships and corporation tax strategies, a well-known platform speaker, and a wealth education innovator. Donald Trump selected Tom to contribute to his Wealth Builders Program, calling Tom "the best of the best." Robert Kiyosaki, bestselling author of *Rich Dad Poor Dad*, calls Tom "a team player that anyone who wants to be rich needs to add to his or her team." In Robert Kiyosaki's book *The Real Book of Real Estate*, Tom authored Chapters 1 and 21. He is a significant contributor to Robert Kiyosaki's new book *Why the Rich Are Getting Richer* and has also contributed to *Who Took My Money?* and *Unfair Advantage*.

Tom has written several articles for publication in major professional journals and online resources and has spoken to thousands throughout the United States, Canada, Europe, and Australia. He has also used his superior relationship and team building skills to advise the Canadian market in the art of investing in the United States by contributing to Philip McKernan's *South of 49* and contributed heavily to his newest book, *Fire Sale*.

For more than 30 years, Tom has devised innovative tax, business, and wealth strategies for sophisticated investors and business owners in the manufacturing, real estate, and high tech fields. His passion is teaching these innovative strategies to the thousands who come to hear him speak. He has participated as a keynote speaker and panelist in multiple roundtables, and led ground-breaking tax discussions challenging the status quo in terms of tax strategies.

Tom has a wide variety of professional experience, ranging from Big 4 accounting, where he managed and led professional training for thousands of CPAs at Ernst & Young's National Tax Department in Washington, D.C., to in-house tax advisor for Pinnacle West Capital Corporation, at the time a Fortune 1000 company. Tom also served as an adjunct professor in the Masters of Tax program at Arizona State University for 14 years where he created the course for teaching multi-state tax planning techniques and taught hundreds of graduate students.

Books by Tom Wheelwright

Rich Dad Advisor Series Books

Tax-Free Wealth

How to Build Massive Wealth by Permanently Lowering Your Taxes

... in Spanish

Riqueza Libra de Impuestos

AN EXCERPT FROM

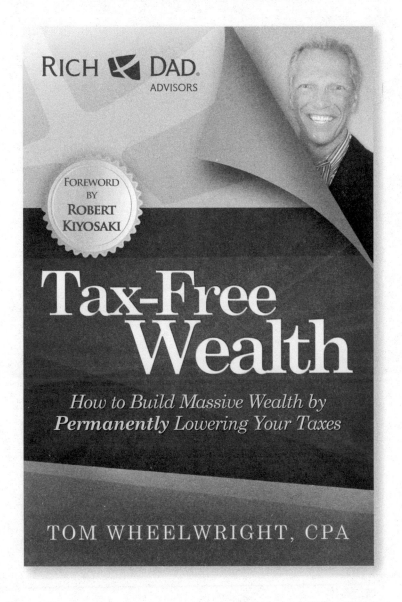

RICH DAD. ADVISORS

FOREWORD BY ROBERT KIYOSAKI

Tax-Free Wealth

How to Build Massive Wealth by
Permanently Lowering Your Taxes

TOM WHEELWRIGHT, CPA

Chapter Twenty-Three

Choose the Right Tax Advisor and Preparer

"Day in and day out, your tax accountant can make or lose you more money than any single person in your life, with the possible exception of your kids."
– Harvey Mackay

The first time I learned about the law was in my business law course in college. One of the local bankruptcy judges taught the course. He was a terrific instructor, and I loved the class. I especially loved learning about how vague the law can be. I'd learned many years earlier that something vague allowed for much more flexibility than something specific and certain. And I liked knowing that the law was flexible.

Like most children, I discovered early on how to manipulate my parents. Sometimes that meant using my mother to persuade my father to let me go somewhere he might not otherwise have allowed. Other times that meant pretending not to hear when they wanted me to do something. Most of the time it simply meant twisting the meaning of what they told me into what I wanted to hear. Then, after I did something they didn't like, I used their words to convince them they'd really allowed me to do it.

Perhaps I was always meant to study the law so that I could use it to my client's advantage. That first business law class really set me on my path to studying the tax law. I was so excited to learn the law that my junior year I signed up to take all of the tax classes available at the University of Utah School of Business. Most of my classmates were waiting to take their tax classes until their senior year, but those classes were so interesting to me that I couldn't wait. To do this, I had to push all of my other upper-division accounting classes to my senior year. I even remember taking both intermediate accounting courses the same semester so that I could fit all those upper-level classes in as a senior. All that work was worth it to me.

The "U" business school had a terrific tax professor, Professor Haney. He was a tax attorney who practiced law full time and taught tax classes on the side. He was demanding, but he understood the law well and was enthusiastic about the subject. When I was thinking about graduate school, the first person I talked to other than my wife was Professor Haney.

I asked him whether I should go to law school or get a master's degree in tax accounting. He told me that if I wanted to spend most of my time working in tax law, I would be better off practicing as a Certified Public Accountant. In his experience, CPAs spent more time doing tax work than lawyers. So on Professor Haney's advice I applied to the University of Texas Master's of Professional Accounting Program.

Since then, I have devoted my life to studying the tax law, teaching the tax law, and using the tax law to help my clients reduce their tax burdens. And taxes really are a burden. As Benjamin Franklin once said, "It would be a hard government that should tax its people one-tenth part of their income." And yet governments throughout the world now routinely take 40 to 50 percent of a person's income.

If you haven't noticed yet, I'm pretty passionate about reducing taxes. And passion is the most important element in reducing your taxes.

RULE #21:	**The more passionate you and your advisor are about reducing your taxes, the lower your taxes will be.**

Every time I speak at a seminar, I'm asked the same question over and over again, "How do I find a good tax advisor?" This is one of the most important questions you can ever ask. A good tax advisor will not only help you reduce your taxes but he'll take the fear out of taxes as well. And most importantly, he'll take the fear out of a tax audit.

I'm asked the same question over and over again, "How do I find a good tax advisor?" This is one of the most important questions you can ever ask.

But being passionate about reducing your taxes is only one of the traits to look for in a good tax advisor. Another is how the advisor looks at the tax law. Is the advisor afraid of the law or does he look at it as an opportunity? Most tax accountants are afraid of the law. They won't even read it. Instead, they read an abbreviated version of the law, such as a simple tax guide. These accountants shy away from anything they don't understand, and they don't understand much.

They shy away from the law because they have never taken the time to learn the law. There is as wide a variety of education among tax advisors and tax preparers as there is among doctors, lawyers, and other professionals. Some tax preparers have only taken a few hours or a few weeks of courses to learn how to prepare tax returns. Others have some schooling, though not very much. It's only the best advisors who have graduated at the top of their classes from the best universities who really understand the tax law. The reason they attended the top schools and graduated at the top of their classes is that they wanted to learn the tax law and all of its intricacies. Like me, they crave learning about the law. The hierarchy of tax preparers is pretty simple—it's based on their level of education, both formal and practical.

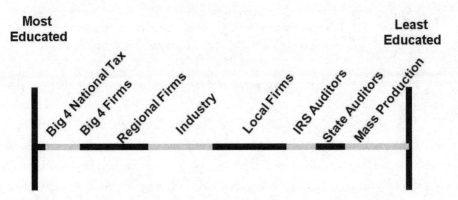

As a result, most accountants, those with less education and understanding, will only take the most obvious deductions and tax benefits when they prepare your returns. And likely you'll only talk to them once or twice a year because they don't have much to tell you. They're likely to make suggestions like maximizing your IRA, RRSP, or 401(k)

contribution. They'll tell you to prepay expenses at the end of the year. Or they'll suggest waiting until a later year to receive some income that you're owed.

What terrible advice. Did you notice how all of this advice is about saving taxes now at the cost of having to pay them later? These accountants are all about tax savings now at the cost of your future. Once, during a training meeting, I asked our staff to explain what's different about ProVision from other CPA firms. Our youngest staff member, right out of college, gave the most insightful answer. She said that she never expected to be working for a firm that focuses on its clients' future rather than dwelling on their past. One of the reasons most tax preparers don't focus on permanent tax savings is because they are only focused on the past and the present. They aren't taking into account your future.

Why do people hire accountants and advisors with such little understanding? Maybe it's because they don't know what to look for in a tax advisor. Or maybe it's just because these preparers and advisors tend to charge less money for their work. What a mistake to hire someone because they charge less than somebody else. The real test of an advisor is not how much they charge you, but how much they cost you.

RULE #22:	It's not how much your tax preparer charges you that matters; it's how much your tax preparer costs you.

Let me give you an example. One of our clients, let's call her Jill, recently reminded me about the amount of taxes we save her each year. Because of our understanding of the law, we've been able to save her $70,000 each year. Invested at 10 percent over 20 years, that amounts to about $4 million in money that she wouldn't have had if she'd stayed with her previous tax advisor. In other words, her previous advisor cost her $4 million over the previous 20 years. Yes, he charged less than my firm, ProVision. We charged about $20,000 to do the tax planning for Jill. But that $20,000 was the best investment Jill has ever made. Her return on investment (ROI) amounts to 350 percent per year. And, since these are income taxes she is getting back, they aren't even taxable. How would you like a 350 percent tax-free return on a $20,000 investment?

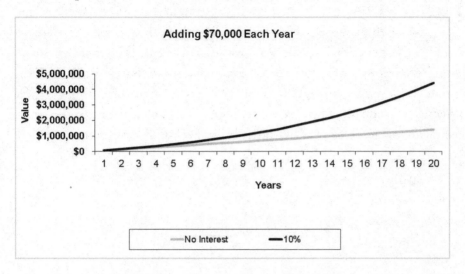

Not every client is going to save $70,000 each year in taxes. Some will save more and some will save less. And fees vary from client to client as well. The key here is to ask which accountant cost Jill more money? The one whom she paid less and who cost her $4 million, or the one whom she paid more and saved $70,000 per year? Pretty obvious, isn't it? Yet most people continue to look at how much their preparer charges rather than how much their tax preparer costs them in excess taxes.

Another tendency for tax accountants is to look at the law as if it runs in a straight line. We call these types of folks linear or left-brained thinkers. Most accountants are like this. They decided to be accountants because they like the certainty and clarity of figures. They generally don't become accountants because they like the vagueness of the law. These tax accountants do okay with routine work such as preparing an accurate tax return. What they won't do is figure out creative ways to use the law in your favor. The challenge is that accountants don't write the tax law. Good tax lawyers hired by congressmen and MPs (Members of Parliament) write the law to carry out those politicians' desires to improve the economy, encourage certain industries, and maintain government revenues. These lawyers tend to not think in a straight line. They're what we would call nonlinear or right-brained thinkers.

The tax laws aren't written in a straight line. The rules of one section of the law will impact the rules of another section of the law, and the connection isn't always obvious. On top of this, there are many interpretations of the law that come from judges in court cases. It's critical that your tax advisor looks at all of the law when figuring out how to best reduce your taxes. If he or she only looks at a single rule, he or she could easily miss out on four or five other rules that could save you money.

Not All Tax Advisors Are Created Equal	
1.	Tax advisors vary in knowledge and experience even more than health care professionals.
2.	Your tax bill will have more to do with choosing your tax advisor than anything else you do.

Of course, the most important trait for your tax advisor is that he or she cares more about you than he or she does about himself or herself. How can you know this? It's simply a matter of whether he or she spends most of the time in your interview answering your questions and talking about himself or herself and his or her services, or whether he or she is more focused on what you need. Let me share a story to illustrate this principle.

A while back, I was having lunch with one of my colleagues at a neighborhood café. I looked at the menu and found a sandwich that looked tasty. I also noticed on the menu that a pickle came with the sandwich. For those of you who enjoy eating pickles, you probably like getting one with your sandwich. But for those of us who don't like pickles, getting one with our sandwich can be devastating.

Pickles are very social. They don't stay in one place. Instead, the juice runs all over, infecting the sandwich and anything else on the plate. I'm sure this is great if you enjoy the pickle flavor. But if you don't, just having a pickle on the plate can ruin the entire meal.

Naturally, when our server took our order, I asked if she could please make sure they didn't put a pickle on my plate. "Of course," she said. "No worries." Still, I was worried. So I asked her about it again when she brought our drinks. She assured me that she'd make sure I didn't get a pickle on my plate.

A few minutes later, she brought us our orders. I looked at mine. There was a sandwich, some French fries, and a *pickle*! I was confused. Why did I get a pickle on my plate after asking twice not to get one? Was I not nice enough? (I thought I was nice enough). Did she forget? Did the cook just ignore her?

As my colleague and I sat there, we wondered what we could learn from this situation. Why did I end up with a pickle on my plate? Our conclusion was that the cook or the server must have been too busy with their normal routine to do something outside of it.

How could this tragedy have been avoided? (OK, so it wasn't *that* much of a tragedy). We thought and thought, and then it came to us. What if our server had asked me if I wanted a pickle? Would I have gotten one? Of course not. *Because that would have meant that it was in their routine to find out exactly what the customer wanted.*

The same is true when you are interviewing a tax advisor. If the tax advisor's routine is for you to ask all the questions, he will (and can) only respond to your questions. He can't find out anything you don't volunteer. If, instead, his routine is to ask you questions about your situation, you can be pretty sure that he'll be looking out for you and what you really want.

Not only that, but the tax you pay depends entirely on your facts and circumstances. Remember my saying that any expense can be deductible in the right situation? If your situation changes, then your tax will change. If your tax advisor is not asking you questions about your situation, how can he or she possibly know what the tax consequences will be to you? He or she certainly won't be able to show you how to change your situation so that you receive better tax results.

The reality is that you have all of the answers. Your advisor should have all of the questions. Don't worry about what questions you should ask your tax advisor. If you have to ask the questions, then you simply have the wrong advisor.

Don't worry about what questions you should ask your tax advisor. If you have to ask the questions, then you simply have the wrong advisor.

TAX TIP:	Hire the right Tax Advisor. This doesn't just require knowing the right questions to ask a potential tax advisor. It means knowing what questions your tax advisor should be asking you.

Also, remember that only you can reduce your taxes. You have to learn enough about how the tax law applies to you so that you can use it to your benefit every minute of every day. Be sure to find a tax advisor who is willing and able to teach you the rules you need to know in order to reduce your taxes.

Many advisors don't actually want you to know the rules. They're afraid that if you know the rules, you won't need their advice. We both know that's not right. If you know the rules, you'll be more successful at reducing your taxes. When you reduce your taxes, you'll increase your cash flow. When you increase your cash flow, you'll increase your wealth. And when you increase your wealth, you're likely to need your tax advisor even more than you do now. So it's really in your advisor's best interest to take the time to teach you the rules you need to know. It's certainly in your best interest.

	Characteristics of a Good Tax Advisor
1.	Fully educated about the tax law
2.	Passionate about reducing your taxes
3.	Embraces the law as an opportunity
4.	Focuses on permanent tax savings
5.	Uses creativity in applying the law in your favor
6.	Considers the entire law when reducing taxes, not just a single rule of law
7.	Cares more about you than himself or herself
8.	Asks you questions about your specific situation
9.	Willing to teach you the tax rules

The last piece of advice I would give you here is to find a tax advisor who will also prepare your taxes. Don't use a tax preparer who isn't also your tax advisor. If you do, it can be a huge mistake. You could get great advice, and then the preparer might not know how to use this advice in preparing your tax return.

You want to be sure that your preparer isn't just accurate. He or she should also be working to reduce your taxes as he or she prepares your return, and he or she should be reducing your chances of being audited. At my firm, we look at tax return preparation as both the final step in last year's tax planning and the first step in next year's tax planning.

Take the time to look for a good tax advisor who can also prepare your tax returns. Prepare for your interview with a prospective advisor by noting the major points we've discussed in this chapter.

Technical Characteristics of a Good Tax Advisor	
1.	Must be accurate
2.	Prepares your tax returns as well as advises you on your tax strategy
3.	Reduces your taxes as he or she prepares your return
4.	Reduces your chances of being audited

Now that you have all of this knowledge about how to reduce your taxes, what are you going to do next? You should work with your tax advisor to put all of this advice to good use and reduce your taxes right away. This will immediately increase your cash flow. Just think about what you can do with all that extra money!

In the next chapter, we'll talk about how you can use that extra cash flow to massively increase your wealth.

CHAPTER 23: KEY POINTS

1.	The tax law is intentionally vague and allows for great flexibility—if you know what it says and how to bend it.
2.	One of the most important things you'll ever do to protect your wealth is find not just a good but a great tax advisor and preparer.
3.	The best tax advisors have a vast understanding of the tax law, can think nonlinearly, and are passionately concerned about your needs.
4.	Never use a tax preparer that isn't also your tax advisor. You may otherwise get great advice that is never used and lose out on great tax savings.

Tax Strategy #23 – Hiring the Right Tax Advisor

Here are the top 10 things to talk about when interviewing a tax advisor:

1. What is your view of the tax law?
2. Who gets the most advantages of the tax law?
3. What made you want to become a tax advisor?
4. What would you like to know about me?
5. Tell me about your team of advisors.
6. Describe your personal business experience.
7. Tell me about your personal investment strategy.
8. Where did you earn your Masters of Tax degree?
9. Give me three examples of how to reduce the risk of an IRS audit.
10. Tell me your thoughts about asset protection.

Here are the top 10 things your prospective tax advisor should discuss with you:

1. Tell me about your dreams and goals.
2. Describe your current and projected family situation.
3. Describe your relationship with your spouse and your children.
4. Describe your current and projected investments.
5. Describe your current and projected business situation.
6. Explain your philosophy of tax reduction.
7. What would you like to learn about the tax laws?
8. How do you learn best? Auditory, visual, tactile, or kinesthetic?
9. In a perfect world, how would you like to work with your CPA?
10. Who are the other members of your team?

Andy Tanner

Rich Dad Advisor on Paper Assets

Personal Background and Entrepreneur Profile

Name   Andy Tanner
Date of Birth   May 10, 1968
Place of Birth   Murray, Utah

Traditional Education
    Snow College – Ephraim, Utah
    University of Utah in Salt Lake City, Utah
    Weber State University Ogden, Utah
    Associates of Science
    (Quit school 12 hours shy of a Bachelors degree)

Professional Education
    None

Grade Point Averages
    High School: 2.36
    College: 2.58

Value of traditional education... relative to becoming an entrepreneur
My experience in athletics while attending traditional schools was
very valuable. Through athletics, I began to experience important
life lessons, such as mission, leadership, and team. I can't really
judge the classroom fairly because it was not interesting to me. I
wasn't very interested in the topics they taught, so I did not study
much, I really don't know if it would have helped me or not. I'm
sure I could have found some good in each class if I had looked
harder, but I lacked the maturity to do so. Additionally, none of

the career choices that traditional school prepares you for resonated with me, and none felt like a calling.

Subject I liked most in school

Phys Ed and Choir. Phys Ed was where my natural talents were. Although I consider myself to be intelligent, I never enjoyed the process of classroom and book learning that focused on taking tests. Additionally, I can't really sing, but I'm glad my parents made me take choir. Leland Flinders was an extraordinary choral teacher. My suspicion is that he was out of the rat race, because he did not teach for money. He taught because he loved music and students. It was his calling. Each year he would teach us students to raise money for an annual senior trip to Hawaii to compete in a choral competition. He demanded hard work and maturity from all of us who wanted to participate. All that work paid off, because in 1986 we won the gold medal at that Hawaiian competition. To this day it is one of my best memories from school.

Subject I hated most in school

Organic Chemistry

First entrepreneurial project

In 1996 I started FamilyParade.com. It was a social networking site like Facebook. I very much wish I would have known what a B-I Triangle was back then!

The key entrepreneurial skill I was *not* taught in school

Leadership—and sales

Why and when I became an entrepreneur and my first major venture

I could not find anything I truly enjoyed other that playing sports. I floundered in some low-paying jobs after I quit school and then discovered I had a love for speaking and teaching. I got into the seminar industry and loved it. The pay was pretty good and inspiring people brought a lot of satisfaction. I learned about stocks because, many years ago, I was asked to teach that topic at a seminar. I started my own education company and created my own artifacts, because I love teaching and I think it's my calling. It is what I am supposed to do in life.

Best Lesson from first business
It is OK to fail. It hurts, but it's not terminal.

What I learned about myself from my Kolbe Index

ANDREW TANNER
Kolbe A™ Index Result

CONGRATULATIONS ANDREW
You Got a Perfect Score on the Kolbe A™ Index

You are uniquely able to take on future-oriented challenges. You lead the way to visionary possibilities and create what others said couldn't be done. You'll say "Yes" before you even know the end of the question – then turn it into a productive adventure.

Kolbe Action Modes®

© 1997-2017 Kathy Kolbe. All rights reserved.

Reprinted with permission from Kolbe Corp.

First, I learned to embrace my nature instead of fighting to change it. Secondly, I learned to embrace the natures of others and not expect them to change. And third, I realized how my Kolbe and my wife's Kolbe complement each other.

My role in the B-I Triangle

My role is to stay focused on mission and communicate to my team.

Skills that are essential for entrepreneurs—but not taught in schools

1. Leadership

I love to speak and teach to help people. This is a part of leadership that I feel comfortable with. Yet I'm still learning how to be a better leader, and it's a skill I'm still developing. Through my own failures in the past and also the challenges I face today, I realize that leadership is a never-ending process of development and not a final destination.

2. Teamwork

Like most people, my time in school made me feel as if I was competing as an individual against my classmates. In hindsight, I can see how this method of teaching robs us of learning how to work as a team. Through athletics, choir, my rock band, and business, I now love being part of a team!

My Most Important Lesson for Entrepreneurs

Spirit. I still consider myself a student. I still make mistakes, I still have challenges. Some days as an entrepreneur are very tough and there is always a battle of some kind to fight. Having an entrepreneur's spirit is not just about having an enthusiasm for freedom or money. I've learned that it is about having a spirit to serve others, to create value for others… and to keep learning, year after year.

How I learned to raise capital

As I stand with the other Rich Dad Advisors, I am in awe of the expertise of Kenny, Josh and Lisa, and Darren when it comes to raising capital. I'm not in their league. Yet I have also discovered there are many people with a lot of money who are looking for places to invest. Knowing that, I can serve these people by having a good investment opportunity for them, and by clearly communicating the potential and risks to these investors. Some businesspeople are better at creating opportunities. Others are better at communicating the opportunity. This is where I have to be very careful, because I can easily use my communication skills to raise a lot of capital. In fact, I often have people approach me wanting me to take their money. For me, raising capital goes beyond the ability to get people to hand over their cash. It is about creating an investor opportunity that is worth investing in. I've watched other people raise money easily—only to lose that money for the investor!

How I learned to overcome fear and failure:

I'm still learning to overcome fear and failure. Every now and then I still get scared to make certain moves. Like everyone else, sometimes I also fear failure. It's something I'm comfortable telling you because I'm human. Even so, there have been times in my life when I have summoned great courage. I have still felt the fear, but calling upon my inner strength has allowed me to move forward anyway.

One of my secret weapons to overcome my individual fears is to surround myself with a great team. I also find that when I focus on my mission and its value to others, I always seem to summon courage to tackle anything. When I have goals worth fighting for, the fear of the fight diminishes. One good example was writing my first book about the problems with 401(k) plans. I was nervous about how it would be received, because I knew I was going against the entrenched thinking of what the government, Wall Street, and society has been advising for decades. I had fears of one-star ratings on Amazon. But when I thought of all the people who would be hurt by the 401(k) system, it gave me courage to speak up and pull no punches. Ultimately, my family gave me the most strength to fight this fear, because I want to create the best life I can give them. There have been times when I have been afraid, but my love for them has driven me past fear.

My personal strength

I can say with total confidence that I am one of the best teachers in the world. I can take difficult topics, such as stock investing, and make it simple and fun to learn. This is the most valuable service I can offer the Rich Dad Advisor team as we support the Rich Dad mission.

My personal weakness

Sometimes I think our culture encourages us to downplay our individual skills and accomplishments. This can result in diminishing the way we view ourselves and how we measure our self worth. Sometimes I fall victim to this myself. While I definitely know my strengths, occasionally I allow my brain to cancel it out with feelings of weakness. When we let the feelings of low self worth overpower our thoughts, I believe it can prevent us from unleashing our full power. So it's a battle that we all must fight every day.

The Entrepreneurial Skills I Teach best

Communication and resiliance

The Entrepreneurial Lesson I Teach

Paper Assets: Strategies for Investing in all Market Conditions and Managing Risks

Paper Assets:
Strategies for Investing and Managing Risk
by Andy Tanner

Market crashes make the rich richer—
and the poor and middle class poorer.
Andy is a member of my team because you need
to know how to make money
when markets are going up...
and, especially, when markets are going down.

– RTK

My role on the Rich Dad Advisor team plays to my strengths, and that is teaching people about paper assets. I'm not surprised when I hear from students that when they increase their knowledge in any of the asset classes – in this case, paper assets – it also helps prepare them (and inspire them) to invest in other asset classes.

By playing Robert's *CASHFLOW 101* game, people instinctively and intuitively learn about a fancy investing term called fundamental analysis. Fundamental analysis is the process of understanding a financial statement, along with assessments of the strengths and weaknesses associated with that statement. I teach thousands of students each year, and my favorite students are those who have already become familiar with the financial statement by playing the *CASHFLOW* game. This exposure makes it much easier to introduce them to real financial statements on the personal level, the family level, as well as the corporate level. This is important when researching a stock to buy, or even understanding what's happening with the financial health of a country that can affect the global markets. Entrepreneurs want to learn fundamental analysis so they can evaluate the strength of their own company or the potential of other opportunities in which they might invest.

In *CASHFLOW 202*, investors are introduced to market trends. When I have the occasion to speak at Robert's side to a group of entrepreneurs or aspiring investors, he often asks me to teach them about trends. Entrepreneurs want to be aware of trends because that's where the market is heading. Trends can go up, trends can go down, and trends can even remain stagnant (what we call a sideways trend). The best part is that no matter what direction the trend is heading, there are good investing opportunities available for educated investors to profit.

The study of trends is called technical analysis. Entrepreneurs have the job of solving problems so that they can create value and profit relative to any trend—up, down, or sideways. In order to benefit, though, the investor must be able to identify the trend and have a way to determine if and when that trend will change direction.

In a nutshell, fundamental analysis and technical analysis are about gathering information and then analyzing it in order to understand what is happening. Once a person has this information and has analyzed it looking for opportunity, the next step is to turn it into cash flow. When it comes to paper assets, there are many ways investors can do this. And many of these methods go beyond the run-of-the-mill, tried-and-true "buy low and sell high" that most people are familiar with. Entrepreneurs can learn how to take a position to generate profits based on the information they have gathered. Some people might take a position for a capital gain (traditional buy and hold), while others might take a position for cash flow (earn money no matter what happens in the market).

I love to educate people on the various positions an investor can take with paper assets, because gaining this education and then applying what they learn can give anyone more control over their investments and more effectively manage risk.

This brings us to the fourth thing I love to teach about paper assets: it's called risk management. One of the beefs that I have with the 401(k) retirement plans is the tremendous amount of risk that is piled on the investor, yet they have virtually no control of that investment to manage the risk. Even if a person is diversified across the stock market, they're still susceptible to a stock market crash – a crash they cannot control. Risk management means that once a person has done their fundamental analysis, their technical analysis, and decides what type of position they want to take, they get to play the devil's advocate. Entrepreneurs always ask *what if?* questions, so that they have a Plan B—or even a Plan C—if markets change unexpectedly.

This is not much different than buying insurance on your house. Insurance allows you to be compensated in case your house burns down due to something that was beyond your control, such as a mischievous neighbor kid playing with matches.

These four areas—fundamental analysis, technical analysis, positions for cash flow, and risk management—make up what I call my Four Pillars of Investing.

I hope you'll keep in mind that these ideas and concepts are not just for people who invest in paper assets. I know that Robert owns some paper assets, but the majority of his holdings are in oil, real estate, and business. Nonetheless, Robert cares about studying fundamentals and trends.

What makes education on paper assets vital, I believe, is that it's the asset class in which most people have invested their money. I would venture to say that many people are looking to have their retirement funded by the value of their 401(k) account, which is made up of mutual funds they've dumped their money in for years and sometimes decades.

What's ironic to me is that paper assets are an area with massive participation, yet with almost no education. Let me say that again so I can emphasize it: Paper assets are an asset class with massive participation... *but almost no one has been educated on how to understand or manage these investments!* In most cases, 401(k) participants hand over a portion of their paycheck to a financial planner or 401(k) administrator and let them worry about it. I see this as a *massive* risk for everyone with a 401(k) account. That's why I am committed to doing all I can to make education related to paper assets and the stock market simple and fun for those who care to learn more about this important topic.

Another thing Robert often asks me to discuss and teach related to paper assets is what this asset class brings to the table for investors like you and me. I've always avoided placing one asset class above another because I think it's a matter of personal preference instead of an issue of "good" or "better." Anyone who bashes real estate has to explain the success of Donald Trump. Anyone who bashes the energy industry has to explain the success of T. Boone Pickens. Anyone who bashes business as being too risky has to explain the success of Sir Richard Branson. And anyone who wants to bash paper assets must first explain the success of the greatest investor of all time, Warren Buffett, who makes billions of dollars a year in paper assets.

More intelligent discussion related to asset classes might focus on the differences among the asset classes and what each brings to the table in terms of strengths and weaknesses; the pros and cons. As I've discussed, this is something Robert often asks me to explain when I'm teaching about paper assets. In the Rich Dad world, diversification is across asset classes, not across stocks or mutual funds.

Paper assets are liquid. This can be good and bad. It's good in that you can turn something into cash almost instantly if you see a better opportunity, or if you see danger where your money is currently invested. If you don't like what you see, you can simply click a button and you're out. If you see the grass is greener on the other side of the fence, you can click a button and you are into a new investment in no time at all.

The downside of liquidity is volatility. This is why you see the stock market's gyrations are much more violent when compared to some other markets. Liquidity gives speed to the supply and demand in the market. That lends itself to incredible booms and earth-shattering busts.

Paper assets are agile. I mentioned earlier that one of the entrepreneurial skills I teach is the ability to identify trends. Paper assets are one of the most welcoming investments when it comes to finding success in a downward-trending market. George Soros, an expert in identifying trends, has become famous largely because of the billions he's been able to make by identifying down trends. In 2013, for example, George Soros made over a billion dollars by taking a bearish position on the Japanese yen, while anyone who was saving yen in a savings account lost purchasing power and value. George Soros, in essence, was borrowing Japanese yen and found tremendous success doing so. Being able to realize a profit or generate cash flow in something that is losing value is a difficult idea for beginning investors to wrap their heads around. Yet it is an important entrepreneurial skill that can keep money flowing into your account no matter what is happening in the market. My job is to make understanding this kind of skill easy, simple, and fun to learn.

Paper assets are scalable. This is another reason I absolutely love teaching people about paper assets. I know there are many people who have read the book *Rich Dad Poor Dad,* but have yet to buy their first rental property or start their first business. I know many of these people would like to have something in their asset column, but for whatever reason they don't have it yet. Paper assets are an amazing way to start because anyone can purchase many of the same assets that are owned by Warren Buffett—even if you're not a billionaire. For example, Warren Buffett owns millions of shares of the Coca-Cola Company. My sons can earn enough money from their lemonade stand to purchase some shares of the Coca-Cola Company as well. They'll even receive a percent return similar to Warren Buffett's, just on a smaller scale. More importantly, they can learn many of the same lessons because they're the same kinds of investments.

If someone has played *CASHFLOW* and now wants to play the game for real, paper assets allow someone to do that on a small scale but still be very much in the stock market "game"—just like in the *CASHFLOW* game. But don't get me wrong here, investing in real paper requires real money, real risk, and the possibility of real loss. But the idea that a person can scale it down to where those losses are minimal can help people learn large lessons without large risk or losses.

Paper assets give you leverage. In real estate the main lever is debt. That's a good thing. In paper, often the main lever is simply a contract. That is also a very good thing. When I first teach people about the options market and they learn how to be a seller of a contract for cash flow, it blows their minds. Selling agreements is an entrepreneurial skill that can be learned and experienced easily in the options market. Taking on massive amounts of real estate debt without proper education and mentorship is unwise, even though it's a good thing for those who are educated and skilled. The exact same thing is true for paper assets. It is extremely risky to begin selling options contracts—even those that can be covered with stocks—without proper knowledge and mentorship.

In my home country the predominant retirement program for people in the E Quadrant is called the 401(k). In Canada it's called an RRSP. In Australia it's called Superannuation, and in Japan it's also called a 401(k). No matter where you live in the world, it's essential to learn about the types of programs that are designed for people in the E quadrant. The Rich Dad mission is about elevating the well-being of humanity through financial education. A large percentage of this population still lives in the E quadrant, and in order to improve their lives I feel a responsibility to tell them about paper assets in a way that the average financial advisor might not. Even if a person decides to remain in the E quadrant and not become an entrepreneur, I still believe they can benefit from financial education on investments like mutual funds or unit trusts. I believe there are massive risks that they are not aware of. I also believe that much of the "big picture" fundamental data we see points to some rough waters ahead for these good people in the E quadrant who are clinging to their mutual funds like life preservers. I'm not saying that mutual funds or unit trusts are a bad investment. What I am saying is to become educated so you can make better decisions for yourself and your family.

I love teaching people about paper assets. I love learning and teaching in general and consider myself a student as well as a teacher. As a Rich Dad Advisor, I think people sometimes see me as someone whose has "arrived" and has all of the answers. One thing I've learned by spending a lot of time with Robert and the other Advisors is that we're all students. We study more than most people think or believe. It's one of the most important ways I learn important new things. And I've learned more as a teacher than I ever did as a student.

Here is my final thought to anyone who wishes to be an entrepreneur: this process means you are also becoming a student as a result of your desire to solve problems and give value to the world. Focus on this and your future will be very bright indeed.

About Andy Tanner

Andy Tanner is a renowned paper assets expert and successful business owner and investor known for his ability to teach key techniques for stock options investing. He serves as a coach to Rich Dad's Stock Success System trainers and as the Rich Dad Advisor for Paper Assets.

As a highly sought after educator, Andy has taught tens of thousands of investors and entrepreneurs around the world. He often speaks to students at the request of Robert Kiyosaki, showing how paper assets can fit into the Rich Dad system of investing. In 2008, Andy played a key role in developing and launching *Rich Dad's Stock Success System*, a program created to teach investors advanced technical trading techniques for profiting in both bull and bear markets.

He is the author of two books: *401(k)aos* and *Stock Market Cash Flow*, a Rich Dad Advisor series book on paper asset investing.

Andy has also created an online investing course called *The 4 Pillars of Investing*. You can find out more about it at www.4pillarsofinvesting.com.

Books by Andy Tanner

Rich Dad Advisor Series Books

Stock Market Cash Flow
Four Pillars of Investing
for Thriving in Today's Markets

Tanner Training Books

401(k)aos
How our Dream of Retirement
Became a Nightmare of Chaos

AN EXCERPT FROM

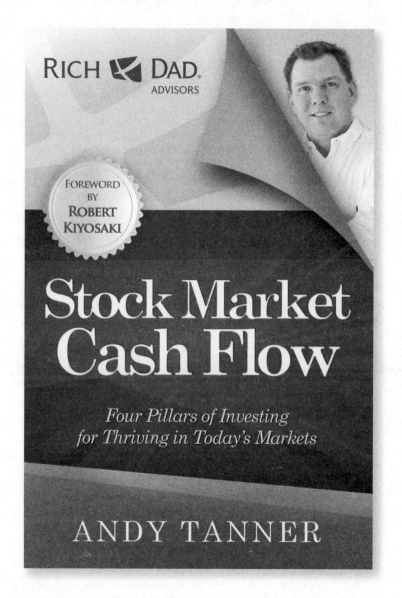

RICH DAD. ADVISORS

FOREWORD BY ROBERT KIYOSAKI

Stock Market Cash Flow

Four Pillars of Investing for Thriving in Today's Markets

ANDY TANNER

Chapter Three

Introducing the 4 Pillars
of Investing

Let me introduce you to the 4 Pillars of Investing. As a student you will find that everything you will ever learn about making money with stocks will fit into one of these four pillars.

In Chapter Two we described wealth building as learning to buy or create assets intelligently. We also saw that the asset classes include business, real estate, commodities, and paper assets such as stocks and options. We learned that each asset class has its own language and nuances.

So how do you learn to buy these things intelligently? How do you make sound decisions when an opportunity presents itself? The answer is in learning the 4 Pillars of Investing. These pillars contain vital information for every type of investor in any asset class, and they are vital whether you are investing for capital gains or cash flow.

In preparing to write this book, I sat down and reviewed everything I had learned from my mentors and teachers about investing. I realized that everything I knew fit very nicely into four categories:

1. I had learned about studying entities (Fundamental Analysis).

2. I had learned how to study trends (Technical Analysis).

3. I had learned techniques to position myself for profit (Cash Flow).

4. I had learned about managing risk (Risk Management).

These categories make up what I call my 4 Pillars of Investing. When you dedicate yourself to studying these four pillars you will learn the criteria that will allow you to look at any investment opportunity in any asset class and make better decisions. These four pillars will support your financial education goals. You will learn to buy assets intelligently and build wealth.

So let's get started by looking at Pillar #1.

Pillar 1: Fundamental Analysis

Fundamental analysis examines the strength of an entity. We need to be able to tell the difference between an entity that is strong and an entity that is weak, be that entity a private company, a charity, even a nation. And we do that by looking at the financial statements. The financial statement tells us the strength of the entity.

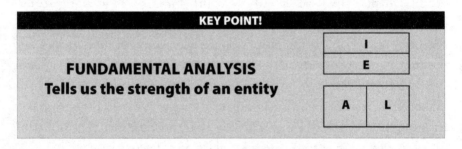

KEY POINT!

FUNDAMENTAL ANALYSIS
Tells us the strength of an entity

| I |
| E |
| A | L |

My college basketball coach was a master when it came to teaching fundamentals. His teams won many championships, and he was well known among avid college basketball fans. People often ask me why I think he was so successful. My answer is always the same: He absolutely demanded perfection in the parts of the game that don't require talent, but do require tremendous effort. Not everyone has the same level of talent, but we all can give supreme effort. There are certain parts of the game that are basic at any level, be it high school or the pros. To have success, you must become proficient in them. My coach was obsessed with the fundamentals, and he coached them well.

The same rigor in fundamentals is needed for financial success, and basic rules apply to every entity—from sovereign governments to corporations to individuals. There are certain financial fundamentals that must be in line for any entity to flourish. In this chapter, you will begin to understand what these fundamentals are. You will also discover how to compare one entity to another and immediately know which one is in a stronger financial position.

Fundamental analysis is the process of looking at some basic numbers and evaluating the financial strength of the entity based on those numbers. I'm going to help you discover what those numbers mean and where you can find them. You're going to discover that as you learn more about how to look at these fundamental numbers you will have an increased ability to make wise investment decisions. You'll be able to set a bar for comparison and then quickly see if the opportunity measures up with your expectation of a good investment.

One helpful way to look at fundamental analysis is to think of it as going to the doctor for a checkup. To analyze your condition, the doctor begins with the basics. She's probably not concerned with the color of your hair or the color of your eyes. These things don't tell the doctor very much about how healthy you are. But she will check your blood pressure and your pulse. She'll tap you on the knee to see if your reflexes are responding properly. She'll use a stethoscope to listen to the beat of your heart and the sound of your lungs. She'll write down your "vital signs." These vital signs represent the fundamental state of your basic health. Collecting and analyzing these numbers is the doctor's first step in figuring out what's happening with your overall system.

When it comes to analyzing a nation's economy or your own financial standing, conducting a fundamental analysis as the first step will give you a quick understanding of financial fitness to see if everything is in order. The financial vital signs can tell us a lot about the health of the entity.

Fundamental analysis also helps us determine value. The more financially healthily the entity, the more valuable it is in the marketplace.

Fundamental analysis is a critical tool for leaders of all kinds. It can be used to discover weakness and, in turn, guide policies for improvement, whether it is being used at the highest levels of government or a for couple at the head of a household. It is a very valuable diagnostic tool.

As we study fundamentals you will learn:

1. How to measure the financial strength of any entity

2. How to see the value of the entity

3. How to diagnose causes of weakness

4. How to change policies to fix weakness and predict change

5. How to see the two sides of any transaction and identify the winner and the loser

6. Why it seems that investors can predict the future

Now, those are things I wish I could have learned in school!

BUILD ON IT

PILLAR #1
Fundamental analysis tells us the strength of an entity.

Pillar 2: Technical Analysis

The second of the four pillars is called technical analysis—"technicals" for short.

Technicals are the story of supply and demand in pictures. Supply and demand creates trends.

KEY POINT!

TECHNICAL ANALYSIS
Tells us the trend

Picture yourself as the owner of a golf course. You've done a great job with every part of your business. Your course is one of the best golf properties anywhere in the world. In fact, there are so many people who want to play on your golf course that there's no way you can accommodate everyone. You have earned the luxury of being in high demand. As a result, tee times on the course are in short supply.

What does this mean to your business? Now you can charge more than your competitors because there's a higher demand for a tee time at your course than anywhere else. On your computer you have a chart that shows the history of your prices as they've climbed year after year. Using this trend, you can forecast where your prices are likely to be in the future. This process of examining a chart and projecting what you expect to happen in the future is called *technical analysis.*

When you buy a share of stock in a company, it makes sense that you will want to carefully examine at least two things:

1. Since you're going to own a share of the company, it feels very natural to want to know how strong the company is financially and how it stacks up against other companies when it comes to the basic numbers (or *fundamental analysis*).

2. You want to see how eager other investors are to buy shares in the company and if there's a high demand for the shares that could drive the company's stock price higher and higher (or *technical analysis*).

It is very important to understand trends because you will see that, with the stock market, opportunity is always present. In the section on technical analysis you will learn:

1. Rules to identify a trend

2. How to read the story the trends are telling

3. That investors use patterns to determine what is most likely to happen next

4. How the use of technical tools helps investors find opportunities and see warnings

BUILD ON IT

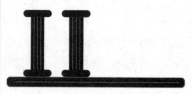

PILLAR #2
Technical Analysis examines the supply and demand (trends) of a stock.

Allow Discovery to Happen

The first two chapters of this book introduced you to the idea of *context*. Those discussions were designed to help open your mind so you can begin to think differently. Now you can feel that we are beginning to move into *content* and some of the important how-to's of investing.

At this point, I want you to give yourself permission to learn about fundamental analysis and technical analysis in a different way. If you do this, your experience will be more fun and enlightening right from the beginning. Here are a few suggestions to keep in mind as you dig into the chapters on fundamental and technical analysis:

Move at Your Own Speed

Unlike school there's no test at the end of the week, there's no grade, so there's no pressure for you to learn everything completely and perfectly the first time you see it.

I remember in college I had to take an organic chemistry class. The material was very complex. But what compounded the problem was that I had to learn it so quickly. I felt pressure because I had to understand everything that was being presented the first time. The stress was brutal and not conducive to really learning the subject. I started to panic because the penalties for not understanding things were so severe and so immediate. I could become ineligible to play ball if I failed the test. It was hard to think of anything but that consequence.

Even after college I found myself reacting the same way, out of habit. If I was in a situation where I didn't understand a concept quickly when it was given to me I became tense, nervous, and stressed out. Now I have learned to relax and let things come to me at my own pace, but it took changing my context. By taking the pressure off, learning has now become one of my favorite activities.

So when you study the chapters on fundamental and technical analysis, please allow yourself—remind yourself—to relax. I'm confident you will do just fine. If you ever do feel anxiety, let that be a signal to take a breath...and relax. Remind yourself that it's okay to read the material more than once, and it's okay to slow down.

I still remember the lesson I learned from a teacher as she used the analogy of learning to drive a car with a manual transmission. We can surely move from ignorance to awareness to competency on the Education Continuum simply by listening to someone else explain the process of letting out the clutch and pushing the accelerator pedal. But proficiency comes when we're actually trying to follow the instructions by sitting in the driver's seat and trying to operate the car. When we try to put those concepts into action, we will inevitably stall the car. But it's not that big of a deal because stalling the car is part of the process. That's how you learn to drive a car with a manual transmission. We learn by making mistakes.

After several attempts, you begin to get the feel of it. You learn how to make tiny adjustments until you get to the point where you can shift from gear to gear, listen to the engine, and know when to up-shift or down-shift,—and even gently balance the clutch and brake when starting on a hill. Before long, you're driving that car without even thinking about it. You have arrived at proficiency.

And just because you stall the car, it doesn't mean you're not learning. I stalled the car when my dad was teaching me. Will I teach my sons the exact same way? You bet I will. It's still the best way to teach. Killing the engine is just part of the process. No harm will come to my sons; I'll be sitting there right next to them until they get the hang of it.

So please remember there's no need to put pressure on yourself as you learn these investing concepts. Take a breath and enjoy the discovery. Once you've built your investing foundation with these first two pillars, it will be time to move on to the third pillar, which is certainly the most exciting one to an investor: cash flow.

Pillar 3: Cash Flow Strategies

Once we see the strength of a company (fundamentals), and the trend of the market (technicals), we then decide how we want to position ourselves to profit.

KEY POINT!

**CASH FLOW
Is about your position in the market:
up, down or sideways**

Some investors put themselves in the position of aiming to profit from a capital gain, which means buying low and selling high, like when you buy and sell a house. Others aim to place themselves in a position of cash flow, like renting a house. To understand one strategy, it helps to understand the other.

The term *cash flow* certainly gets everyone's heart beating a little faster. Ultimately, that's what we really want as investors. Because as money freely flows into your account through smart investment decisions, you will experience what true freedom feels like. The goal of this book is to help you begin to feel confident and comfortable in your ability to draw cash from the stock market on a regular basis—no matter the direction in which the market moves. That's the beauty of it: You'll learn how this can be done in markets that go up, down, or sideways.

Cash Flow Is a Solution to the Problem of Expenses

Everyone has expenses like food, clothing, shelter, taxes, and recreation, among many others. Expenses are the basic financial problem of life. We can solve that problem in one of four ways:

Employee

Self Employed

Business Owner

Investor

If you need $5,000 each month to solve your expense problem, then to move from the left side of the quadrant to the right side, your financial statement must change from this:

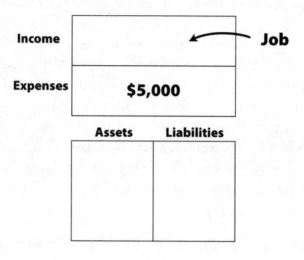

to this:

The Best Cash Flow Is Not Dependent on Bull Markets

Many people who work at a job put money away into some sort of a contribution retirement program such as a 401(k) or an individual retirement account (IRA). The money put into these accounts finds its way into the stock market through mutual funds or unit trusts, depending on the country in which you live. Whether or not you make money is often directly dependent upon the performance of the overall stock market. Due to the fact that these strategies are almost entirely focused on the long term, they are not a source of current cash flow for the investor. But here's the problem: The stock market doesn't always (or only) move in a steady upward direction. It can—and definitely does—travel upward, or downward, or remain stagnant for long periods of time.

In the United States the predominant account for retirement investments is called a 401(k). Unfortunately, the value of these investments is dependent on a bull market. So rather than being designed to grow cash flow, they are designed to grow net worth. As the market fluctuates, so does net worth.

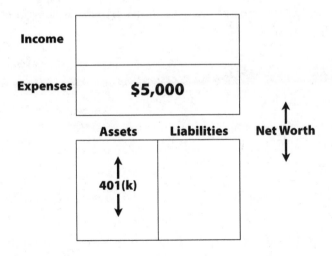

When I think about 401(k) accounts they remind me of Aesop's fable about the goose that laid golden eggs. Most contribution retirement plans rely on money earned in the past (what I call "old money") to solve expense problems in the future.

GOLDEN GOOSE
Generates "new money"

GOLDEN EGG
Relies on "old money"

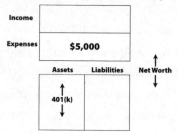

The plans that rely on old money are in a risky situation. Instead of having monthly cash flow that could last indefinitely, the investor is left with what feels like two hour glasses. One is filled with money and the other with time. That's why one of the main fears people have is running out of money in retirement. This wouldn't happen if they knew how to generate "new money."

I want to introduce you to a totally new way of thinking—one you may never have considered before. These new "golden-goose" ideas are different from what you experience when you let your money sit in long-term retirement accounts.

When it comes to purchasing stocks, fundamental analysis is the process of gathering information about the strength of a company, and technical analysis is the process of gathering information about the supply and demand for that stock. When you have that information, you can use it to determine whether you're investing your money in a golden goose or a golden egg. You're going to discover there are a variety of ways to *harvest* what you see in fundamental and technical analyses.

In the chapters on cash flow strategies you're going to see some examples of how to turn this information into potential profit, as well as some of the rules that we follow when we execute a certain investing strategy. I'm also going to give you some insight into how to choose one strategy over another and some methods to give you confidence in the decisions you make to help you move toward your money and lifestyle goals.

Learning many different cash flow strategies is like having many different colors available to you when painting a picture. With a variety of colors in front of you, think of how much more effectively you can mix and match those colors to help that painting match your vision of what you want it to be.

To their detriment, many investors develop fundamental and technical criteria that limit them only to capital gains. Moreover, many limit their toolbox to bullish strategies only. As a college athlete, I had to learn many different offensive schemes and had many plays in my playbook that could address many different situations. I would take what the defense gave me and find ways to win, no matter what.

The same can be said of taking what the market gives you—be it a trend up, down, or sideways—and addressing it.

By learning different ways to position yourself for cash flow (or even a capital gain, for that matter), you are beginning to understand that there are opportunities for profit no matter what the market does.

Some of what you will learn in the section on Cash Flow:

1. How to get a capital gain when the market goes up

2. How to get a capital gain when the market goes down

3. How to get leverage without using debt

4. How the stock and option markets can work together to generate cash flow

BUILD ON IT

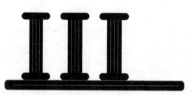

PILLAR #3
Cash Flow is about choosing a position in the market.

Pillar 4: Risk Management

Whether you invest in real estate, stocks, or any other asset class, you have to remember: Things can change suddenly.

KEY POINT!

RISK MANAGEMENT
Helps us deal with uncertainty or when we're just plain wrong.

If the market crashes and your retirement is lost, do you have a plan B?

If you save money and the dollar crashes, what will you do?

If there is a flood and your home is lost, do you have insurance?

No matter what you do, there are always some things that are beyond your control and others you can always control. Risk management is using the things you can control to deal with those you can't. I can't control the flood, but I can control whether or not I buy insurance.

The Relationship Between Risk and Control

You might want to pause for a moment and consider this key point: Risk is related to control.

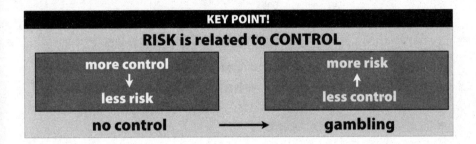

Whenever someone is about to invest money or use debt as an investment lever, they would be wise to consider how much control they have over the outcome of the investment. The question of control is equally important for people who have placed large amounts of money into traditional retirement plans that are broadly diversified across the markets. How much control do they have over the outcome? It is a sobering question to consider.

An investor has no control over the first two pillars we discussed, fundamental analysis and technical analysis. When we look at a company's numbers, we understand that its performance is beyond our control. We don't make the day-to-day decisions inside the company. We are not out there selling its products. We may own some shares of the company, but we have little to no impact on company policy. Likewise, when we look at the chart of that company's stock and see the trend of the share price of the stock, we realize that the direction of the stock price is beyond our control as well.

No matter how badly you might want the price of the stock to go up, it's completely out of your control. The same is true with the company's earnings. We can't control these things any more than we can control the weather or the lottery.

Remember that the first two pillars, fundamental analysis and technical analysis, are about gathering and analyzing information—not about controlling that information.

BUILD ON IT

PILLAR #4
Risk management is using what you can control to deal with what you can't.

Things You Can Control

After you've gleaned some vital information by conducting a fundamental analysis (looking at the financial strength of a company) and technical analysis (looking at the supply and demand for that stock), it's time to consider a cash flow strategy and how you want to manage the risk associated with that strategy. Again, you have no control over the first two pillars. But you have total control and full responsibility for your actions with the last two pillars.

In other words, you really can't control what the weather's going to be, but you do get to choose how you'll deal with it. You can't control a hurricane that's coming your way. But if you gather information that shows a hurricane is coming, you can benefit from that information and begin selling emergency supplies to those who need them. You can also manage your risk by purchasing insurance to protect your own home. These actions are entirely up to you. The same is true with your cash-flow investing.

You also control the level of your financial education. In Chapter One we discussed the importance of investors becoming serious students. It is entirely up to you how far you want to go with each of the 4 Pillars of Investing. That's very good news. Because if we realize that our lifestyle goals are related to our money goals, and that our money goals are achieved when we reach our education goals, then the 4 Pillars of Investing become a clear pathway to success. We now know what to study and what to work on. We know how to grow our very own orange trees with endless supplies of delicious fruit.

Some of what you will learn in the section on risk:

1. You will learn about many different kinds of risks investors face.

2. You will expand your financial vocabulary.

3. You will learn about exit strategies.

4. You will learn about hedges.

5. You will learn about position sizing.

The 4 Pillars in the Education Continuum

Paper assets are a great place to start learning the 4 Pillars because of its advantage in scalability and liquidity. But it would be a grave mistake, for example, to think that real estate investors do not need to understand technical analysis in their day-to-day business. I have heard Rich Dad Advisor Ken McElroy declare many times that his real estate business is a trend business. The 4 Pillars offer a foundation for any financial education.

Now that you have a basic understanding of each of the four pillars, it's time to become more *aware* of what they are. It's time to begin to become more *competent* in each pillar. As you desire to become more competent, your mind will automatically search for mentors and ways you can practice to become more and more *proficient* because of the law of attraction. Because this is simply how your brain works naturally.

The Education Continuum™

Ignorance → Awareness → Competency → Proficiency

Focusing on your education goals more clearly identifies the people and the opportunities that will help you achieve your goals. This increased focus and desire to identify solutions will give you the feeling that these people and opportunities are being drawn to you.

As you study the 4 Pillars of Investing, I encourage you to think about your progress in each pillar along the Education Continuum. It's a good way to evaluate where you are in your learning. There's a big difference between being aware of what a financial statement is and being proficient in conducting a fundamental analysis of that statement. There's a big difference between being aware of technical analysis and being proficient in reading stock charts. The process of moving toward proficiency in the Education Continuum is even more important with the last two pillars: cash flow and risk management. Because this is where your decisions and actions will directly impact your profits.

Cash flow strategies and risk management are double-edged swords: You can do the most good for yourself, but also the most harm. As investors, our goal is proficiency with these pillars. As you take this journey, enjoy the discovery of each pillar and remember that success is the natural order of things. Just let it happen.

Chapter Summary

Let's review some of the important points of Chapter Three:

1. Fundamental analysis helps us know the **financial strength of an entity.**

   A financial statement reveals the financial fitness of an entity. You can use those numbers to see its value, diagnose its problems, and better forecast the future.

2. Technical analysis helps us **identify trends.**

   By reading stock charts we can identify trends. We can see changes in supply and demand. We can see patterns that tell us what is likely to happen next. We can see warning signals in the market.

3. Cash Flow strategies are how we choose to **position ourselves to profit.**

   Learning all the cash flow and capital gain strategies gives you the opportunity to take what the market gives you and have profit potential in any market—be it up, down, or sideways—instead of being at its mercy.

4. Risk management is about **dealing with the unexpected.**

   Every serious investor needs countermeasures to deal with the unexpected or to protect themself when they're wrong.

5. The 4 Pillars are not just for stock investors, they are for **all investors**.

   No matter the assets class, proficiency in the 4 Pillars makes for better decision-making!

Darren Weeks

Rich Dad Advisor on Raising Capital

Personal Background and Entrepreneur Profile

Name   Darren Weeks
Date of Birth   June 14, 1968
Place of Birth   Edmonton, Alberta Canada

Traditional Education
University of Alberta
Degree: Bachelor of Commerce
Started CPA Program, but dropped out

Professional Education
None

Grade Point Averages
High School: 2.45
College: 2.2

Value of traditional education... relative to becoming an entrepreneur
In my opinion it was not useful at all. I use very few of the lessons taught at University. If I had to do it all again I would not have attended University.

Subject I liked most in school
Social studies and current events.

Subject I hated most in school
Math. Once they introduced the alphabet—all the xs and the ys—into math class, I failed continuously. Prior to that, I was one of the best math students in my class.

First entrepreneurial project

When I was a young boy I would shovel snowy sidewalks for neighbors, cut their grass, and deliver newspapers.

The key entrepreneurial skill I was *not* taught in school

Biggest missing link is how to sell

Why and when I became an entrepreneur and my first major venture

I always wanted to be rich, so I would do whatever I thought could forward my objective. I invested in mutual funds in grade six and also had my first business card for selling guppies in that same grade.

First major venture was selling Inuit Art in Canada. I quit my full time government job to do so and continued to buy more real estate. Everyone thought I was crazy. To me, this experience was much more valuable than my Bachelor of Commerce degree.

Best Lesson from first business:

Wow! So many. The realization that I wasn't going to receive a paycheck every two weeks and that I needed to have more discipline. I realized I needed to spend time looking for customers, instead of avoiding that task. I was scared to sell and didn't know how to go about learning this important skill.

I also had no idea how to build a team or use leverage to my advantage. I didn't use anyone else's time, skills, or money. I was the typical S—with no leverage.

What I learned about myself from my Kolbe Index

DARREN WEEKS

Kolbe A™ Index Result

CONGRATULATIONS DARREN
You Got a Perfect Score on the Kolbe A™ Index

You are uniquely able to take on future-oriented challenges. You lead the way to visionary
possibilities and create what others said couldn't be done. You'll say "Yes" before you even
know the end of the question – then turn it into a productive adventure.

Kolbe Action Modes®

©1997-2017 Kathy Kolbe. All rights reserved.

Reprinted with permission from Kolbe Corp.

I am a typical entrepreneur and can spot opportunities easily but
do not like to follow through with the necessary details.

My role in the B-I Triangle

My roles relate to Communication and Mission. For 16 years I
have been communicating the Mission of Rich Dad to thousands
of people around the world and am living proof that the strategies
Robert and Rich Dad have taught work.

Skills that are essential for entrepreneurs—but not taught in schools

- Communications skills and primarily sales skills
- How to spot opportunities—which are literally everywhere
- How to build a team

My Most Important Lesson for Entrepreneurs

I've learned that money is plentiful for investors who have a plan and a team. Money—or the lack of it—should never hold you back. I've also learned that while banks are very profitable businesses, relying on them can hurt your chances of entrepreneurial success.

How I learned to raise capital

I had an attitude that I would not fail. So after a bank turned me down for a loan, I thought of then asking my friends, family, and associates if they wanted to team up with me for my project. And it worked—for all of us.

How I learned to overcome fear and failure

When I was six years old I was a determined kid. I knew I would be rich so I didn't have a lot holding me back.

Also, after my first, full-time Inuit Art business, I realized that my effort level needed to increase if I wanted to achieve my financial goals.

My Personal Strength

Perseverance and mindset. When I set my mind to something I am damned and determined to succeed.

My Personal Weakness

Laziness. Not working to my full potential, especially as I search for my next real mission on earth.

The Entrepreneurial Skill that I teach best

Communication skills necessary to raise capital.

The Entrepreneurial Lesson I Teach

Communication: The Key to Raising Capital

Communication:
The Key to Raising Capital
by Darren Weeks

Rich dad said, "Only lazy people use their own money to get rich."
Entrepreneurs who want to be rich learn how
to use OPM—Other People's Money—responsibly.

– RTK

About a decade ago I joined an exclusive membership organization that included various entrepreneurs from my hometown of Edmonton, in Canada. In order to qualify for membership you had to own a company that had annual sales in excess of $1.2 million USD. The group was formed so that successful leaders could help one another learn about business and personal development. We meet monthly and in small groups with 10 of our peers.

In one of these meetings, a man who owned a very successful furniture store said something to me that I have never forgotten. He said, "Darren, of all our 80 members in Edmonton, you are truly the most entrepreneurial!" I was shocked at this comment and listened as he continued to speak. He said he had never met someone who could start a business, literally from scratch and with no family or financial help, and grow it to one that had sales of over $1.2 million.

Looking back, I now see that my entrepreneurial spirit has been strong since I was a young boy. I knew I always wanted to be "rich" and my will has always been strong. When I first read *Rich Dad Poor Dad* I immediately saw an opportunity to teach others financial literacy through the *CASHFLOW* game. That realization was all it took for me to begin the path as a teacher. I found that you just need to believe you will be successful and start taking steps in the direction of making that thought a reality.

From that day forward, I did something every day to further

my belief in being a successful entrepreneur using the CASHFLOW game as my tool to create a vibrant business. And fifteen years later I completed that chapter in my life when I sold my seminar business.

I believe the strongest attribute that I bring to the Rich Dad family is my ability to identify entrepreneurs and guide them based on my experiences and their goals. Whether it's someone who has no money to start a venture, wants to buy their first rental property, lacks revenue growth, wants to hire an employee, or simply doesn't see their own potential, I believe I can help that person.

Many people call this "gift" experience. And that's a huge piece of it. I can see—and have trained myself to see—things most people cannot see or simply aren't looking for when it comes to business. I've found that I can create things out of nothing. Most importantly, I can see the potential in people who need a helping hand with a word of encouragement or a gentle nudge of awareness that they need to focus or get back on track.

Lots of people who know me and my background may be thinking that "Darren is all about Raising Capital," and I have not yet mentioned that. I have raised a lot of money over my career. Over $500 million that was then invested in more than 5,000 apartment units, raw land, cruise ship terminals, and much more. Even *I* look at that number and am impressed with all of the zeroes! But, in my opinion, raising capital is not my primary strength. My true strength, I believe, is putting together all of the pieces that will make a business successful. The analogy I use often is that a business is like a large, complicated jig saw puzzle. It takes skill to put the pieces together in the right sequence so a complete picture is created.

Mastering the skills to build that masterpiece is what I like to do and believe I do very well. Raising Capital is only one of those pieces. Can I show you how to raise capital? Absolutely. But prior to taking steps to raise capital, you need to have a strong mission, be able to lead people, have a strong brand, and know how to communicate so your business can grow. And, of course, you need a track record of success that shows potential investors that you have the skills and experience that people want to invest in.

How do I help people with developing these skills? Practice, practice and more practice. I roll up my sleeves and practice with people. I show them the way. The way I have been doing it for 30 years or more. Over the last few years, I have dedicated my time to helping entrepreneurs all over the world improve their entrepreneurial skills. I have seen amazing transformations of entrepreneurs who practice in a safe environment with other entrepreneurs. Then when they are unleashed and enter the real world, that practice pays off as they achieve fantastic results and their businesses flourish.

Are the results always positive? No. That's reality. And life in the real world. Many times when I am working with an entrepreneur, something doesn't work as well as they had hoped. But when you can communicate with someone who has been down that road before, someone who understands that part of the process is correcting and adjusting as you go, it is magical when we debrief the experience and turn it into a positive… and they try it again. Practice, implement, learn, practice, and implement again. It's the circle of an entrepreneur's life.

It has been an amazing journey as I look back to when I first read *Rich Dad Poor Dad* in 2001. I have met tens of thousands of positive people at seminars all over the world. And I have become a better person in the process, as I realized that personal development is just as important as business training. I am forever grateful to have become a Rich Dad Advisor and be among a group that holds both education and personal development in such high regards.

In 2001, when I hosted my first *CASHFLOW* game event, only four people showed up. Never in my wildest dreams did I believe that one day I would speak on the same stage as Robert Kiyosaki and become friends with him, Kim and their Advisors. Robert and Kim have been amazing mentors and incredible supporters over the years.

My closing words: Keep working on the skills you need to be

a successful entrepreneur and I am sure you will find that, in the process, you will become a better and stronger person. I know it has worked that way for me.

About Darren Weeks

Darren Weeks has always had a passion for investing. In grade six he began investing in mutual funds. By junior high school he moved on to penny stocks. In high school, Darren was investing in physical commodities, including silver bars. Using his investment profits, Darren bought his first rental property as a business student at the University of Alberta and he still owns that property today.

Finishing with a degree in accounting, Darren continued to add more rental properties as opportunities appeared. Once he graduated from university, he was sidetracked from investing. For several years, Darren did what everyone else was doing—working 9 to 5 to make ends meet and looking forward to the weekends. He worked in accounting and sales roles for a variety of organizations and kept investing in real estate on the side. Darren slowly added more doors to his real estate portfolio while feeling increasingly limited and stifled by the traditional career path.

Everything changed in 2001 when a friend recommended that Darren read a book called *Rich Dad Poor Dad* by Robert Kiyosaki. The book so perfectly articulated all of his beliefs about money that it reignited the passion for investing he had in his youth. Shortly after reading the book, he made the life-altering decision to start Fast Track to Cash Flow, a company that would teach Canadians the principles laid out in the book in addition to the lessons Darren had learned about money over the years. Best of all, Fast Track's seminars would be free of charge! This venture allowed him to give up the traditional career path and focus on his business and investing full-time.

Fast forward to the present. Darren has amassed an investment portfolio consisting of over 4,000 rental properties across North America, tens of millions of dollars in energy interests, and hundreds of acres of land. He is also the largest individual shareholder in the world's largest cruise ship terminal, the Port of Falmouth, which is operated by the Royal Caribbean Cruise Lines.

Darren and his team are still providing events and conferences designed to expand the financial contexts of Canadians. Events about everything from budgeting, real estate, investing, entrepreneurship, raising capital, networking, marketing, personal development and much more.

More than 350,000 people have now attended the Fast Track Group events throughout the country. From a simple idea, the company has branched out to include several divisions. The success of the company has positioned the Fast Track Group amongst Canada's business elite, having been ranked on the PROFIT 200 list for three consecutive years.

Darren was named a Rich Dad Advisor for raising capital in 2013. He sold the FastTrack Group in 2016 to focus once again on learning, teaching, mentoring, and investing. His passion to help others remains as strong as ever as has his belief that financial literacy makes financial freedom possible for everyone.

Books by Darren Weeks

Rich Dad Advisor Series Books

The Art of Raising Capital
for Entrepreneurs and Investors

... in Spanish

El Arte de Recuadar Capital

AN EXCERPT FROM

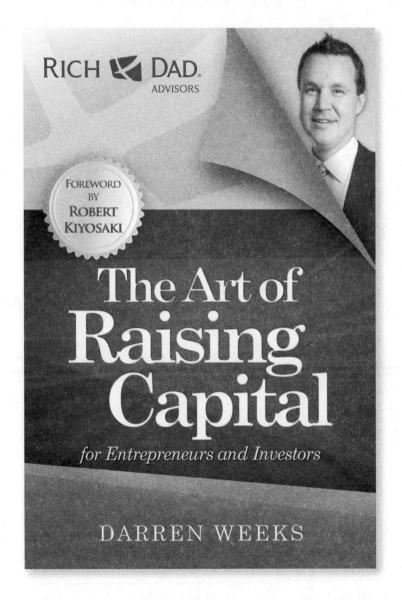

RICH DAD. ADVISORS

FOREWORD BY ROBERT KIYOSAKI

The Art of Raising Capital

for Entrepreneurs and Investors

DARREN WEEKS

Chapter One

Starting Out Right

Before you start reaching out to investors and partners to secure funding, there is some preparation that needs to be done. Trust me, the time you put into this preparation is going to pay off big time once you start approaching people for investment capital.

A lot of the preparation is mental. The idea of using other people's money isn't a natural step for many entrepreneurs. My theory is that part of the reluctance is due to the business owner's fear of losing the business to unscrupulous partners with high-powered lawyers. We can all picture the scenario—and Hollywood helps us in this—where the hard working entrepreneur loses control of everything in a legal loophole and sees his vision corrupted. I don't know where the entrepreneur's lawyer is on reviewing the contract in this scenario, but that's not the real irony of this common fear.

The irony is that these same owners who fear partnering or selling private shares are the same people who have significant portions of their business and home pledged to the bank as collateral for loans. Banks aren't famous for their patience on late payments and, yes, they have no shortage of high-powered lawyers to take ownership of assets that are collateral against loans in arrears. I'd argue that partners willing to put money into your business will be much more understanding about the ups and downs, especially if you are communicating with them about their investment. More on that later.

The other part of my theory on why entrepreneurs generally don't raise capital is that those who do—and are successful at it—often gloss over that part of their growth story. When people talk about Warren Buffett, long one of the world's richest men, they mainly talk about his career after acquiring the failing textile mill, Berkshire Hathaway. What gets glossed over is the fact that Buffett made his first millions by running investment partnerships he created with private capital from qualified investors. Funds from those partnerships were used to purchase Berkshire Hathaway, which he turned into a multibillion dollar holding company for his acquired businesses.

I am not trying to minimize Buffett's achievements. Anyone who has read his shareholder letters knows that Warren Buffett is one of the finest financial minds of all time. What I am trying to draw attention to is the fact that, without raising capital, Warren Buffett's success wouldn't have happened as rapidly as it did. Buffett needed money from private investors in order to become the world's richest investor. Without that money, he'd still be the world's greatest investor—but not the richest.

You can find the same theme of other people's money hidden in the background of most success stories. We like to read the fairytale version where the young entrepreneur fights his or her way up the ladder without a helping hand from anyone. But it is just that—a fairytale. I don't want to hit you over the head with example after example of well-known entrepreneurs who used other people's money to get where they are–there are enough to fill several books. I am simply trying to make the point that raising capital for your business isn't a sign of failure. It is a sign of success. When your business needs more money than you have on hand in order to grow, then you are doing something right.

The Power of Capital

Before we get too deep into crafting your pitch, filtering prospects and the other nuts and bolts of raising capital, it is worth looking at what capital can and cannot do. Capital in all its forms–dollar bills, silver coins, bars of gold and so on–is time made tradable. When a business is well capitalized, it can survive the bumps and bruises of the market better than other businesses with less capital. For example, if your business has $10,000 in capital and your business takes $5000 a month to operate, then you can survive two months of little or no profit. This is oversimplified, but the capital can buy you two months of time to make a profit. As any entrepreneur can tell you, time is the most valuable commodity there is when you are building a business.

The power of capital to help buy time during tough times is important, but the ability of capital to compress time is even more exciting. When you have capital, you can scale up your business sooner, grow faster, and do more. Imagine how long it would take a business to grow if it could only use its profits to fund expansion. You could spend months of saving up enough profit for a new piece of equipment and years saving up enough to pay an employee or open a new office.

There are many points in your business where an injection of capital is necessary: you may need new equipment, better software, a bigger oven or any of a thousand other things that you don't have the money on hand to cover. Rather than raising capital in these situations, most entrepreneurs go to the bank or get short-term funding from friends and family. When these sources are tapped out, those businesses fold up and disappear. And this might not be a bad thing because there are limitations on the power of capital.

Is Capital All You Need?

One thing capital cannot do is turn a failing business into a strong business. If your business is flawed and the profits are just not there, then all capital can do is allow you to continue operating longer than you could have without it. In these situations, capital gives you the time to waste more of your time (and money). Whether or not you should be raising capital at all is an important question. It is also a sensitive one because we all believe that our business idea is sound or else we wouldn't be putting our own time and money into it. But you have to ask (and honestly answer) the following question, "Is a lack of capital the only thing holding my business back?"

When I speak at conferences, this is the question I throw back at people who tell me they are struggling to get their fantastic business (more often a business idea) off the ground. When we actually talk it through, it usually turns out that a lack of capital is not the most pressing issue facing these well-intentioned people. Instead, they are struggling because they don't have a clear path to profitability or are too focused on making a product rather than selling it, or don't have any partners, and on and on.

Some people, however, do have a clear capital problem. In general, they have businesses that have a clear plan to become profitable and are run by a strong team. If a business is already turning a profit and can provide returns on invested capital, then it is all but screaming for more money to grow, whether or not the business owner can hear it.

The Investor's View

The ability to provide excess returns on invested capital sounds like it should be the most important point to your investors. After all, if I invest money in your pizza business to help you buy a new oven, I'm not doing it out of the goodness of my heart. If I want to feel good, I will give my money to a charity, not a business. My goal as an investor is to help you scale up your business because there is money in it for both of us. If a new oven helps you make more pizzas to sell and that increases your profits, I am expecting you to pay back my investment plus a healthy bonus. In the real world, however, the amount of return you can provide on invested capital is often the least important thing to your investors.

The most important thing to investors, especially the ones that invest capital into private partnerships and joint ventures, is whether or not they can trust you to deliver on what you say. If you and I have no prior relationship, I don't care whether you promise me a 10% return or a 1,000% return. I am not giving you money because I don't know you from Adam—or Bernie Madoff for that matter. If, however, you show me how you've produced profits in the past and introduce me to your team, I am probably going to hear out your business proposal. That is, I will if you've put the effort into preparing and carrying yourself like a professional.

Creating Your Professional Persona

When I first started coaching entrepreneurs on raising capital, I was tempted to skip over the part about creating a professional persona. After all, most of the people attending were already professionals and business owners. When my first students arrived, many in sneakers and jeans—and over half without business cards—I realized that creating a professional persona was the most immediate lesson to be learned. Without it, you will be fighting an uphill battle for respect and trust. So, before you go and make your first pitch, there a few basic tools you need to have in place.

Your Appearance

One of the most powerful things you can give someone is presence, which is another way of saying confidence. We have done the onstage transformation at some of my events where we focus on one small variable—the wardrobe a person wears—and improve it. It is a deceivingly simple thing to take someone wearing casual clothes and have them dressed in a high quality suit and groomed by professionals, but it truly does make a huge difference in how they carry themselves. They take the stage with an entirely different gait, they stand with their shoulders back and their body open to the crowd, they smile more—essentially, they send all those important signals that make us respect and trust them. They send these signals with their body language simply because they *feel* different in a suit.

When I started raising capital from investors, I was still in my 20s and cursed with a baby face. I say cursed because I was trying to convince people that I had the experience needed to deliver on my business plan for a particular property. When potential investors saw me face to face, they probably doubted I had the experience to drive a car without an adult in the vehicle, let alone run an investment property. Right from the beginning, I knew I had a trust deficit to make up because I looked even younger than I was. However, I made up that deficit and it was suits that helped me do it.

I was not a savvy shopper, nor an overly fashionable person, but I was able to find a men's clothing store with a manager who was both. I invested—yes, invested—in three suits and received the most exceptional fashion education you can in an hour. I left the store with my suits and tips on how to "break up" my new wardrobe with blazers and nice jeans to create three looks of professional, polished, and business casual. I wore those suits for all they were worth. I wore them to meetings with investors, I wore them to meetings with tenants, I wore them to meetings with the bank, and I wore them to trade shows. I became comfortable in a suit and tie, and people interpreted that comfort and my appearance as a sign of maturity.

I am not saying you need to invest thousands in a wardrobe just to talk to investors, but it is important to understand that the clothes you wear and the time you put into your appearance is a visual cue for everyone you meet. For better or worse, you are giving them information that they are interpreting either positively or negatively. People invested billions with Mark Zuckerberg, but they did it despite his trademark hooded sweater because he had already distinguished himself as a programming and business phenom. His known talents trumped any opinions people may have had about his appearance, although his wardrobe was the focus of many media headlines. The chances are good that you are an unknown quantity for many of the investors you meet, so it is well worth your time and money to make sure that your appearance isn't digging you into a hole before you even get a chance to open your mouth.

And, for what it's worth, I still wear a suit to most meetings even after over two decades and hundreds of millions raised—although I've finally gotten away from the tie. Most of the time.

Your Business Cards

In the age of LinkedIn, Facebook company pages, Quora, and the 15 new social media services that will pop up as you are reading this, I get a bit of grief on my insistence that people carry business cards. Now and for the foreseeable future, the business card is the global standard for sharing contact information and is a part of our business etiquette. I have seen too many people ruin a good conversation by pulling out a smartphone instead of a card. They spend the next few minutes seeing if they have a compatible app for sharing their information. Then they spend the rest of the conversation discussing the merits of their particular phone or scrolling through alerts while pretending to hear what the other person is saying.

Whether you input all of the cards you receive into your smartphone later is your business, but in a networking situation your smartphone kills conversations. Instead, spend the money to get physical business cards printed out. I find that the most effective cards are ones that clearly state the business you are in and give the most relevant contact information.

For example, if you are raising capital to do real estate deals, then your card should say Real Estate Investor right below your name and give your email, website and phone number. I have found that there is a lot of value in having your card professionally designed by people who understand complimentary colors and can speak to difference in spacing between font families, but all that really matters is that you have **functional business cards that you carry with you at all times**.

When it comes time to hand over your card, make sure that you receive a card for every one you give. This is good business etiquette, but it serves a practical purpose as well. All too often, you'll have a promising conversation with someone and realize you didn't grab their card at the end, meaning you are left with a one-way connection and no possibility of following up.

Another technique you can use to expand the impact that your card is to write a dollar figure on the back like $500 or $1,000. When you hand the card to someone, hand it to them with the dollar figure showing. When they ask you about it, let them know that is the referral fee you pay if they connect you with someone who ends up investing in a property with you. This ensures that they will keep your card and remember you while also increasing your chances of getting an out of network referral.

More Business Card Tips

- No logo is better than a confusing one or clipart.

- Keep it readable:

  o Vary the font size, not the font.

  o Use centered text sparingly and default to aligning left.

Your Website

Like your business card and your wardrobe, your website will always be a work in progress. A website is a must-have from the perspective of raising capital because we are all googling to find out more. A web presence lends authority and credibility, provided it is done right.

The core of any website is the content. At a minimum, your website needs:

- An information ("about") page that describes your business

- A bio page that highlights your journey to what you are doing now

- A contact form that the user can fill in to receive more information

- Photos or videos that provide a visual introduction of yourself

With a basic site like the one outlined above, it can also help to put your phone number in the header or footer of every page just to make certain people can get from your site to you.

This type of site is not going to cost you a lot to have built and, with a bit of patience, you can throw it together yourself through Google Sites,

Wordpress or any of the hundreds of other free website builders out there. If you are going to spend the money on having a website built, it is worth considering your brand. For example, the colors on the website should reinforce those on your business cards and any marketing materials. Your brand is also going to inform the type of content you'll be offering people as you build out the website from its basics.

Giving people free content through your website is a win-win when it comes to establishing your credentials. People that you have networked with offline can go to your site and see the article you wrote about "Tips For Increasing Real Estate Cash Flow" or "The Most Important Metrics For Evaluating Investment Properties" and see that you know what you are talking about. Adding content to your website will also help you rank on the search engines and turn that content into a marketing tool that brings in more potential investors than you could ever personally meet in a lifetime.

A deeper content base for your website will also pay off in making the creation of monthly newsletters and mailouts much easier in the future. We'll talk more about the importance of growing and systemizing your communications infrastructure throughout the book.

Basic Website Tips for the DIYer

- Pick one font and stick to it. Arial is a good default.

- Try to have a few content types, including videos, photos, podcasts and written articles.

- Resize photos for quicker load times or use a web service like Google's Picassa to do it for you.

- Maintain a professional tone when writing or recording (I hope checking spelling and grammar goes without saying by now).

- Don't hesitate to get help. The resources on YouTube alone are staggering.

Your Online Presence

Despite my impassioned defense of business cards, it is becoming clear they will be replaced in the future in all but physical networking events. People will take your business cards but they are most likely to use it to put your name in a search engine. This is something most of us have done just for interest sake, but it is now something that you'll be doing regularly as part of your online reputation management.

Your online presence will include your website, as well as all the other online platforms you utilize. The size of the online presence is, of course, directly related to how much content you are putting out there. Much like people were once expected to have business cards, we now expect to see at least a LinkedIn account, if not Facebook and Twitter as well. Depending upon how common your name is, you may not even see your own information popping up unless you add in your city or other identifiers. When you've been in business longer and been a contributor to different media pieces and the subject of others, your ability to influence your online presence actually gets harder because you are not the originator of most of it.

When you are just starting out, it is important to have something rather than nothing. There are different schools of thought on how much work you should put into social media and the value that those primarily personal networks like Facebook can generate, but for the purposes of raising capital, it is at least worth having a LinkedIn profile and even a company page with a few professional photos of yourself and your team. As you focus more on raising capital as your primary business and begin to tell your story, sending that content out on more platforms is great for increasing reach.

Some sharing of content that would interest the type of investors you want to work with will help you define your online presence as you build it, but I would caution against spending too much time on it. At the end of the day, people are checking your online reputation after meeting with you in person, so you actually have to be networking and meeting with investors before maintaining your online reputation becomes a necessity.

Your Context and Your Content

Your context is another one of those intangibles like your appearance—people will pick up on it without any conscious effort. Your context refers to the mental framework you use to understand the content you are exposed to. If you are going to be successful in business, you need to expand your context and increase the range of content you are comfortable with.

When I started out as a landlord, I had a decent context. I knew I wanted renters to pay off my properties so I could buy more. I also knew that real estate could be the foundation for significant wealth. I had a conceptual framework for what I wanted to do, but I didn't know much of the actual content. I didn't know how to calculate cash flow or how to write off repairs against rental income. I didn't know how to create a rental contract or screen tenants. I was missing the content that I needed to fill out my context.

It took me months of reading and attending seminars to become comfortable with the systems and lingo used in real estate investing. By the time I ran out of my own capital and started raising money from investors, I could talk at length about appreciation, curb appeal, renovation tax breaks, and nearly every aspect of running a real estate business. As you can imagine, my knowledge put investors at ease.

To raise capital effectively, you need to master the content of your business and the world of finance. Most people know their business to the smallest detail, but they struggle with translating that knowledge into something that investors can relate to. If you are offering people a chance to invest, you need to present your opportunity in terms they can recognize and compare to other opportunities. This means proposing a term, setting a target return on investment (ROI), disclosing dividend triggers, and so on.

We'll look at all these in later chapters, but there is much more context and content that will help when speaking to investors. To pitch effectively to investors, you need to understand their current investments and their real rates of return so you can quickly evaluate what your particular deal can offer that their portfolio currently does not. I encourage you to absorb as much financial content as you can. The fact that you are reading this book is a good sign that you are already working on both context and content, so keep it up. Your education is one of the smartest investments you can make.

Chapter Review

- The purpose of this book is to get you thinking of your capital needs more creatively.

- Capital can't fix a bad business. Capital helps good businesses grow bigger and better within a shorter timeframe.

- Rather than selling people on a specific deal, raising capital is about selling people on you as someone who can do what you say.

- Selling people on you requires an investment of time and money into:
    - Maintaining a professional appearance
    - Developing basic marketing materials like business cards and a website
    - Creating an online presence on platforms like LinkedIn
    - Growing your context and adding more content

Josh and Lisa Lannon

Rich Dad Advisors on Social Capitalism

Personal Background and Entrepreneur Profile

Name	Josh Lannon	Lisa Lannon
Date of Birth	August 24, 1974	December 16, 1970
Place of Birth	Long Beach, CA	Brookings, SD

Traditional Education

JOSH

University of the Nations

Kailua Kona, Hawaii

Degree: School of Hard Knocks

Highest level completed: 10th grade

LISA

Black Hills State University

University of Nevada Las Vegas

Degree: Bachelor of Arts, Criminal Justice

Highest level completed: BA Degree

Professional Education

JOSH

Masters Degree, AKKI Senior Professor of the Arts

Special Operations USASOL graduate, Levels I, II, and III

LISA

Commissioned Law Enforcement Officer – LVMPD

Grade Point Averages

JOSH	High School: don't know
LISA	High School: 3.2
	College: 2.8

Value of traditional education... relative to becoming an entrepreneur

JOSH: The basics are very important—reading, writing, arithmetic, etc. But once the basics are achieved, the school system should allow the student to pick their areas of interest. My challenge was that I was not interested in the topics being forced upon me. Honestly, it was confusing, boring, and felt like abuse. This led me to dislike the traditional school system.

At that time I was very interested in BMX (bicycle motocross). If the teachers could have related to a topic of interest, I would have plunged deeper in the study. For example: "a Mongoose bike can support a 180-pound rider. However, the Mongoose attorneys will not allow this data to be posted on their website. Let's explore the load capacity and why you think the legal team would not allow this to be posted." Now you have my interest.

What the traditional education system did for me to become an entrepreneur? Not much

LISA: It was useful in providing the basics of education. But, looking back, I wish I would have made some different choices at university, paying more attention in basic accounting and economics. That may have given me a better basic understanding when I took on financial education later in life.

Subject I liked most in school

JOSH: Math... until it did not relate to life.

LISA: English – because it was easy and I was a teachers aide my junior and senior years in high school. That allowed some freedom during the school day—and that was the goal back then. Freedom. So I guess not much has changed...

Subject I hated most in school

JOSH: English. I'm dyslectic and had a difficult time following in class. Anytime we had to read out loud, I had a panic attack. I would count the number of paragraphs and estimate the short

ones to see what section I had to read. I would read it over
and over in my head, waiting for my turn. Then some smart A
students would read more then they should have and I had to re-
compute and start all over. It was painful. I was doing 10 times
the work!

LISA: Algebra – it didn't make sense. I had to take it three times
in university before I passed.

First entrepreneurial project

JOSH: Buying, training and (yes!) stealing BMX bikes. We ended
up with an entire bike shop (40+ bikes) in the garage. Once my
father caught on to what we were up to, we got shut down. It was
a great lesson on regulation and how authorities can shut down
your business.

LISA: Selling Girl Scout cookies. While it wasn't my own
business, I look back on it as being "self-employed," similar to
an MLM.

Next would be building Journey Healing Centers with Josh. I
was always taught to go to school, get good grades, and get a
job (preferably with the government), so entrepreneurship was
not something I thought about or had many ideas about in
my childhood years. While I always had questions about who
owned different buildings and real estate, I did not grow up with
entrepreneurs around me.

The key entrepreneurial skill I was *not* taught in school

JOSH: How to think outside the box

LISA: I was not taught that it's OK to make mistakes. School
made me fearful of making mistakes. It was not OK to risk raising
my hand if I wasn't sure of the answer. The class would laugh and
kids would be embarrassed, and making a mistake was frowned
upon. Even on tests, a wrong answer meant a lower grade or
failure. In most cases, wrong answers were never discussed and

we didn't review or talk about why an answer was wrong or try to learn from our mistakes. Only the students with the highest scores got into good universities and would be successful.

Why and when I became an entrepreneur and my first major venture

JOSH: Vending machines. I worked for my father in the nightclub business. He did not really pay me anything. He's also an entrepreneur and I'll never forget when I questioned him for paying me so little, he said, "Son, if you want to make more money, the answers are all around you." He was right and I got into the vending machines in the club, pool tables, etc. By thinking outside the box, I was free.

My "why"… Good question. Because if I wanted to make more money, it was up to me… no one else.

LISA: I became an entrepreneur in 2002 with Josh, building Journey Healing Centers. We grew JHC to six locations in two states.

The "why" was because we had been through addiction and knew we could make a difference. When Josh quit drinking, I knew he couldn't go back to working in the nightclubs; we had to make an environment change. Opening our own behavioral health facilities made sense to us. We had been introduced to *Rich Dad Poor Dad* and we were ready to take control of our lives and achieve financial freedom, along with making a difference in the world.

We sold JHC in 2013 to a large, private equity-backed company, EBH and went onto our next major venture: Warriors Heart.

Best Lesson from first business

JOSH: Looking back, I think it's pretty funny it was cash management. Lisa and I would have hundreds of dollars in quarters. The banks hated them and it was a pain to roll them. We started cashing them in at the local casinos. They started kicking us out. So we then started filling up the casino's buckets with our quarters and taking them to the cage to cash in. On the way (holding as many buckets as we could) we would tell the people playing that this was the best casino in Vegas! We acted like "winners"—and tipped the cashier. Ha!

LISA: Personal development and staying mission-focused was a key lesson. Being an entrepreneur is a roller coaster ride. Being able to handle the emotions of a business is key. Issues like the loss of steady income to handling employees and upset customers can cause a wide range of emotions. Taking on personal development and developing myself not only made me a better leader, but also assisted me in handling the emotions that arise.

Years ago I committed to being a person who was always learning, always taking personal development courses, and always seeking coaches and mentors.

What I learned about myself from my Kolbe Index

JOSH LANNON
Kolbe A™ Index Result

CONGRATULATIONS JOSH
You Got a Perfect Score on the Kolbe A™ Index

You are uniquely able to take on future-oriented challenges. You lead the way to visionary possibilities and create what others said couldn't be done. You'll say "Yes" before you even know the end of the question – then turn it into a productive adventure.

Kolbe Action Modes®

Fact Finder   Follow Thru   Quick Start   Implementor

4   3   8   4

©1997-2017 Kathy Kolbe All rights reserved.

Reprinted with permission from Kolbe Corp.

JOSH: I'm a Quick Start. I'm really good at start up. I can drive hard, pull teams together, and get it done. However, once a business is operating, I get to step out and let the strong Follow Thrus and Fact Finders run the operation.

My Kolbe also taught me a lot about communicating with people. For example: as a Quick Start, I can't push a Fact Finder into action until they have done enough data work. We joke about it in the company. But now we know and it helps communication and working to complement each other's strengths.

What I learned about myself from my Kolbe Index

LISA LANNON

Kolbe A™ Index Result

CONGRATULATIONS LISA
You Got a Perfect Score on the Kolbe A™ Index

You're terrific when juggling rapidly changing priorities. You are known for taking risks that are grounded in practical realities. You don't mess around with what has always been done, but temper your trial-and-error approach by strategizing options.

Kolbe Action Modes®

©1997-2017 Kathy Kolbe. All rights reserved.

Reprinted with permission from Kolbe Corp.

LISA: I loved learning about the Kolbe. It validated how I do things and why I struggle when doing something that is opposite of where I am on my Kolbe chart.

My strengths are being a Quick Start and Visualization (Implementor category). I love creating new businesses and new investments. This is exciting to me, jumping into something new and making innovative changes in business. Taking risks, creating urgency on projects, and working under deadlines are natural to me.

When I have a project, sometimes I get frustrated about why I don't start it until the last minute and I was always looking at ways I could change this. Seeing my Kolbe—and learning that I work well under pressure and with deadlines—relieved a lot of the pressure of feeling I had to change the procrastinator in me. That went against my grain.

I'm a big picture person, I can see what things should look like or visualize how it's supposed to be.

I don't have to be hands on. One of my gifts is finding new properties for our businesses. I can see what they'll look like and how it will work. This works really well for new projects and creating the future. Building a strong team that complements our Kolbe strengths is also key.

My Role in the B-I Triangle

JOSH: The outside of the B-I Triangle—100%. Clearly communicating the Mission, building the right Team (which includes the defining and supporting the culture) and Leadership. I'm always working to improve my stills and abilities to lead.

LISA: We utilize every part of B-I Triangle in our businesses. As Social Entrepreneurs, building businesses that have a social aspect, our role on the Advisor team is in the Mission, Team and Leadership areas. Having that strong "why"—or purpose—is the foundation of Social Entrepreneurs, so we really focus on Mission.

Skills that are essential for entrepreneurs—but not taught in schools

JOSH: For employees—which is what the school system produces—learning not to make mistakes is good. For instance, we want to train our employees well, and have them follow policy and procedures. But for entrepreneurs, we are the ones who create the policy. And that only happens though trial and error. A better idea: Reward the kids in an entrepreneur program for making mistakes. That's how we learn. And the bigger the screw-up, the better the story!

LISA: Three things...

Perseverance – Schools focused on the A students. The praise went to the top students and athletes and it's really about bringing out the best in everyone. We all have a skill, a gift, and school should be about assisting students in finding their strength so they can succeed at whatever they want to be or do… versus just focusing on the best.

The kids who aren't the best in school are sometimes led to believe they will be losers in life and will not succeed. If they aren't taught to persevere they can take on these beliefs and not attempt to do their best or find their gift in life.

It's OK to make mistakes – I talk about this earlier in what I was not taught in schools. I believe it's an essential skill that we deserve to be taught. We learn through after-school sports programs that practice makes us better, so why is this not also taught inside the classrooms? Most after-school sports are taught by the same teachers who say it's not OK to make mistakes in the classroom.

When I was an employee, I was trained for a job and got in trouble (even written up sometimes!) if a mistake was made. This can make a person even more fearful of making mistakes. Learning that it was OK to make mistakes provided some of my biggest lessons in business. While I want to do my best to limit mistakes because they can be costly, it's a part of life that we all make mistakes sometimes.

When an employee makes a mistake, we look at it and see if they need more training or if the cause was something else. As long as they learn, we have learned to be forgiving. If the same mistakes are repeated, then obviously a lesson isn't being learned and other measures have to be taken.

Team – In business it's crucial to have a strong team. A team that's aligned with the same mission, values, and vision. In school, it's an individual game. We can't collaborate on tests, and homework is done independently. There are very few classes or assignments where it's OK to work as a team.

Learning to play on a team and working together is essential. Especially when different personalities are introduced into a workplace environment or a business. If we could learn this in school, it would be easier to work together in business.

How I learned to raise capital

JOSH: It started by asking Mom and Dad for money! If you have kids, train them in different sales techniques and ways to improve their pitch. Reward them for not giving up easily. I like to see parents who don't crush their childrens' spirits for asking for money. This "raising capital" skill is one to be honed, practiced, and rewarded.

LISA: We learned to raise capital by making a lot of mistakes. In our first business, we attempted the traditional route: banks. And we were turned down over and over again. Eventually we went to a private investor and were able to raise the $1.5 million we needed to start our business. This took several attempts, with many revisions of a bad business plan. Looking back, we've realized that we made a lot of mistakes that first time, but our investor took a chance on us. What I'm most proud of is that even after being turned down several times, we never gave up.

How I learned to overcome fear and failure

JOSH: I wanted a girlfriend. And I had to overcome fear and just ask her out! Then, when I got dumped (it really happened!)... learning how to overcome failure and rejection. It hurt, but I learned something each time. (Don't tell Lisa... We met when I was 19, and she thinks she was my first girlfriend!)

LISA: There will always be fear and failure, and personal development was key in learning to control fear and be OK with failure. When stepping into something new, like our new business—and even though we have done it before—we are tailoring towards a specific niche and going into what is unchartered territory for us. There is still the fear of the unknowns and the fear of failure. The best way I've learned to deal with fear is to break it down into chunks I can control, and do some fact finding to make some of the unknowns known.

In Law Enforcement, there is always the fear of danger. Not knowing what the next situation might entail and the fear of being physically hurt or killed. It was the practice of our defensive tactics and training that eased these fears. With failure, it's learning to be OK with failure and *learning from it* so the same mistakes aren't repeated in the future.

My personal strength

JOSH: I am always willing to go for it! Heck, why not? If you have a vision, dream, goal…. go after it with everything you've got. That's my strength. I believe we should dedicate our life, our energy, our money, and our time to achieving what we want in life.

LISA: My personal strength is perseverance and being a protector… a warrior. I am a Warrior at heart. Going into Law Enforcement to protect and serve, taking a stand for my marriage, and our current business—Warriors Heart, healing our nations warriors—reflect the protector in me.

My personal weakness

JOSH: I can drive people too hard. I'm very critical of myself and expect others to act the same way. I'm learning to be more gentle (on myself and others) and support people in becoming better, versus demanding it.

LISA: I work really well with deadlines, but until I have them I am a really good procrastinator. At times this is a strength, as I'm very good under pressure. That said, without pressure, like a deadline, I don't always jump to get things done. I've learned that I have to set deadlines—and tricking myself with false or arbitrary deadlines doesn't always work.

The Entrepreneurial Skills We Teach Best
LISA and JOSH: Mission

The Entrepreneurial Lesson We Teach
LISA and JOSH: Capitalists can be good people and Business Models that Target Social Needs

Business Models that Target Social Needs
by Josh and Lisa Lannon

*The world is filled with greedy people
who will do anything for money…
but you don't need to be one of them.
Josh and Lisa prove you can be
social capitalists, entrepreneurs with a heart,
and make a lot of money.*

– RTK

Josh:

Lisa and I are believers that one must be in alignment what he or she does and teaches. In other words, it's difficult to respect the advice from a financial planner who's broke. Or respect an overweight nutritionist. They may be great people, but they're out of alignment in their area of expertise. They're simply not practicing what they preach.

That's one of the reasons why we love learning with the Rich Dad team. Each and every one of Robert and Kim's Advisors are living what they teach each and every day. It's part of the Rich Dad Code. Robert, Kim and the team of Advisors have built, destroyed, and rebuilt businesses all around the world. They speak from experience and have the battle scars and the bank account to show for it. To us, that's integrity. Robert often quotes R. Buckminster Fuller, as do we, and here's what he has to say on the subject: *"Integrity is the essence of everything successful."*

We will do our best to stay within our area of focus. The entrepreneurial skill that we best teach—and live—is Mission… hands down, 100%. We are mission driven, from how we invest, spend time, and build and operate businesses to how we choose to live. Having purpose in life and in business brings focus to our labor and fulfillment from it.

Lisa:

We have been successful in applying the Rich Dad principles in our personal and professional lives. We found the principles both straightforward and common sense... and interesting in that no one else, in our experience, has been able to frame up teachings like the Rich Dad team has. For example, Rich Dad's lesson #1 is The Rich Don't work for Money. At first it's difficult to understand the depth and simplicity of the principle. If the rich don't work for money, then what do they work for?

One of the reasons why we love this current project, *More Important Than Money,* is because for us, this lesson has always been embedded within the Rich Dad message. With this book revealing the very core of Rich Dad's work, this could be the most important project to date.

Money is important, very important... but it's not the "most important" aspect of our lives. If we allow money to be the most important focus, the "why" you are in business or have a job, well then... you're screwed. There is so much more to life.

Josh:

For example, since 2002 Lisa and I have dedicated our lives to the behavioral health field. We have built and operated seven successful drug and alcohol treatment centers in a number of states. Being in the addiction field, people show the same characteristics and behaviors around money as a heroin addict does around their drug of choice.

If money is the *most important*, thing in your life, then you're addicted to it. Money is your drug. We're not making it wrong, but let's just call it for what it is. Do you get a sense of euphoria (a high) when a check comes in? The larger the check, the bigger the high? Do you feel anxious when you see the bank account deplete? You may never have looked at it this way before, but peel it back, and assess an addiction.

You can hear it in the words people use. "I have to make at least $80,000 a year. You don't understand, I have kids to feed, bills to pay, school loans, debt…" We've all heard it… and it goes on and on.

If you want to see if you're addicted to money, take away your paycheck for a year, or even a month. See what happens. Will you go through a violent detox? Will you shake, kick, and scream after losing your job? If so, this is the book for you.

First Step

Our area of focus is Mission, freeing your mind from the bondage of addiction. In AA (Alcoholics Anonymous) this is called the First Step. *We admitted we were powerless over alcohol—that our lives had become unmanageable.*

It usually takes a great deal of suffering for an alcoholic to get to Step One. In order to take the first step in recovery, it is necessary for the individual to be humble enough to admit that they need help. Some people view humility as a type of weakness, but this could not be further from the truth. It just means that the individual owns up to the reality that they do not have all the answers. Humility also means that the individual becomes willing to accept help for their problem.

With the Rich Dad Advisor team, we practice humility on a regular basis and show each other our personal and business financial statements. Because all of us, at one time to another, found "our financial lives had become unmanageable." Like in AA, we practice rigorous honesty with each other. The standard is not honesty—it's *rigorous honesty*—and it's important to understand the distinction between the two. Truth is what drives honesty, where truthiness (the quality of seeming or being felt to be true, even if not necessarily true) is the motivating force behind rigorous honesty.

This rigorously honest look into our financial lives, holds us accountable to the integrity of… *Are we truly practicing what we teach?* As students, are we able to apply the principles in our own lives? If I were still a drunk, would you send your loved one to one of my treatment centers to get sober? Hell no! So why do we take advice from broke people?

This is a peek into the code of conduct of Rich Dad and it all ties to Mission. We practice integrity, rigorous honesty, vulnerability, and positive competition. At this level of vulnerability it strengthens the team and creates an extremely high level of trust. Who on your team do you trust? Who will hold you accountable to living on purpose without taking advantage of you?

If you're ready to start, find a mentor that you trust and reveal your personal financial statement. That's taking the first step: "We admitted we were powerless over money—that our lives had become unmanageable."

Step One from the Big Book of AA (page 21) is *No other kind of bankruptcy is like this one. Alcohol, now become the rapacious creditor, bleeds us of all self sufficiency and all will to resist its demands. Once this stark fact is accepted, our bankruptcy as going human concerns is complete.*

We could easily replace *alcohol* with the *lack of financial education* as the "rapacious creditor" that "bleeds us of all self-sufficiency and all will to resist its demands." Once this stark fact is accepted, our bankruptcy as going human concerns is complete.

I got sober in 2001, and at the same time Lisa and I started studying Robert and Kim Kiyosaki's books. It was personal for us… and I was not going to let any drug control me ever again. Being a student of recovery, Rich Dad's lesson #1, the Rich Don't Work for Money, spoke to my soul.

The rich work for assets… and, for me, that asset was sobriety!

Lisa and I joined hand in hand, as we did in marriage, and began our social entrepreneurial journey. No longer were we going to work for money. We had found our mission in life and in business. Our future endeavors were going to use business as the force for good.

Lisa:

Before Josh got sober in 2001, we were employees with job security. Josh was working for his father in his nightclubs and I was in Law Enforcement working for the Las Vegas Metropolitan Police Department. To the outside world, everything looked great. Middle-class home, nice cars, and a few bucks in our pockets... but internally we were falling apart. This was evident in our marriage (which was about to implode), Josh's deteriorating health, and cash getting sucked out of our accounts from all the late night partying.

Being in the Vegas nightclubs for years, Josh's drinking was destroying him. Working with addiction in law enforcement on a nightly basis, it was taking its toll on me. I was dealing with it both at work and in my marriage. After several years of dealing with the emotional rollercoaster, I had to give him the ultimatum: divorce or rehab. I was done.

Josh was also ready for the madness to end. We had been playing this game for years. He would say, and try, "I will only drink on the weekends" or "This time will be different." You name it, he tried it. This time the gig was up. No more broken promises; I was at my wit's end. Thank God he chose rehab, because we were at a point where the decision was really about life or death.

After he got out of rehab, Josh did not want go back to the nightclub industry. He did not want to be part of the problem anymore. Their business plan was simple: get the patrons drunk, help them have a really good time, and keep everyone safe. It worked. The club was #1 in Vegas and people loved it there. But even after working so hard for years to create the #1 country honky-tonk in Vegas, he was done. He was ready to walk away from his father's business, a business that someday could have been his.

We had to make changes. It was time for a new Mission. Even though Josh had stopped drinking, he was still early in recovery and in the same environment. The environment was tempting and crushing at the same time. Our friends thought we were crazy to leave. The club business was doing well, with 1500 people a night through the doors, and I had a promising career in law enforcement. And, once again, to the outside world, our life looked great. But for us, personally and spiritually… we knew it was time to get out.

As the proverb says: "When the student is ready, the teacher will appear." That was certainly our experience with the Rich Dad messages. They came at the right time and it changed our lives. With sobriety as the foundation of our mission, we decided we would open our own rehab facility. We had a strong "why," a strong mission in entering this field and that proved to be a solid foundation.

As Josh said, we were entering the world of Social Entrepreneurship.

Josh:

This is what Social Entrepreneurs do. We tap into passion, into a *why*… to solve problems. Simon Sinek says it best in his book *Start with Why – How great leaders inspire everyone to take action.* He writes: *"The more organizations and people who learn to start with WHY, the more people there will be who wake up being fulfilled by the work they do."*

Why start with *Why?* Sinek's words again:

"The ability to motivate people is, in itself, not difficult. It is usually tied to some external factor. Great leaders, in contrast are able to inspire people to act. Those who are able to inspire give people a sense of purpose or belonging that has little to do with any external incentive or benefit to be gained. Those who truly lead are able to create a following of people who act not because they were swayed, but because they were inspired.

"For those who are inspired, the motivation to act is deeply personal. They are less likely to be swayed by incentives. Those who are inspired are willing to pay a premium or endure inconvenience, even personal suffering. Those who are able to inspire will create a following of people —supporters, voters, customers, workers—who act for the good of the whole not because they have to, but because they want to.

"People who love going to work are more productive and creative. They go home happier and have happier families. They treat their colleagues and clients and customers better. Inspired employees make for stronger companies and stronger economies."

Money and power (although tempting) was not our why. Our motivation was deeply personal. Our marriage was more important than money. Our happiness was more important. My sobriety was more important then money. We were willing to pay the premium and endure the personal suffering of opening a business. We took the leap of faith.

Social Entrepreneurs use business as a force for good. Rich Dad's B-I Triangle provided the outline to develop our business plan and we put our thoughts into action. We will not go into all the details here, but if you're interested in learning more, I encourage you to read *Rich Dad's Retire Young Retire Rich.*

It's no surprise that the foundation of the B-I Triangle is Mission.

With Mission as the foundation to build upon, it only made sense (to us, anyway) that a business is designed to be mission driven. Individuals can harness the power of enterprise to make this world a better place *and* make a profit.

Social Entrepreneurs are not driven by money; we are inspired by purpose and our motivation is deeply personal. The goal: Build sustainable businesses with a higher purpose.

If you look around, I'm sure you'll see countless problems to solve. Why not use the power of private enterprise to address these problems? From the lack of financial education to addiction, fighting sex trafficking, child abuse, clean water, crime, food, housing… the list is endless. Private enterprise can deliver solutions to social issues, but it's going to take people like you who are willing to take a stand and be the change. Simon Sinek's words are worth repeating: "For those who are inspired, the motivation to act is deeply personal. They are less likely to be swayed by incentives. Those who are inspired are willing to pay a premium or endure inconvenience, even personal suffering."

Lisa:

This is why our key strength is in Mission-driven companies. Our current facility, Warriors Heart, is mission driven. Our niche is serving our warrior population—military service men and women, veterans, law enforcement, firefighters, EMTs, and other first responders. We assist them in overcoming addiction and PTSD (Post Traumatic Stress Disorder) along with other disorders that are a result of traumas that include anxiety, grief, injuries, and depression.

So ask yourself: What gets you up and motivated in the morning? What problem do you see in the world? Sometimes your motivation comes from something intensely personal, like ours did. Other times it might just be something that pisses you off and you *know* you have to do something about it.

If you are interested in becoming a Social Entrepreneur, your time is now. This is why we wrote the book, *The Social Capitalist*. You can learn from other Social Entrepreneurs and turn your passion into a profitable business. You can do good in this world *and* do well financially.

We believe that we are entering in a stage of corporate accountability and responsibility. A time when customers, stockholders, and employees are demanding transparency. This is a new age and many Social Entrepreneurs are leading the way for change. This is what we teach at Rich Dad; the Mission of Building Sustainable Businesses—by applying the Rich Dad principles, passion, *and* profits. We are Social Entrepreneurs.

About Josh Lannon

Described as "a driven person with out of the box insights," Josh Lannon has successfully opened and operated seven licensed and accredited healing centers in three states and has held a CEO position from 2002. His latest mission, Warriors Heart, has a bold vision to bring 1,000,000 warriors home from addiction and PTSD. Warriors Heart is leading the way in private chemical dependency treatment for our warriors.

Josh has extensive experience in leadership, business development, behavioral health, licensing, accreditation, real estate, investing, public speaking, social entrepreneurship, business coaching and strategic planning. His life experience and career path have run the gamut from construction foreman (Kohala Ranch in Hawaii) and general manager of a chain of nightclubs (Dylan's in Nevada) to founder, with wife Lisa, of Journey Healing Centers (Utah and Arizona), an accredited dual diagnosis, drug and alcohol treatment center. Over the course of 12 years, between 2000 and 2013, JHC expanded to six locations in multiple states with a professional staff of 100 and successfully treated thousands of clients. In late 2013, all six of JHC locations were acquired by EBH Elements Behavior Health, a nationwide provider and financially backed by Frazier Health Care.

In 2014, the Lannons launched Warriors Heart in Bandera, Texas. Warriors Heart is a dedicated, licensed and JOINT accredited 40-bed, residential treatment center for the healing of our nation's warriors. Its focus is on serving the men and women who are our veterans, military, law enforcement, firefighters, medical first responders, and other warriors.

Josh is a LUF Navy SEAL SOT-G Leadership Course graduate and a Special Operations USASOL (Levels I, II and III) graduate.

About Lisa Lannon

Lisa Lannon is a Social Entrepreneur, author, investor, international speaker and Mom.

Described as a "protector with compassion," Lisa has a bold passion in building businesses and providing safe, world-class healing environments assisting warriors in sobriety and healing. Her current mission is Warriors Heart, a healing facility for our warriors—veterans, active military, police officers firefighters and other first responders and protectors.

Lisa is the co-Author of the Rich Dad Advisor Series book *The Social Capitalist*. As a successful entrepreneur, she has built and sold six private addiction treatment facilities, JHC, with her husband, Josh. She is the Founder of Brooke Property Management with investments in residential homes, commercial buildings, and apartment complexes and holdings of over 2,600 units.

Prior to becoming an entrepreneur, Lisa was a commissioned Law Enforcement Officer with the Las Vegas Metropolitan Police Department. Lisa and Josh, have been inseparable since 1995 and are proud parents of two amazing children. They've dedicated themselves to building businesses that make sense and addresses social problems.

For nearly two decades, Lisa has been empowered by the belief that doing good and making money do not have to be mutually exclusive. She believes that the world is crying out for entrepreneurs to take a stand, create jobs, and solve problems. Her life has been an inspiring story, of turning problems into solutions, and Lisa is a visionary who builds purpose- and value-driven organizations that create positive change.

Books by Josh and Lisa Lannon

Rich Dad Advisor Series Books

The Social Capitalist
Passion and Profits—An Entrepreneurial Journey

... in Spanish

Emprendedores Sociales

AN EXCERPT FROM

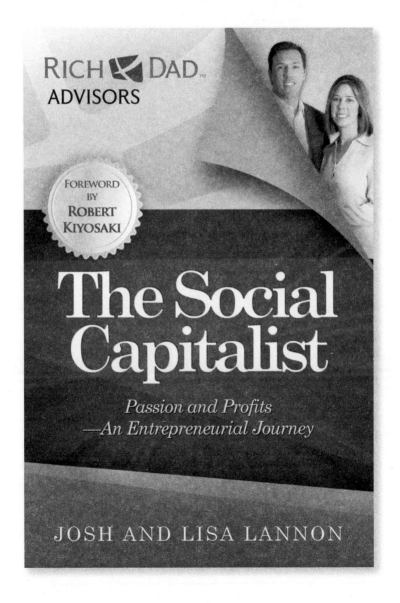

RICH DAD™
ADVISORS

FOREWORD
BY
ROBERT
KIYOSAKI

The Social Capitalist

*Passion and Profits
—An Entrepreneurial Journey*

JOSH AND LISA LANNON

Chapter Two

Understanding
Social Capitalism

"Indeed, for anyone who has ever said, 'This isn't working' or 'We can do better!'—for anyone who gets a kick out of challenging the status quo, shaking up the system, or practicing a little entrepreneurial 'creative destruction'—these are propitious times."

—David Bornstein, *How to Change the World*

Perhaps to best define the concept of Social Capitalism, we should turn to one of its pioneers.

J. Gregory Dees, adjunct professor and founding faculty director of the Center for the Advancement of Social Entrepreneurship (CASE) at Duke University's Fuqua School of Business, is considered an academic leader in the area of social entrepreneurship. In 2006, at a gathering hosted by New Profit Inc., Dees said that the term "social entrepreneur" conveys "this blending of sectors—a mixture of the social purpose we typically associate with nonprofits and the kind of entrepreneurial orientation we associate with business, particularly with the most creative and dynamic aspect of business."

In other words, social entrepreneurs build businesses that make sense while accomplishing social missions.

Of course, the concept of becoming social entrepreneurs wasn't anywhere on our radar in late 2001. Once we'd made our decision to creating a new life for ourselves, that was just the beginning of the journey. As any entrepreneur in any industry can tell you, bridging the gap between the glimmer of an idea and getting a successful, full-fledged business up and running is where most new businesses fall short, social or not.

Once we'd realized that we wanted to create this new life for ourselves *and* be financially free, we had to come to grips with the idea that we had a long, hard road ahead of us. We didn't have to change a few things in our lives... We had to change *everything*, from the self-defeating thoughts we had to the words we used, the friends we spent time with and the things we did in our free time. For that moment in our driveway, we felt as if we'd figured things out, which was a relief. We were ready to embrace change, no matter how difficult the road that lay ahead.

But then the full weight of what that decision implied fell upon us.

As much as we would like to say that we were so moved by my experience in rehab and the idea of taking control over our lives that we instantly knew our lifelong passion, it wouldn't be the truth. We didn't decide to open rehabilitation centers as we were driving back to Las Vegas from Southern California. What we were most passionate about was rebuilding our lives and our marriage.

We were just two people heading back from a rehab center to a clean start, determined not to let the clubs and money and destructive lifestyle we'd fallen into reclaim us. But I was still my father's right-hand man, employed at a nightclub, and as much as I didn't want to live that life anymore, I had no idea what life I *did* want. And sharing this with my father, a man who would likely take such an admission as an act of weakness, was simply not an option that I saw as viable. I was terrified to return to work, but terrified not to.

I'd been home for only a couple of days when I found myself standing on the floor of Dylan's, surrounded by the more than 1,500 people celebrating New Year's Eve, 2001. All night I had been wondering what the hell I was doing there. I felt beaten and trapped. I watched the smiles and laughter of the people partying around me, and as the night wore on, it became clear to me that it was all fake, a big lie. I don't know, perhaps I was projecting my issues onto them, but at that moment, it occurred to me that very few of those people were honestly happy. As I watched the ball begin to drop in Times Square on the big-screen TVs on every wall, and heard the seconds counting down to the beginning of a brand-new year, I felt my fear of separating from my father's business eroding in the face of the fear I felt about spending another year in that place. Nothing, *nothing*, not the threat of my often-violent and temperamental father, not the threat of financial ruin, not the uncertainty about my future career or the potential estrangement from my family, none of it was worth living like this, in the midst of that toxic environment. *I had to GET OUT.* Immediately.

Meanwhile, Lisa was facing her own fears as the clock ticked down to midnight and she walked the Vegas Strip in uniform with her fellow officers that New Year's Eve. The crowds, hundreds of thousands strong, could have easily been dangerous enough, but Lisa's fears had more to do with what was happening to me, a very newly recovering alcoholic, in a nightclub, on this night in which it seemed the entire world was focused on drinking and partying. She knew I had to get out of the nightclub business, because all it would have taken was doing one celebratory shot with a customer to drag me back. She carried a knot of worry around in her stomach all night.

After the night wound down and the sun began to rise, our shifts came to an end and it was time to finally clock out. When we were both home safe and sound from our jobs, she was surprised, relieved, excited, and nervous to learn of my decision on the morning of New Year's Day to begin my extracting myself from my father's business. We made the decision that morning to start fresh. This was it. We didn't know what we were going to do, but we *did* know that if we didn't act right then and there, we might never get out. We spent New Year's Day joyfully brainstorming the possibilities that might await us. It felt somehow taboo for me to consider doing anything else besides working in my dad's nightclub business, or for Lisa not to be a commissioned officer, but yet it also felt so right, so thrilling to

> *Your environment can be supportive or destructive to who you are and what you want to do. If you want to change, you get to look at your environment and make it one that supports you.*

realize that a whole world of possibilities was out there for the taking. Lisa and I just threw everything that popped into our heads onto the table for discussion that day, no holds barred.

Then, in a flash, my discussion with Spencer popped into my mind – Spencer, the former restaurateur who decided to open rehab centers when he realized that the restaurant business no longer suited his sobriety.

Could that have been a sign? Did we dare to dream a similar life for ourselves? Yes, we did. Because as soon as I shared the memory of that conversation out loud with Lisa, we both grew silent and looked at each other, completely serious. We recognized what felt like a calling. After all, we knew what it was like for other people grappling with addiction, and we also knew what their loved ones were going through. The puzzle pieces of our lives all seemed to come together right at that moment, and we could see how everything that had happened to us might have happened for a reason.

Because *of course* it made sense. I had done rehab several times, I knew what worked and what didn't. Lisa and I had both known the pain of addiction, the difficulty in returning to life sober, the systems that must be in place to stay clean and sober. It would be incredibly rewarding to share what we knew in order to keep others on the straight and narrow, to give families back the peace that Lisa and I were just coming to know and love.

We made the decision to sleep on it, and to call Spencer the next morning. I did, first thing. I shared with what we had been experiencing— my feeling of being trapped at the nightclubs and my certainty that, spiritually, it would be suicide for me to continue to work there. I told him how it was just a matter of time before I succumbed to that environment again. I shared how Lisa felt the same way, and was in full support of my decision to leave.

I told Spencer that we wanted to be part of the solution, and could no longer be part of the problem. Then, I asked Spencer if he could teach me about the rehab business, and told him I would appreciate his support and guidance.

"Are you serious about this?" he asked me.

I assured him that, yes, I was absolutely serious.

"Well, okay, great!" he said. "Be in my office Monday morning."

Without any idea where Spencer was leading us or whether there was a hidden agenda, I drove back to Southern California to meet with him and gather every little bit of insight and advice I possibly could from this man who had walked the same path that Lisa and I wanted to embark on.

Our meeting lasted all of ten minutes, during which time he handed me a stack of policy and procedure manuals for his rehab centers, and said, "Here. This is how you open a treatment center." In fact, he shared proprietary information with me, to the dismay of his staff.

"Getting licensed is one of the hardest things to do in this business," he said, handing me some more paperwork. "Here's how you do it."

I stood there, gracious but in shock, holding the growing stack of 3-ring binders Spencer's kept piling on me. When he'd handed over everything, he said, in a tone that sounded as if he were giving an order to an employee, "I want you to fly to Florida to see my treatment center there. Okay? I'll be there in a few days, so I'll see you there and we can talk some more." And without so much as a handshake to wish me well, he was out the door to his next appointment.

"How'd it go?" Lisa asked me when I returned home later that night.

"Well, it was a great ten minutes," I told her, stunned by how good I still felt in our plan, and buoyed by the tools Spencer had provided to me and his seeming confidence in my ability to pull it off. He hadn't seemed to question me or our decision at all. "Lisa, maybe it's because we asked for his support rather than just taking from him. I don't know. But now, we get to go to Florida."

Fortunately, she trusted me and this new mentor of mine, Spencer, enough that she was willing to hop on board a plane to Florida along with me. There was absolutely no hesitation from either of us. We booked our flights for a week in Florida with our own money, and completely, willingly submitted to Spencer's directives. Later we discovered that he and his associates had only scheduled about one full day's worth of meetings for us, involving travel to several locations around Orlando and talks with many people who were experienced in the addiction treatment industry.

Looking back, we're convinced that this was Spencer's test to determine how serious we actually were about this decision. And it appeared that we'd passed.

By the end of the day, we were only more convinced of our decision, and were eager to hit the ground running. However, we had booked a week in Florida. So after the day with Spencer was complete, we decided to take a few days out for ourselves before this new venture and visit Disneyworld. It was during this time that our daughter, Haley, was conceived. We took it as a universal sign, the third in a series of signs that included my near-death experience and my dad's providential Christmas gift, that told us we were about to begin the life we were meant for.

We had years of management and leadership experience between the two of us, a solid foundation of financial education through *Rich Dad,* the policy and procedure manuals containing information about licensing, a supportive colleague and mentor, and, I was shocked to realize, my father's blessing to separate from his business and begin our own. Everything seemed to be pointing us in this direction.

The Foundation for Success

Over the next couple of years, we were involved in the long process of establishing Journey Healing Centers. We set about on a challenging journey that included securing capital, finding a location for our business, becoming licensed as a treatment facility, establishing a niche market, finding and growing a clientele, enhancing our variety of services, and expanding our territory by adding locations. How that all happened is a story we'll be sharing with you.

We were successful, eventually, but we had to make a lot of mistakes along the way. We faced a lot of challenges and had to continually remind ourselves of what we wanted and why. We had to recommit dozens of times – times when it would have been a lot easier to throw up our hands and say, "Forget it, let's do something else."

But when it came right down to it, what we cared most about was being part of the solution by serving the roughly 140 million people around the world who struggle with dependence on alcohol. In 2002, when we were in the beginning stages of creating our business, we found that more than 80 percent of people who needed addictions treatment didn't receive it.

Many people give up before they reach their goals, learn to find your strength and determination to keep going. Evaluate how serious you are about your passion and dreams and make sure it is what you truly want.

We found that addiction affects every culture and every socioeconomic class; it does not discriminate. This mission was deeply personal for us, and we had a strong "why" for building this socially conscious business.

From that passion and deep sense of personal commitment grew a series of steps that we believe to be the foundation of a social enterprise:

- **Discover your "why" – build upon your passion.** Our "why" wasn't instantly clear to us. But after going through the clarifying process of rehab (others may find the experience of personal development seminars similarly helpful), it became very clear. Then, our "why" was all we had, and it was the reason we got up every morning and kept working on this business. That's still true today. Your "why" is everything. Having a strong "why" will keep going when times get tough, as they will from time to time in your business.

- **Make and clarify your commitment.** We'd made the commitment to open a treatment center. We clarified our commitment by uncovering research, both from Spencer and data we collected on our own about the legalities of doing this kind of work, what it took to be licensed, the facts about treatment and recovery, and what did and didn't work in terms of running a successful facility. We invested every free hour of our time in research, and turned our home office into a "mission control" center where we collected all the pieces of information we uncovered and filed away for later use. And we assessed our own strengths and weaknesses, taking into account how our own personal experiences could show us what values weren't currently being met in the world of addiction treatment.

- **Find the right support system, mentors, and coaches.** We already had Spencer in our corner, mentoring us and offering us wisdom when he could. We would encounter many more mentors and supporters in the coming years, and they would prove to be invaluable for us. The right support system, mentor, and coach will push you to be uncomfortable. He or she will push you beyond what you thought was possible, get you to think differently. This is a sign of a great support system. If they aren't supporting your vision and pushing you along the way, you deserve someone else, because otherwise you may never achieve what you want out of life.

- **Dedicate and invest in yourself.** We invested a tremendous amount of time, money, and energy into personal development. Your business and your life will be a reflection of you. Mahatma Gandhi once said, "For things to change, first I must change." A business will only grow to the capacity of the owner's context. You can suppress the growth of your business or you can lead it to success. We have never stopped dedicating time to improving ourselves and the work we do. This wasn't something we did in our free time; it is part of the business plan.

- **Get a financial education.** When we were first starting out, the two of us knew very little about what money really is, how to raise capital, how to make investments, or the difference between active and passive income. The key to beginning our financial education was *Choose To Be Rich*, but that was only the beginning. Bottom line, it became clear very early on that regardless of your social mission, you can't run a successful business without respecting the power of financial education. Continue to learn as the business grows; as the world and economies change, there is always more to know.

- **Build a business plan.** Here's where you really get to think through the business design. Is the business leverageable, financeable, expandable, and predictable? No one will give you capital to build your business if you cannot show (on paper, at least) that you have invested time, energy, and resources into thinking through your business, its mission, the team members involved, and how you are going to return investors' capital. This is where the rubber meets the road in terms of a social enterprise's viability.

As it turns out, the steps we took to lay a solid foundation in our business align pretty neatly with those recommended by many of the major players in the social entrepreneurship sector.

In fact, in a November 2002 report by CASE entitled *The Process of Social Entrepreneurship: Creating Opportunities Worthy of Serious Pursuit*, Authors Ayse Guclu, J. Gregory Dees, and Beth Battle Anderson say that personal experience usually drives the formation of social enterprises. That is followed by a determination of social need, or "the gaps between socially desirable conditions and the existing reality." Then, because a social needs assessment often over-emphasizes the negative, social entrepreneurs determine where the assets are that can be "leveraged to create wealth." Finally, they create change, and are constantly inspired by it, seeking opportunities to have a positive social impact.

"Successful social entrepreneurs embody this 'how can' attitude, particularly in the idea generation phase," say Guclu, Dees, and Anderson. "Effective social entrepreneurs carry this orientation into the opportunity development process, engaging in continuous innovation, adaptation, analysis, and learning along the way."

Really, this is, and was, a major key to our success—this process of "engaging in continuous innovation, adaptation, and learning along the way."

Mirjam Schöning, the head of the Schwab Foundation for Social Entrepreneurship, a global organization whose mission is to highlight and advance leading models of sustainable social innovation, has identified seven basic tenets or pieces of advice for social entrepreneurs, after having worked in the sector for ten years:

1. Follow your passion – it's the most important ingredient, and it's what will keep you going in the tough times.

2. Balance your passion with rationale. Are you addressing a real, substantiated need?

3. Brainstorm – generate a thousand ideas, and don't be afraid to consider them, refine them, dismiss them, or replace them.

4. Carefully choose your business model, and articulate your vision, mission, and systems for evaluation and measurement from day one.

5. Study approaches that lead to the same impact you're trying to achieve. Is your idea really as unique as you think? Consider the competitive landscape.

6. Consider franchising your social enterprise – it's arguable that what we need most is for entrepreneurs to take their brilliant ideas to other parts of the world.

7. Give yourself a minimum of three years (or 36 months, which sounds shorter) to get your enterprise off the ground and into calmer waters.

Perhaps, for us, the fact that the life we were leaving behind would have killed me eventually is what kept us at it night and day, working on this business despite the obstacles. We literally felt as if we had no choice. Like a frog in tepid water that is slowly cooked as the pot works its way to a boil, I could see myself dying a little every single day I remained a nightclub employee. And despite Lisa's respectable profession and the contribution she made each day, as an officer, to the social good, it often left her unsatisfied and craving a more significant outlet in which she could improve our lives and the lives of those around us.

So, perhaps, that's the real key to a successful social enterprise: The fact that doing *nothing* about a problem or injustice, or failing to address it properly, affects a lot more people than just you.

For-Profit or Nonprofit?

You certainly don't have to create a business to begin solving problems. Plenty of people join the Peace Corps or Doctors Without Borders. It's wonderful to donate money to, or volunteer for, the Sierra Club, The Nature Conservancy, Feed the Children, Feeding America, The Green Children Foundation, or any other charitable organization, and lots of amazing people do this. It's much needed, and we would hate to disparage those important efforts by indicating somehow that this kind of selfless act should be supplanted by a for-profit business model with profit being the ultimate goal.

Journey Healing Centers stemmed from our desire to create an environment that supported life and made us a living while we were doing something important to assist others. But that's not to say that the efforts of volunteers and nonprofit organizations are somehow less worthy.

We will say, however, that the desire to give back to the world or to solve a social problem need not be relegated to the nonprofit or non-governmental organization (NGO) realm. What many people, like us, are discovering is that not only are the desires for being of service and earning a profit no longer mutually exclusive, but that in many cases, the for-profit model is more sustainable and powerful over the long term. After all, anyone who controls your funding ultimately controls you. By having a for-profit, we can expand the business to be more responsive, provide a much-needed service to humanity in all socioeconomic class, and give more easily to other charities through doing our work in a free market with fewer regulatory constrictions.

One believer of this premise is Michael Holthouse, a Texas-based philanthropist and longtime entrepreneur who was founder and president of Paranet, Inc., a computer network services company established in 1990. He was an *Inc. Magazine* Entrepreneur of the Year and two-time "Inc. 500 Fastest Growing Company" winner. After selling Paranet to Sprint in 1997, Holthouse channeled his energies and financial resources into philanthropic projects, including the Holthouse Foundation For Kids, a foundation that focuses on proactive and experiential programs for at-risk youth, and Prepared 4 Life, a nonprofit that operates Lemonade Day, an experiential, community-based program that develops life skills; and teaches youth about the skills and values of entrepreneurship through the formation of lemonade stands.

"There are lots of 501(c)3's out there that are currently operating off the kind of model that says, 'I'm doing good in the world, but I've got to go to foundations and get money from them in order to keep doing what I'm doing,'" says Holthouse. "But that model is a dinosaur, and it isn't going to last much longer. Every group that wants to address a social issue is going to have to operate like a real business. They'll have to operate with budgets, revenues, and services that they provide. They'll have to operate as any business would. The profits may not be distributed to shareholders, but would be reinvested back into the organization so that it can increase the number of people it serves or improve the quality by which it serves people."

"I think social entrepreneurs share the trait that we don't think we should need to starve to make a difference," says R. Christine Hershey, president and founder of Hershey Cause, a strategic communications firm that works with social entrepreneurs and corporations to build brands and create campaigns that help advance social change. "One of the reasons we haven't solved the world's biggest problems is that folks in those sectors are underfunded."

It's why Hershey suggests that any social venture still be grounded in business best practices. "It's almost as if, in the old days, in the nonprofit model, there was a virtue that nonprofits didn't need to be vigorous, or think strategically. I think that's turned into a crutch. And I think that's why a lot of them are barely limping along. I think they need rigorous best practices to figure out how they'll survive and make a bigger contribution."

The Obama Administration has set forth world food security as a top priority in its foreign policy plans, but rather than relying on NGOs to handle this, the administration has shared that a for-profit philosophy can be the change-maker. A February 2011 article in Voice of America News (VOANews.com) relates a story about Mozambique's poultry farming practices. Because farmers there couldn't afford medicines or enough food to properly raise chickens, the chickens they produced were often spoiled or too thin to compete on a global scale with other foreign producers.

When TechnoServe, a non-governmental organization based in Washington, D.C. that provides business development assistance to aid in breaking the cycle of poverty in third-world countries, and Cargill, an agribusiness corporation, got involved with financial, regulatory, and business development support, the quality of poultry raised in Mozambique drastically improved. It created jobs, improved incomes for farmers, and ultimately improved the quality of poultry that Cargill could then sell, which in turn bolstered its bottom line. The motive for profit became a win-win-win – for farmers, for industry, and for consumers – while ultimately accomplishing a major step in the fight for world food security.

What we found as we started Journey Healing Centers is that we really prefer to have control over ourselves and how we run the business. We decided to run it as a true, revenue-generating business so that we could continue to reinvest in the very best services and treatments for our customers. How could we expect to attract the very best addiction counselors and doctors by relying on the nonprofit model of relying on kind donations of time from busy professionals?

The triple-bottom-line philosophy comes up frequently in discussions of social entrepreneurship. The three prongs of this triple bottom line are typically referred to as "the 3 P's": People, Planet, and Profit. Social enterprises aspire to a bottom line that achieves social mission, benefits or does no harm to the planet, and still earns a profit.

For us, our triple bottom line morphed into **"social value, profit, and freedom"**—that is, providing social value, profit that enables us to continue doing it, and freedom from the shackles of addiction and a destructive lifestyle, not only for ourselves but for those we treat as well. And, as we learned more about moving from employees to business owners and, ultimately, investors, we earned financial freedom as well.

It's important to note, though, that the term "Social Capitalist" might imply that we were somehow all about money—that because we embraced the *Rich Dad* philosophies of growing wealth, we were somehow looking to capitalize on others' misery in order to grow wealthy.

The truth is that if money were our motive, I would have stayed in the nightclub business. It certainly could provide a lavish lifestyle. I could eventually have taken over for my father and run and expanded a very successful nightclub operation. Lisa and I volunteer for Journey Healing Centers; we have never taken a paycheck from the company.

From Day 1, we have invested money back into the business to improve, expand, and enhance its offerings. And we have established a toll-free, 24-hour addiction hotline, run by a call center that operates 7 days a week and takes calls from anyone looking for support, advice, or resources, regardless of whether the callers are seeking treatment from JHC.

And the truth is that it's okay to be profitable while helping the world. In fact, as global trends seem to indicate, it may be preferable.

Chapter Thought

How would you characterize your relationship with money? Do you curse it because you don't have enough? Do you speak poorly of those people who have it? Money is only an idea. If you change your thoughts about money, you can change how you relate to it. Money was designed to serve you, not for you to serve it.

PART THREE

Mastering the B-I Triangle

*"Choose your team—and your teachers—wisely.
Who's on your team?"*

— *Robert Kiyosaki*

Mastering
The B-I Triangle

Like the human body, Rich Dad's B-I Triangle

is a system of systems.

When one system is weak or failing,

the entire body is impacted. The same is true in business.

In this section, the Rich Dad team explains the importance

of each of the 8 Integrities of a Business...

the eight critical components of the B-I Triangle.

MISSION
Mission Is Spiritual
by Kim Kiyosaki

Mission is spiritual, the soul of a company. Robert and I are mission-driven and so is The Rich Dad Company. We live and breathe our mission: to elevate the financial well-being of humanity.

If there is one thing that has become crystal clear as The Rich Dad Company has evolved over the past two decades, it's that mission is sacred. It is spiritual—and it shapes the culture of an organization. It is the foundation of our brand, just as Mission is the foundation of the B-I Triangle. Mission—coupled with Leadership and Team— create the framework for the five elements that are critical to the success of a business. And it all starts with, and builds upon, Mission.

At military school and in the Marine Corps, Robert learned the spiritual power of mission. In Vietnam he learned the importance of having a team united by the same mission. He has often shared the fact that having a strong mission—whether at Kings Point or in the Marine Corp or at Rich Dad—provided discipline and made him a stronger member of the team, a stronger and more effective leader.

My role in the Rich Dad B-I Triangle, related to Mission, is as Keeper of the Spirit. The spirit of a company is what connects us with the minds and hearts of everyone associated with the brand— employees, partners, fans and followers. Spirit fuels the passion that makes us fearless and tireless as we pursue the goals and dreams we have for our businesses.

There is an incredible energy in our company… and that spirit is reflected in our entrepreneurial culture, in the contrarian nature of our brand, and in those people around the world who have embraced the Rich Dad messages and taken action in their lives. In Asia, they call Rich Dad 'The Purple Storm'… as it has swept across the world with power and passion and purpose.

It wasn't until Robert and I were clear on our mission and saw how we could serve in addressing the pressing need in the world for financial education, that we talked about product development.

Each day, as we hear from people around the world whose lives have been changed for the better by the messages of Rich Dad and the work of the Rich Dad Company and its partners around the world, our spirits soar. We know that we have put our talents and gifts to good use in serving a global community that is hungry for knowledge and open to learning more about money and how to make it work for them in their lives.

Kim's Kolbe Index

KIM KIYOSAKI

Kolbe A™ Index Result

CONGRATULATIONS KIM
You Got a Perfect Score on the Kolbe A™ Index

You are uniquely able to take on future-oriented challenges. You lead the way to visionary possibilities and create what others said couldn't be done. You'll say "Yes" before you even know the end of the question – then turn it into a productive adventure.

Kolbe Action Modes®

©1997-2017 Kathy Kolbe All rights reserved.

Reprinted with permission from Kolbe Corp.

LEADERSHIP
Life as a CEO
by Mike Sullivan, Esq.
CEO of The Rich Dad Company and Serial Entrepreneur

Leadership styles vary considerably from company to company, based upon a wide variety of things. The personality of the leader, certainly, but also the culture of the company, the business climate, and the industry. In today's fast-paced Information-Age world, markets and market-condition changes are fast and furious. Procrastination or indecisiveness can be a killer—and give competitors an edge or an opening. Strong leaders, I've found, trust their instincts when it comes to cultivating a leadership style that serves their company and brand, the marketplace, and their customers, as well as their own personal strengths and the corporate culture. Steve Jobs, it's said, was very much of a micro-manager… with a leadership style very different from that of Tim Cook. Warren Buffett, on the other hand, is known for taking a hands-off approach toward leadership of the companies he owns or invests in, trusting his managers to know how to achieve the performance he expects.

I'd describe myself as a hands-off leader with an easy-going management style. Those who have worked with me know that, outwardly, I come across as very hands-off… but, behind the scenes, I'm really very hands-on. I have a gift, I think, for cultivating relationships—with our managers, our team members, our strategic partners and all the stakeholders of the business. That helps me to know what's really going on in the business, and that's a key advantage. I'm able to zero in on problem areas and make sure our leaders have the resources and guidance they need to do their jobs well. I'm a guy who deals directly with issues and problems that arise and I believe in cutting your losses quickly. If you don't, the indecisiveness compounds the problem and poisons the team. They deserve a leader who has a clear vision for the future, who understands that we hold each other accountable for meeting the expectations and standards we set, and who calls it as he sees it—even when it's a tough call.

That said, I set high expectations for management and our teams and come down hard when expectations aren't met. Or when we aren't delivering to our potential and the brand standards of The Rich Dad Company. I set the rules for how our team will operate and it doesn't take long for people to understand that they have one shot to step up and deliver. I don't pull punches; I deliver honest direction on how we'll operate and do my best to deliver serious and thoughtful feedback that will help our team grow and thrive. And, by extension, the business will thrive. And if teams or individuals are underperforming, they'll get fair warning that things need to change. And if they respect the culture of our organization and want to continue to play on a first-rate team, they usually do.

Later in this section of the book on Mastering the B-I Triangle, Shane writes about the role of technology in business today. When I took the reins of leadership at The Rich Dad Company, one of the first things I realized was the power of the brand globally. It was beyond belief. And, immediately, I knew two things: one was that I needed someone who was a visionary when it came to technology and other was that we needed to make staying connected to the massive, world-wide community of raving Rich Dad fans a high communications priority.

When I was first introduced to Robert and Kim and our conversations led to the role I would take with The Rich Dad Company, I knew that I couldn't accomplish all that the job would require without an IT whiz-kid. And lucky for me—and The Rich Dad Company—I had just the guy. My long-time business partner Shane Caniglia. A young gun who had embraced all the opportunities that technology could deliver in our existing businesses, Shane has a healthy skepticism for the status quo and doesn't think twice when it comes to questioning everything and challenging the way we think and do things today. Very "Rich Dad"… even before he took on the role of President at The Rich Dad Company. Shane will be sharing his thoughts about Team and Systems, related to the B-I Triangle, later in this book.

I'm often asked how my leadership style has evolved over the years. Experience provides both context and perspective and in nearly five decades of work in entrepreneurial businesses I've seen a tremendous amount of change. Most for the better—and much of it opening the door for new opportunities, new ways to do things, more efficient and profitable ways to operate and serve your customer base. One thing I've seen is that, regardless of the company or the product or the industry, the same problems arise again and again. And I knew there was a message in that.

Experience is a great teacher and my years of experience have helped me to make decisions faster and with more confidence. I think the mark of a strong leader is that he or she can deliver strong and constructive feedback—feedback that will make both the individual and the team better.

One of the strengths I bring to Rich Dad as its CEO is that I work hard to see both sides of issues and problems. While I might not agree with everyone, it's important that I understand and appreciate other points of view. Robert often talks about a coin having three sides: your side, my side and the 'edge,' for which we can see both sides. I've learned to keep a lot of my thoughts and thought processes to myself as I take in and process information… and people rarely know exactly what's going on in my head. A little mystery is good… and keeps everyone on his or her toes. Don't get me wrong: I'm open and honest in my communications. I just don't always put all my cards on the table in terms of how I might think or act in the future. That strategy has served me well over the years, as I've observed, listened, and processed what I see and hear.

Part of the Rich Dad culture that has really resonated with me is that making mistakes is how we learn. As a leader, I think it's important to let people know that it's OK to make mistakes. Just don't make the same ones over and over again! There's a lot we can learn from mistakes, if we're paying attention and applying what we learn. That's usually a tough leadership lesson to learn… since society conditions us to believe that mistakes are bad or reflect poorly on us or our ability to do the job "right."

I've been called a serial entrepreneur—and that's describes me well. I've learned that CEOs of all large companies all face the same challenges—and nobody reinvents the wheel. It's always about people and money. The key is to hire good people, train them, and support them. Set clear expectations around the mission of the company and their role on the team. People work best, in my experience, when they're clear on objectives, focused on common goals, and know that they are valued and appreciated. The rest is up to them.

The biggest challenges I've faced as an entrepreneur and leading entrepreneurial organizations have revolved around raising money. Securing the money that lets you do what you need to do. If you're always up against the wall financially you're always thinking about money—instead of outpacing your competition, building a world-class team, and growing the business. Being strapped for cash takes your focus off your vision for the future and often means you're not hiring the best talent or cutting corners or delaying growth strategies… for which you'll eventually pay a price.

In addition to being a serial entrepreneur, I'm kind of a sports nut. So I thought I'd close with a quote from Lou Holtz, famed Notre Dame football coach: "It's a fine thing to have ability, but the ability to discover ability in others is the true test." That's a key role of a leader—to discover and nurture talent that can propel an organization into the future.

What words of wisdom on leadership would I share with entrepreneurs? That's easy: don't get caught up in the minutia, the little stuff that can bog you down. Things like: do we have the right name? The right logo? Should we set the business up as an LLC or a Corporation? Those decisions are best left to the specialists—your Legal and Communications teams—so the leader can focus on the big picture and the future.

I've worked with many companies, large and small, and the one thing that is a constant is money. I mentioned it earlier. Having the money to do what you need to do—to launch a business or grow one—is critical. I see entrepreneurs fall into the same trap time and time again. They have their business plan (and it might be a killer business plan) but without the money behind it… the odds of stellar success are against them. They may have that million-dollar idea… but not the financial wherewithal to create the business that will make them millions.

If I were to choose three words that would sum up my leadership legacy, they would be these: plan, execute… and change. A plan is only as good as a leader's ability to stay the course and correct and adjust over time.

Mike's Kolbe Index

MIKE SULLIVAN
Kolbe A™ Index Result

CONGRATULATIONS MIKE
You Got a Perfect Score on the Kolbe A™ Index

You are excellent in situations that require strategic organization of information. You set priorities and put them into appropriate sequences. Your talent with both strategies and tactics makes you essential to any massive effort.

Kolbe Action Modes®

Reprinted with permission from Kolbe Corp.

TEAM
There Is no I in TEAM
by Shane Caniglia
President of The Rich Dad Company

Team—along with Mission and Leadership—are the three elements of a business that frame the B-I Triangle. They make sure it holds its shape, its structural integrity. If these three of the 8 Integrities of a Business are not rock-solid, the foundation is shaky. And it's tough to build anything that can stand up to all the challenges businesses face if you have a weak foundation.

Robert and Kim set the vision for The Rich Dad Company, and its Mission. Mike Sullivan, Rich Dad's CEO and a guy I've known (and been business partners with) for many years, is a strong leader who lives the entrepreneurial sprit. He appreciates and respects the culture at Rich Dad and gives our team the room to learn and grow. My role, related to Team, has been multi-faceted—with responsibilities for business rules, systems and processes, technology, and talent. My experience with building teams has taught me that there are parts of the process that are universal—the same for all organizations, regardless of the type of business or industry sector—and parts that are truly unique to our business. For me, that's what has always been the appeal and the challenge in hiring, shaping, and growing strong teams. It's part science and part art—tangibles and intangibles. And when you get the mix just right, it's an amazing experience to be a part of.

I would describe my management style as 'flat'—we're a team and we all contribute to creating the very best outcomes. And while titles are important for the outside world, they divide people internally. Additionally, they can pigeonhole an individual and his or her thought process (and actions) to be based only on their responsibility or skill set or 'job description.' This thought or division in the brain tends to stifle both the team and individual creativity. At Rich Dad, we apply the rule that team members need to always communicate and when it's your time to speak you respectfully present your thoughts and prepare for feedback. We build upon the feedback until the ideas begin to come to life. It's a great process and we've all learned to give—and take—helpful and well-intended feedback.

When building or expanding our team, we always assess interpersonal skills in the interviewing process. We believe that we can teach a new team member any skill set. And we will quickly learn whether a candidates strengths and skill set match what he or she has said they are.

If, during the interview process, we hear the I-word a lot, it is a clear sign of someone that is more worried about individual credit than overall team success. It also tells us that they're not a good listener… and that they are more interested in how great *they* are than in how they will complement the team. No one can do everything all by themselves. No matter what you do, it takes someone else to help you along the way. We live and work by this principle: There is no I in TEAM.

We look for individuals with a passion for learning and who can be humble about failures that are sure to be part of the process of building brands and businesses. It's important that we're aware of lessons learned along the way—and that we don't repeat the same mistakes. Mistakes aren't necessarily bad. In fact, we say, "fail hard, fail fast." Sometimes they can teach us a lot—if we're paying attention. It's when we miss the lessons and repeat mistakes that 'mistakes' become an issue.

As we look to expand our team, someone who demonstrates knowledge of the Rich Dad brand certainly has a leg up in the hiring process. It tells us that they prepared for the interview and gave some thought to how their skills and strengths could support the brand and its mission.

Red flags in the team-building process? One that we believe is a sure 'tell' related to how good a fit someone will be is that 'I' word… People who interrupt, don't listen, go on and on without making a point or answering a direct question are not a good fit for the team we've built and how we operate. The team at Rich Dad is committed to supporting each other and delivering—whatever the project or program or challenge—at the highest level. We set the bar high and expect that everyone on the team is willing to play their A game. And we *never* say "… that's not my job."

Team-building in an entrepreneurial company is both challenging and exciting. We are always pushing ourselves to think differently, creatively, entrepreneurially. That's the culture at Rich Dad. Communication is critical. We teach and live by the golden rule: Teams cannot over-communicate. When something falters or fails, it invariably comes down to the communication—no communication, poor communication, or too little communication. We communicate internally and to the outside world—and our communications need to be consistent. The same levels of respect and clarity apply whether we're developing a new product launch, strategizing with our business partners, or communicating with the millions of people around the world who follow Robert and Rich Dad on Twitter and Facebook.

We operate as a team, supporting and holding each other accountable. We over-communicate and always have our teammates' backs, and vice versa. We don't seek acknowledgement and we win or lose as a team—not as individuals. It's because of that mindset that you'll never hear anyone at Rich Dad say "… not my job."

We must remember first and foremost that we are hiring and teaching *humans*. One thing I like to teach is that you are hiring humans to do the work, not the other way around. So learn to manage people, not just the work. And they have personal issues and goals, as well as professional goals. Those personal priorities are usually hidden from a company's management and their co-workers. Great leaders teach and help every person on the team dig deep and get in touch with themselves so they can believe in themselves and their potential. By doing this, leaders on the team help them develop confidence in things they didn't know or didn't think they could do.

That growth is key to pushing someone farther than they thought they could go. And the success in making that happen always comes down to effective, consistent communication.

Our goal is to build and grow a world-class team… a team that has high standards for communication and accountability, a team whose goal is to keep learning and growing.

Shane's Kolbe Index

 SHANE CANIGLIA
Kolbe A™ Index Result

CONGRATULATIONS SHANE
You Got a Perfect Score on the Kolbe A™ Index

You have an uncanny talent for coming up with unique strategies, prioritizing opportunities, and dealing with the unknowns in complex problems. You thrive when quantifying an opportunity and prospecting for ways to enhance it.

Kolbe Action Modes®

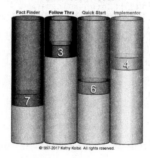

©1997-2017 Kathy Kolbe. All rights reserved.

Reprinted with permission from Kolbe Corp.

PRODUCT
Why Product Doesn't Matter
by Robert Kiyosaki

I hear it all the time: "I gave a great idea for a product." If only it were that easy. Most of us, at one time or another, have a really great idea. It's getting it to market—with ALL the moving pieces of a business working in perfect harmony—that separates the proverbial business men from the boys.

As we've stated in the opening sections of this book, many people have had a million dollar idea. The problem is most of us do not know how to turn that million-dollar idea into a million dollars.

That's where a team can make all the difference.

The diagram my rich dad called the B-I Triangle represents the eight components of every business. He called it the B-I—Business-Investor—Triangle because it is for those who operate on the right side of the CASHFLOW Quadrant, Businesses and Investors.

When an entrepreneur "builds a business," what they build is a B-I Triangle.

If the entrepreneur cannot put all eight of the components, the integrities, together, the business fails or suffers financially.

Notice that the product, or the idea, is the least important part of the B-I Triangle. One reason why most entrepreneurs fail, even those with genuine million-dollar ideas, is because all they have is the top of the triangle. The Product. Most are missing one or more of the other integrities.

Many people agonize over finding a great product or service. Many think a great product or new service will propel them into entrepreneurial heaven. That is delusional.

As you may guess, the primary reason why nine out of 10 entrepreneurs fail in the first five years is because they are unable to put the eight pieces of the entrepreneur's puzzle together. Many crash and burn because one or more of the eight pieces is missing, or weak, or mismanaged. For example, when I started my first big business, my nylon-and-Velcro surfer wallet business in the 1970s, I had a great product—the wallets—but I did not go to the step below Product... Legal. Because I did not have much money, I did not spend the $7,000 for attorney's fees to patent the product. After a year of hard work, making the nylon wallets a raging success, my wallet was ripped off by many manufacturers in Asia. Soon the U.S. market was flooded with cheap "knock-offs" of *my* hot new product. I could not do anything about it because I failed to spend the money to make my product "proprietary"—an asset that I owned and controlled. The word *proprietary* comes from the word *property.*

The problem with most entrepreneurs is they work to make a lot of money, not develop property. At least that is what I did. I was in such a hurry to sell a few wallets, to make some money, that I failed to create property—the real asset. It is property, not money, which makes entrepreneurs rich.

If you have ever watched the TV show *Shark Tank*, you will often hear one of the sharks ask the entrepreneur, "Is your product proprietary?" These sharks have zeroed in on level two on the B-I Triangle: Legal.

Proprietary could refer to your product's patent, copyright, or trademark. Or whether or not your product or your IP—intellectual property—can be licensed. That means someone would pay you to use your property. Simply put, proprietary is similar to legal real estate. Today, The Rich Dad Company licenses the rights to use my *intellectual* property to more than 50 businesses around the world.

That is why I am a rich entrepreneur. I make a lot of money without working, because the *property* I created is working for me.

The young girl who was a successful baby-sitter would probably not become a rich entrepreneur because she was working for money, rather than developing property.

I know a few of you are still wondering about why product is the least important of the 8 integrities of a business. Let me answer that question now. Whenever someone wants to debate the importance of a product, I ask, "Have you ever eaten a McDonald's hamburger?" Regardless of where I am in the world, most people tell me they have. Most people, at one time or another, have eaten at McDonald's.

I then ask, "Can you make a better hamburger than McDonald's?" Most say they can.

I then ask, "Can you build a bigger and richer business than McDonald's?"

Obviously, most say, "No."

I end by saying, "That is why product is not that important to being an entrepreneur." The ability to build a business is. Rich entrepreneurs work to build businesses, not hamburgers. They build assets.

Once Kim and I were clear on our Mission we began product development. Once the prototype of the *CASHFLOW* game was beta-tested, and *Rich Dad Poor Dad* was in manuscript, the next step in the B-I Triangle was Legal. We needed a patent and trademark attorney to turn my products into property, branded products.

I had learned my lessons from rock and roll. Rather than be the entrepreneur with the factories, employees, overhead, and other miseries of business, The Rich Dad Company was designed to be a brand. That is why the core Rich Dad company is a small organization. We do not own factories, printing presses, or warehouses. We make our money by allowing businesses all over the world—businesses such as book publishing companies—to exercise the legal right to produce our products, and pay The Rich Dad Company a royalty. In some ways, it's like money for nothing.

Obviously, I make it sound easier than it really is. For Kim and me, it was a trying process. Today, Rich Dad is an international brand working cooperatively with partners all over the world. In many ways Rich Dad is much like Coca-Cola. We own the brand and our partners own the printing presses that produce our books, seminars, and games under our license.

If you want to learn how to build a better product, like a better hamburger, get a cookbook. This book is not for you. This book is about assembling your team—your B-I Triangle business structure—that will support and drive your business.

Robert's Kolbe Index

ROBERT KIYOSAKI

Kolbe A™ Index Result

CONGRATULATIONS ROBERT
You Got a Perfect Score on the Kolbe A™ Index

You are terrific at stepping into tough situations and concocting daring solutions, making the seemingly impossible, possible. You lead the way out of dilemmas as you blaze uncharted trails and improvise inventions until you get them working.

Kolbe Action Modes®

Reprinted with permission from Kolbe Corp.

LEGAL
Getting Legal in the B-I Triangle
by Garrett Sutton, Esq.

In the B-I Triangle, Legal is found just under Product at the top of the pyramid. There is a good reason for Legal to be one of the 8 integrities. As we discussed earlier, the influence of law and regulations affect every entrepreneur and investor.

You will need attorneys who specialize in the areas you enter. If your field of endeavor is highly regulated you want an attorney who specializes in those regulations. If you are going to create ideas and products you want an intellectual property attorney to protect your creativity with patents, trademarks and copyrights. But in all scenarios you will be building and growing your assets. Accordingly, you will always need asset protection.

It is a requirement that we all follow the law. It is a benefit when you understand and follow the laws that allow for—and encourage—wealth building. Viewing Legal as not a burden, but rather a benefit is the mindset of successful people. Growing your own wealth is proactive. You are the one to make it happen. As you do this you must also engage in a protective activity. Again, you alone must make it happen. The government doesn't care if you protect yourself or not. Instead, you must be proactive in setting up your asset protection structure. You must work with your attorney to establish the right mix of LLCs, corporations, and trusts to protect your assets.

Asset Protection Defined

Asset protection is a strategy used to prevent loss in our litigious society. It's based on the principle that assets in your name can be seized by a judgement creditor (someone who has sued and won in court). Assets held not in your name but rather in a corporation or LLC are better protected. But you must meet the legal requirements to have those protections in place. There are some states (such as California) with weak protection laws that require additional planning. You have several choices to make when it comes to business structures (collectively called "entities.") That's why it's so important to gain assistance on which entity and which state is best for your specific situation.

There are eight things you should know about protecting you assets.

1. Plan Your Asset Protection Strategy Before You Get Sued

People in business and investing get sued all the time. While it is quaint to think it won't happen to you…

Once a lawsuit arrives, it's too late to put protections in place. Just as you can't get insurance after a fire, you can't protect yourself once you've been threatened with a lawsuit. Either your structures are in place or they are not. This means you've got to set up your LLCs, and corporations not only before you get sued but before you know of a problem. The only possible way to be safe is to do it right from the start.

2. Keep Your Personal and Business Assets Separate

If you don't insulate your own assets from those of your business, you could be in trouble. You don't want to operate your business in the form of a sole proprietorship or as a general partnership. These businesses are not registered, protective entities. They are just you doing business as an individual. Your personal assets are not insulated from those of your business. Instead, they are one in the same, and easy for someone to reach. Not having separate bank accounts is also problematic. You can't do business or invest through a personal bank account without exposing your personal assets to attack.

3. Remember that it's Risky to Be a Sole Proprietor (and Even Risker to be a General Partner).

If you're a sole proprietor and an angry customer sues you, any personal assets you own such as your house or car are not protected. Financial assets such as your bank account and some retirement accounts are also not protected. These can all be taken should a judgment be entered against you. With entities we have the good, the bad and the ugly. A sole proprietorship is the bad entity, offering no protection.

The ugly entity is the general partnership. It is liability times two. While they are very easy to form—a handshake will do—the consequences to you are dramatic. You are now personally liable for not only your mistakes but for your partner's errors and mistakes as well. Stay away from the bad and ugly entities.

4. Use a Good Entity for Asset Protection

To protect yourself, use one of the four good entities, listed below. These entities are chartered with your state (or the strong state you choose such as Wyoming or Nevada). These four good entities for limiting your liability are:

- C Corporations
- S Corporations
- Limited Liability Companies (LLCs)
- Limited Partnerships (LPs)

C corporations and S corporations are both corporations chartered with a state. The difference is in how they are taxed. A C corporation is taxed at the company level and the shareholder level, thus "double taxation." The S corporation has flow through taxation at the shareholder level. For more information please see my book *Run Your Own Corporation* or visit CorporateDirect.com.

5. Follow the Corporate Requirements So That Legal Protections Remain Intact

Chartering a corporation or LLC does not mean you are forever protected without effort. You must follow on going requirements to stay protected. You'll need to keep your company's registration up-to-date and sign any documents as a corporate officer and not as an individual, among other requirements. This is known as maintaining the corporate veil of protection. We provide this service to many of our clients. If you fail to follow these simple formalities (which apply to all good entities) a judgement creditor can pierce the corporate veil and seek your personal assets to satisfy a corporate debt. Piercing the veil claims succeed in almost half of all cases. Clearly, not enough people are following the rules.

What are some of those formalities? They include:

1. Perform all annual filings with the state and pay any fees.

2. Have a resident agent in your state of formation and any state your company qualifies to do business in.

3. Maintain a written record of all decisions (meeting minutes).

4. Provide the world with corporate notice (using Inc. or LLC on contracts and checks).

5. Ensure the corporation is sufficiently capitalized.

6. Maintain separate bank accounts and tax filings.

If you haven't followed these formalities the time is now to do it right. Corporate clean up services are available at Corporate Direct.

6. Obtain the Proper Insurance Coverage

Insurance coverage is the first line of defense for all of us, in both our personal and wealth building activities. In business you want insurance in place for your entrepreneurial activities and your real estate holdings. As an individual you want insurance on your home and automobiles. From that policy you can obtain umbrella insurance coverage extending your personal coverage by a million dollars or more.

Attorneys know how to get insurance monies. They have a tougher time getting LLC or corporate interests. With enough insurance in place they are less likely to go after your investments held in protective entities.

What should you look for in an insurance policy? Here are a few things to consider:

- The liability insurance should cover injuries to third parties on your property.
- If you have people working as your employees, you must have Worker's Compensation insurance.
- Weigh whether your insurance should have "increased cost of construction" additions if your building should become damaged or require reconstruction. This means you'll be covered at today's construction prices instead of those of previous years.
- If you are a landlord, "loss of rents" riders can help you recover costs in the event your building is damaged and uninhabitable so that you can pay relocation costs or receive income from the property while it's being rebuilt to offset losses.

These are only a few issues to consider. A good insurance broker should be one of your trusted team members. That said, be realistic. Insurance companies have an economic incentive not to cover every claim. They find reasons to deny coverage. So while you will have insurance, you will use entities as a second line of defense to protect your personal assets from your business claims.

7. Transfer Property Into the Entity Name

Too many people setup an LLC for their real estate holdings and think they are finished. There is another crucial step.

You must transfer the title of that property from your name into the name of your new LLC. If the LLC exists but it is not on the title at the county record's office you have no protection. Someone suing over the property will bring a claim against the owner of record. Without a transfer to the LLC that is still you personally. Oops.

Once you set up the LLC make sure you file a grant or warranty deed (and not a quit claim deed) transferring ownership into the LLC. There are several other issues involved in the process, which are covered in my book, *Loopholes of Real Estate*.

8. Can I Set Up Asset Protection After I Get Sued?

The short answer: No. You will not be able to set up asset protection after you get sued.

Asset protection is a privilege, and not a right. Before you can protect your assets with an LLC or corporation it must be set up in a timely manner. If you get sued on Tuesday and set up an LLC on Wednesday, you are not protected. A judge can ignore your new LLC that showed up late to the party.

A few years ago, a California woman approached me to ask how much it would cost for our incorporation services. She was the owner of several duplexes and had been renting them out to various tenants. She felt the price of protection was too high (in part because the state of California charges $800 per year per entity). She decided not to set up an LLC as a buffer between she and her tenants.

A few months later she called our office. She had been sued by a tenant who slipped on the stairs. She asked if there was anything we could do for her. Unfortunately, there was not.

Because she did not have her asset protection in place, all of her assets were fair game for the plaintiff and his attorney, including her home equity, bank accounts and all of her duplexes.

The worst part is, this is a common story. In fact, 50% of business owners across the country are being held personally responsible when their businesses or investment holdings are sued because they either aren't incorporated or are not in compliance with corporate formalities.

That is why it is so important to put protections in place before you start growing your wealth. And just as important, you must follow the formalities to continue those protections.

Garrett's Kolbe Index

GARRETT SUTON
Kolbe A™ Index Result

CONGRATULATIONS GARRETT
You Got a Perfect Score on the Kolbe A™ Index

You're terrific when juggling rapidly changing priorities. You are known for taking risks that
are grounded in practical realities. You don't mess around with what has always been done,
but temper your trial-and-error approach by strategizing options.

Reprinted with permission from Kolbe Corp.

SYSTEMS
Systems = IT
by Shane Caniglia

President of The Rich Dad Company and IT Wizard

Today's business marketplace worships at the altar of IT—Internet Technology. It has changed the way the world does business and provides a wealth of opportunities for those who embrace its power. On the flip side, the evolution of technology is constant and fast-paced and demands that we are both vigilant and proactive. To do anything less, today, is business suicide.

In today's world, Systems in the B-I Triangle is IT. Technology has become the core of business infrastructures and impacts every aspect of a business, from Legal and Cash Flow to Product and Communications. Especially Communications. It represents big-time rewards, as well as some risks.

We use systems for two main things: communication and analytics. We have systems for communication, both internal and external and, as I wrote about in the Team section… teams cannot over-communicate. I can't stress it enough. Communication is essential and constant, both internal and external. We use technology and systems to make sure the team is focused on ideas and products. We also use systems to tell us what did—or didn't—work in regard to our messaging and marketing. There are tools that help our marketing teams learn what we need to do to tweak or adjust what we communicate or how we position messages and products. We tweak, assess… then try again. It always comes back to communication.

(Which by the way is a component, of its own, in the B-I Triangle: Communications. No surprise there!)

The B-I Triangle is really a system of systems that are all connected. The key function of internal systems is to leverage technology to paint a story of what is happening in the marketplace and how you can use it to your advantage.

Today, technology impacts every facet of every business—from web presence to accounting, HR, and business systems. It's changed how we approach sales and marketing, build and manage databases, how we store and retrieve information.

In today's world, if you do not have a strong customer-facing web presence people will not take you seriously. And this presence must be seamless, no matter what device a person is using—mobile, laptop, desktop. The same is true for internal systems. They must meet the same level of expectation for your employees so they can focus on new ideas and products—and not whether something is working or not. It's a mixed blessing, since systems and processes must evolve regularly, as we keep up with today's ever-changing business world.

The opportunities are incredible, and there are new ones emerging all the time. Today, entrepreneurs and businesses have access to the world! A decade ago, a small or start-up business would focus on its local area. Not today! And by utilizing free tools such as Facebook, Twitter, and Instagram we can communicate directly with people in the ways they want to be communicated to.

Businesses and brands have the ability to perform tests and experiment with their communities. We can get to know them, read the data related to what they are telling us about what they want and how they want it delivered.

Our strategy: Listen until we get it right. It's a win-win for both the company and its audiences.

Change has become the one thing we can count on, as technology continues to evolve and become more sophisticated. Social media now gives everyone a voice and forum to say whatever they want, however they want to say it. We must stay on top of this. With a strong internal team that is humble and focused, it will become natural for you to stay in tune with your communities. And they will notice.

There are exciting things on the horizon. Automation, in certain industries, is already happening. And while this is certain to affect some jobs, it creates others. It sure makes the case for why teams, and businesses, can never stop learning and growing!

The future belongs to those who know that the only constant is change. Our strategy for staying in front of tomorrow's innovations and tools is to designate members of our team, on a rotating basis, to research new tech and how we might be able to use it. We do this— non-stop!

Shane's Kolbe Index

SHANE CANIGLIA
Kolbe A™ Index Result

CONGRATULATIONS SHANE
You Got a Perfect Score on the Kolbe A™ Index

You have an uncanny talent for coming up with unique strategies, prioritizing opportunities, and dealing with the unknowns in complex problems. You thrive when quantifying an opportunity and prospecting for ways to enhance it.

Kolbe Action Modes®

Reprinted with permission from Kolbe Corp.

COMMUNICATIONS
How PR and Marketing Drive Sales
by Mona Gambetta
Director of Plata Publishing and Public Relations

In Part One of this book, Robert wrote about building a brand. A key element of that process is brand awareness—making your product or service the one, the *brand*, that comes to mind when people need something—whether it's a copy machine, tissues, glass cleaner, burgers, or tires.

There are many ways to drive brand equity and brand awareness. All of them fall into the Communications section of the B-I Triangle.

Let's focus first on external communications. The Internet has changed the way people communicate and offers a wealth of new opportunities. It has also leveled the playing field, as a low-cost way to build community, share messages, and stay connected. The days of needing to hire a high-power ad agency and have an ad budget with lots of zeros are over. That doesn't mean it's gotten any easier or requires less focus or discipline. The vehicles have changed, and with them the rules and parameters for how we communicate. Today it's more about targeted messaging, creating value, and respecting the fact that you have only minutes—if not seconds—to get someone's attention. That's a tall order.

All that said—and apart from huge changes in delivery systems—not all that much has changed in terms of how businesses message and market. Marketing components still include sales, advertising, and public relations. Robert has often shared what his rich dad had to say about sales: Sales=Income.

According to Robert's rich dad, sales is the #1 skill an entrepreneur needs to be successful and everyone in an organization must sell, internally or externally. If they don't, it's unlikely that the business will succeed. It will mean the company will need a boatload of money for advertising... when a focus on sales could be more efficient and deliver a better ROI.

Advertising can get expensive. Whether it's a Google ad or an ad in the *Wall Street Journal*, it means hard dollars in play and no guarantee of success or sales. That's where public relations, the outreach that drives publicity, comes into play.

Both advertising and public relations require an investment in defining your target markets and crafting messages that resonate with those audiences, but the cost differentials can be significant. In many cases, public relations can be more soft costs than hard ones... and with start-up businesses, owners often have more time than money. Generating publicity takes time and consistent effort, but the return on those investments can be huge.

If you take the time to research and target media outlets that are the most fertile fields for your messages, you and your publicists can actually become a service provider—a reliable source of information that serves their audiences and delivers real value. There are more media outlets today than ever before—24/7 programming, social media channels, website content, podcasts, blogs—in addition to traditional print, radio, and television outlets. And they all need quality content to keep their audiences engaged and active—and experts who are great communicators and have strong messages are in high demand.

As Robert wrote about in his section on Branding, The Rich Dad Company has spent little to nothing on advertising over the past two decades. You might ask: *How can that be? How did the brand grow to be the global powerhouse that it is today?*

You've probably guessed it: Communications. In the world of communication, there are three primary means of promoting and selling your products or services. I referenced them earlier: public relations, advertising, and sales.

Over the years, The Rich Dad Company has spent a lot of time (yet relatively little money) on public relations. It started in 1997, when *Rich Dad Poor Dad* was published. Robert and Kim used a service that booked authors on radio shows across the country. Every week, Robert would get on the phone with radio show hosts and tell the story of *Rich Dad Poor Dad.* He was not *selling*… he was telling his story. He was a great guest—articulate and animated, with a story that resonated with audiences around the world. By telling the story, he got people to want to *buy* the book.

Inevitably, at the end of every interview, the radio show host would ask, "Where can our listeners find your book?" Robert's answer was always the same: "at bookstores everywhere."

People went into bookstores, asking for *Rich Dad Poor Dad.* They *wanted to buy.* The bookstores didn't need to "sell" the book—because we let publicity drive sales.

And those sales—the direct result of PR outreach and interviews—propelled *Rich Dad Poor Dad* on to *The New York Times* bestsellers list. It caught the attention of Oprah Winfrey, in 2000, and after an hour as her guest on *Oprah!* Robert and Kim understood the Oprah Effect. When the world was introduced to Robert Kiyosaki and the messages of Rich Dad, the energy that Robert and Oprah shared—two big personalities, both passionate about education— catapulted both Robert and his book onto the world stage. It made Rich Dad a household word and a world-class brand and set the stage for Robert and Kim as outspoken advocates of financial education.

Why was a 10-minute radio interview more powerful than a 60-second, $1,000 radio ad? Because Robert was not selling. He used publicity to drive buyers to bookstores. His objective was to get into the hearts and minds of the listeners by telling the story of his rich dad and his poor dad and a young boy's struggle with two opposing points of view about money. The listeners came to understand why he wrote the book… and why financial education is so important.

There is another advantage of publicity—PR outreach and media coverage—that is often overlooked. It's what could be called a 'third-party endorsement.' If a reporter chooses to interview and quote Robert in an article on personal finance—or the foolishness (today) of saving money, or how to use debt responsibly, or how to get smarter with your money—he or she is communicating that Robert is an authority, an important voice in the personal finance space that merits our attention. The same is true when he's part of a panel on FOX News or CNN or MarketWatch with other well-known and respected experts. It makes a statement about him, his messages, and his credibility. One that money can't always buy. That's the power of PR.

Social media channels and the success of companies like Facebook and Twitter and Instagram have had a huge impact on how the world communicates today—and made a case for the importance and value of Communications. Social media has made communication efficient and fast—and much less expensive.

Just as important, and critical to the Communications section of the B-I Triangle for a business, are internal communications. They deserve as much attention and consistency as external. To echo Shane's words: we *cannot* over-communicate. Internally, we communicate with team members, management, company owners and stakeholders—as well as strategic partners, vendors, and affiliates. Successful entrepreneurs will attest to the fact that clear, concise, and respectful internal communications build strong teams, brands, and businesses. Strong internal communications can make all the difference in the success of a new campaign or product launch… or something as mundane (but important) as updates to the company's healthcare program. In today's fast-paced world—with shorter attention spans and less patience in ferreting out messages—we need to communicate in sound bites and cut to the chase. Strategies for relationship building and brand building can be added in layers, when appropriate, once a strong connection is made—internally or externally.

Over the years, Robert has done thousands of interviews and contributed hundreds of articles to dozens of media outlets around the world. He's been featured on the covers of so many magazines that I've lost count. The buzz about Rich Dad and *Rich Dad Poor Dad*—which today ranks as the #1 Personal Finance book of all time—continues and is influencing new generations. The communication mediums may be a bit different—email messages and Facebook posts over a print interview in the *Chicago Tribune*— but the power of Communications, like the messages of *Rich Dad Poor Dad*, stands the test of time. It is a critical component of every business's B-I Triangle.

Mona's Kolbe Index

MONA GAMBETTA
Kolbe A™ Index Result

CONGRATULATIONS MONA
You Got a Perfect Score on the Kolbe A™ Index

You are fantastic at making comparisons, documenting information, and defining priorities. You can be counted on to research historical details, become an expert in areas of special interest, and make strategic decisions.

Kolbe Action Modes®

Reprinted with permission from Kolbe Corp.

CASH FLOW
Sales = Top Line...
Cash Flow = Bottom Line
by Tom Wheelwright, CPA

Once you have your Leadership, Team, and Mission in place and operating in tandem, it's time to turn to Cash Flow. Cash Flow is the life-blood of any business. Without it, the business fails. With it, the business and the owners of the business thrive. So where does Cash Flow come from and what is the best way to make sure cash flow continues to increase and is always available for the needs of the business and its owners?

Cash Flow comes from multiple sources and can be attributed to three broad categories. These categories make up the most important of the company's financial statements, the Statement of Cash Flow. The Statement of Cash Flow explains where cash flow came from for a given period (month or year) and where it went.

First, cash flow can come from operations. This is the best way to generate cash flow. It starts with sales (see Communications in the B-I Triangle). Sales create income. Income can be in the form of cash or it can be in the form of accounts receivable. If you sell your product to a customer and allow that customer a certain number of days or months to pay, you have an account receivable from that customer. The accounts receivable don't turn into cash until collected. One challenge for many business owners is when they see they have positive income on their income statement (profit and loss statement) and they don't have the same amount of cash coming into the business. This is likely because their accounts receivable are increasing, so there is plenty of income and no cash.

Of course, sales are just the beginning of the cash flow from operations. Once cash comes in, it is often gobbled up in expenses. Here is where the savvy business owner pays a lot of attention. The successful business owner pays as much attention to expenses as they do to income. Let's look at a simple example. Suppose your profit and loss looks like this:

Profit and Loss Statement			
100	Sales	140	40%
- 80	COGS	- 112	80%
20	GP	28	
- 16	Expenses	- 22.4	16%
4	Net Income	5.6	40%

You decide you would like to increase your net profit by 40%. One option, of course, is to increase your sales by 40%. This would look like this:

40% Profit Increase		
100	Sales	140
- 80	COGS	- 112
20	GP	28
(14.4)	Expenses	- 22.4
5.6	Net Income	5.6

Another option is to decrease your expenses. In this example, you would only have to decrease your expenses by 10% in order to increase your net profit by 40%. It looks like this:

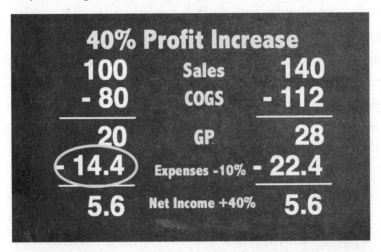

So which is easier—increasing sales by 40% or decreasing expenses by 10%? Of course, decreasing expenses by 10% is always easier. The way to do this is to examine each expense with the question, *Will this expense increase my income?* The purpose of any expense should be to increase income. Any expenses that will not increase income should be eliminated. For example, many companies now provide food and drinks for employees. This can be a sizeable expense. If this works to increase the employees' productivity and, as a result, income goes up, then it's a good way to spend money. If the employees just get fatter from it and it doesn't do anything for productivity, then get rid of the expense and find another way to increase their productivity.

Every expense should be analyzed in this way. Start by looking at your income statement for the past 12 months. Sit down with your CPA or business partner and examine every single expense category. What expenses make you money and what expenses could be eliminated with little or no effect on the business?

The next place you can get or spend cash flow is investments in assets. The purpose of assets is to generate cash flow. You could have lots of cash flowing in and be spending it on furniture, equipment, and other assets so you have no cash flow at the end. This is okay, as long as you manage it properly.

Just like you did with expenses, look carefully at every asset you have on your balance sheet. Your balance sheet includes your assets (what you own) and your liabilities (what you owe) as well as what's left over for the owners (equity). If an asset is not producing income, get rid of it. Sell it or donate it to a worthy cause. (If you donate it, at least you will receive some cash flow in the form of a tax write-off.)

If an asset is not producing income, it really is no longer an asset. It's just sitting there on your balance sheet doing nothing. We call this an *un-utilized* or *under-utilized asset*. These assets must go. It doesn't matter if you end up selling the asset at a loss. This is a resource that is not producing income and must be converted to an income-producing asset.

Decide first what is an acceptable return on investment (ROI) for your assets. Any asset that isn't meeting this ROI should be challenged. Is there a way to improve the asset's ROI? If so, then take the actions required to improve the ROI. If not, get rid of the asset. In my accounting firm, we had a number of clients several years ago that were not producing much revenue for us. So we sold the clients to another accounting firm. That freed up our staff to focus on stronger clients.

The last way to increase cash flow is through financing. This includes equity financing from investors as well as bank financing. You could be showing a lot of income on your profit and loss statement and wonder why you don't have any cash and the reason could be that you are using the money to pay off debt. So your net equity is increasing at the expense of your cash flow. This isn't necessarily bad.

Just like you did with expenses and assets, you must regularly look at your liabilities (*liabilities* are the accountants' and bankers' term for debt) and challenge whether they are doing their job. The purpose of any liability is to create an asset. If you have liabilities that are not producing assets, these liabilities are bad debt. Liabilities that produce assets (which in turn produce cash flow) are good debt.

Business owners who pay attention to their cash flow and follow these basic principles rarely run into trouble. They routinely look at their Statement of Cash Flows and regularly examine their expenses, assets, and liabilities to make sure their expenses are producing income, their assets are producing cash flow, and their liabilities are producing assets.

One last area that is crucial to Cash Flow is taxes. With the exceptions of cost of goods sold (the cost of producing the products you are selling) and labor (your employees or contractors), taxes will be your single largest expense. Fortunately, the tax law in all countries is set up to benefit business owners.

The government also wants to make sure that your expenses are producing income. In fact, that's one of the tests for whether a cost is deductible as a business expense. Is the expense necessary to your business? Will the expense either increase income or increase your market share? If so, and if you properly document the expense, the government will allow you to deduct it against your income. Remember that you pay taxes on your net income, so any expense you deduct reduces the amount of taxes you pay.

How your business is set up legally will also have a big impact on your taxes. How you are set up is called your *entity*. Garrett covers this in the Legal section of the B-I Triangle. Which entity you use—whether it's a partnership entity, corporate entity, or limited liability entity—will have a big impact on how you are taxed. The government will reward you with lower taxes if you are set up correctly. In the United States, this means you likely want to be an S Corporation for an operating business or a limited liability taxed as a partnership for an investment company (such as real estate rentals).

Of course, the most important part of reducing your taxes and managing your cash flow will be your team members. Your Cash Flow team member should be a CPA, a certified public accountant, or the equivalent (a "chartered accountant" in many countries is equivalent to a CPA in the United States and Canada). Your CPA can help you with your financial statements as well as your tax returns and should be an integral part of your Cash Flow team. For more on how to find a good CPA and tax advisor, I invite you to read chapter 23 of my book *Tax-Free Wealth* in Part Two of this book.

Tom's Kolbe Index

TOM WHEELRIGHT

Kolbe A™ Index Result

CONGRATULATIONS TOM
You Got a Perfect Score on the Kolbe A™ Index

You are uniquely able to take on future-oriented challenges. You lead the way to visionary possibilities and create what others said couldn't be done. You'll say "Yes" before you even know the end of the question – then turn it into a productive adventure.

Kolbe Action Modes®

Reprinted with permission from Kolbe Corp.

IN CONCLUSION
Robert Kiyosaki

This book was a team effort. And I'm reminded, yet again, of the wealth of talent and experience in the team Kim and I have assembled. I hope it will inspire you to seek and find the talent you need to build a world-class business team.

Start today in building your team. Create your Code of Honor and hold each other to high standards. This will help you attract the quality of clients, partners, mentors, and advisors that can make the difference between a business that struggles and one that thrives.

Embrace the power and the lessons of the B-I Triangle and use it as your guide for creating and supporting 8 strong integrities of your business—ones that will stand up to the tests all businesses face.

I'm proud to have this opportunity to share my team with you. I know that the lessons and stories they've shared will help you avoid some of the mistakes I made early in my business career. And I think you'll agree that they are great assets—and more important, even, than money.

Our closing thought for you is a question: Who's on *your* team?

Kolbe Corp's mission is to help people succeed by having the freedom to be themselves. This begins with the Kolbe A™ Index, which is an assessment that measures what no other assessment does—your conative strengths. Conation involves a third part of the mind that you don't hear much about. To put it simply, it's the part of the mind that dictates what you actually WILL or WON'T do when you're solving problems. Think of it as your "gut instincts."

By understanding these instincts and how you naturally solve problems or what situations cause you stress, you can more easily succeed in business and your personal life.

Kolbe helps businesses place the right people in the right roles, reduce workplace stress and help teams work better together— all by identifying natural strengths. Once you understand your instincts and those that drive your relationships with a friend, partner or spouse, you can more easily discuss your differences, laugh about them and develop techniques for dealing with them. The same applies with your children and helping them tap into their instinctive strengths.

Start by taking the Kolbe A Index on Kolbe.com

Rich Dad's
B-I Triangle